"Within the storms of life, sobriety becomes the lighthouse that guides us safely to the shores of serenity."

*Exercise:
Choose bright and vibrant colors as you color the page. With each stroke, visualize your future becoming brighter and more filled with hope.

*Exercise:
Embrace your inner champion as you color, using colors to depict your victories.

*Exercise:
While coloring, reflect on how alcohol masks pain but doesn't heal it. Use each stroke as a step towards acknowledging and addressing emotional wounds.

*Exercise:
While coloring, reflect on how alcohol may have stolen joy and left regret in its wake. Use each stroke to symbolize reclaiming your happiness, one color at a time.

Welcome to

'Mindful Mandalas for Sobriety.'

This unique coloring book is your
companion on the path to sobriety and
personal growth. Each page provides a
creative outlet for self-expression and
mindfulness, featuring exercises and
inspirational quotes for reflection.

Coloring is a therapeutic tool that can
help you stay focused on your journey
to a healthier, alcohol-free life.
Dive in, savor the process, and celebrate
your progress one stroke at a time.
Whether you're on the path to recovery
or simply seeking a creative way to
nurture your well-being, this coloring
book is here to support and inspire you.

This book belongs to:

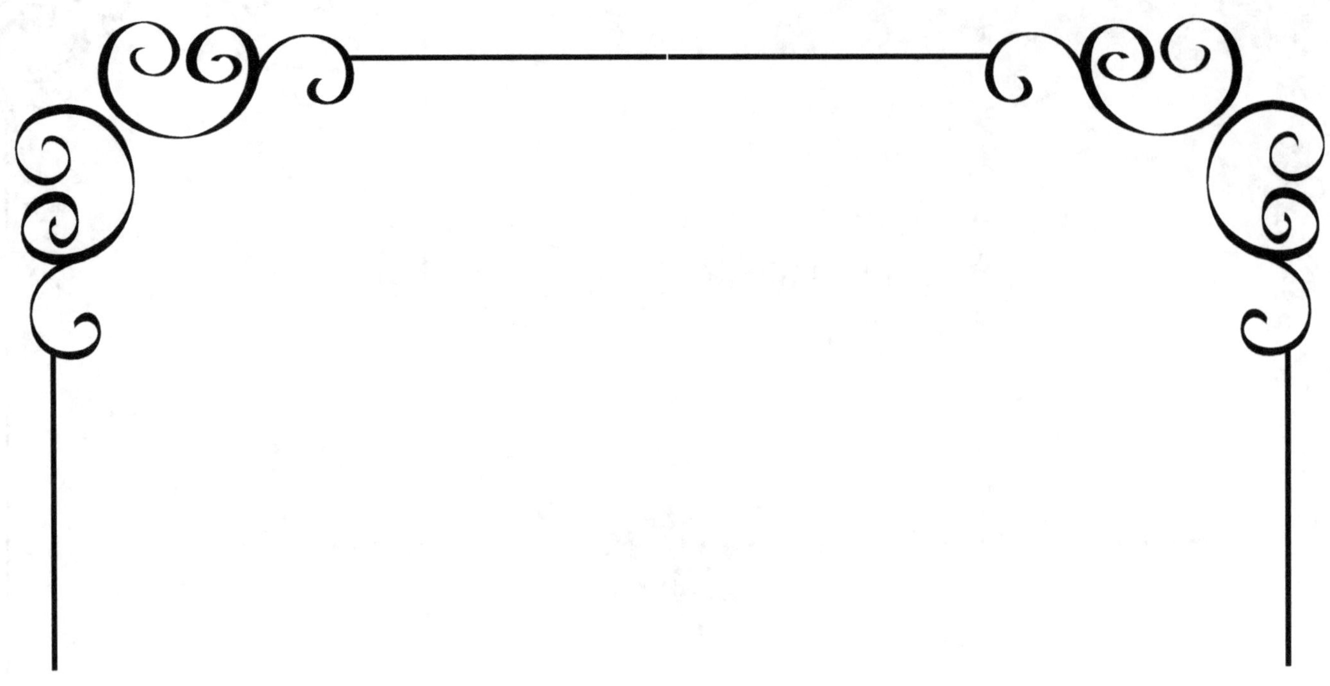

Recovery is possible.
I believe in my
strength
to overcome.

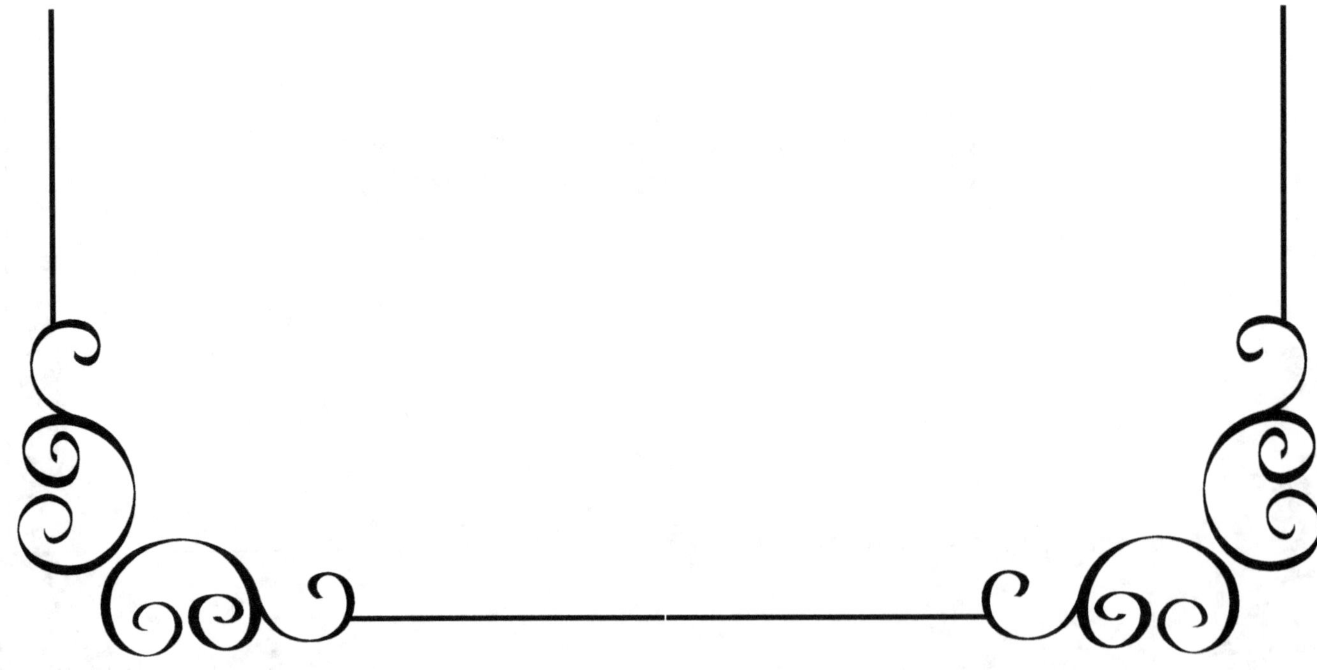

*Exercise:
As you color, imagine each stroke of your coloring pencil
reinforcing your inner strength. Visualize your strength
growing with each color you add to the page.

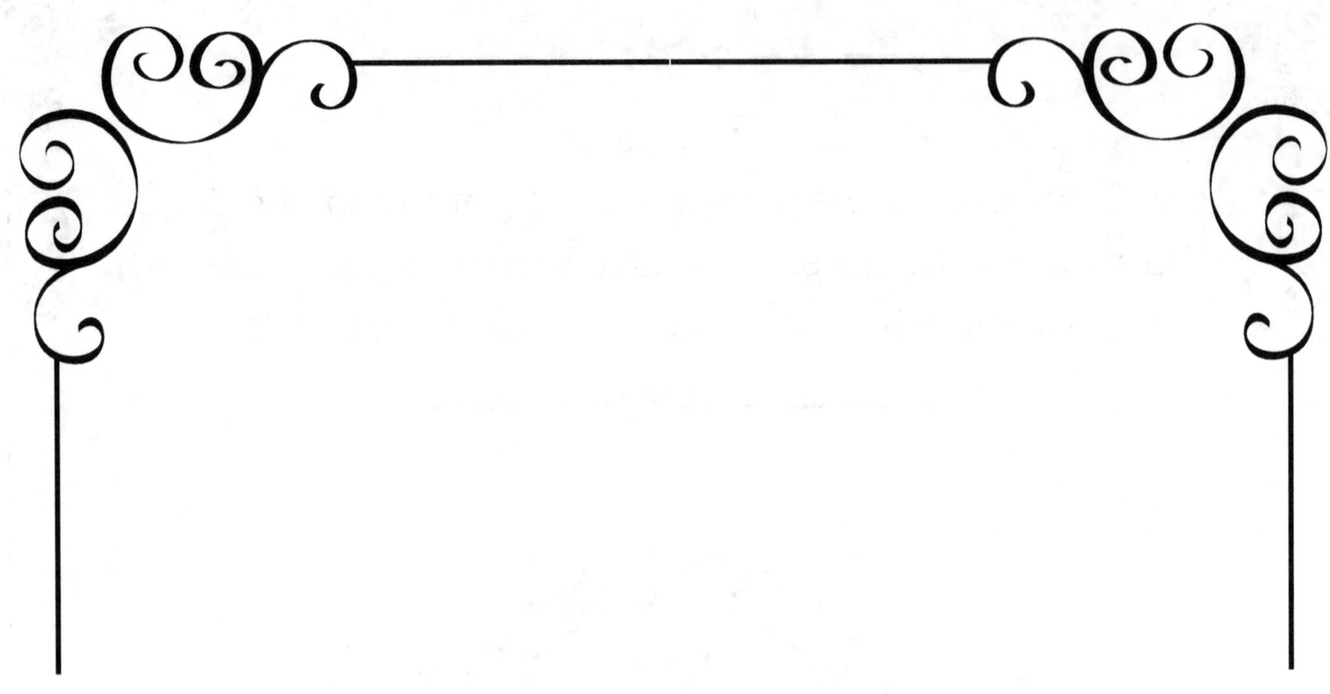

Every sober day
is a step
towards a
brighter future.

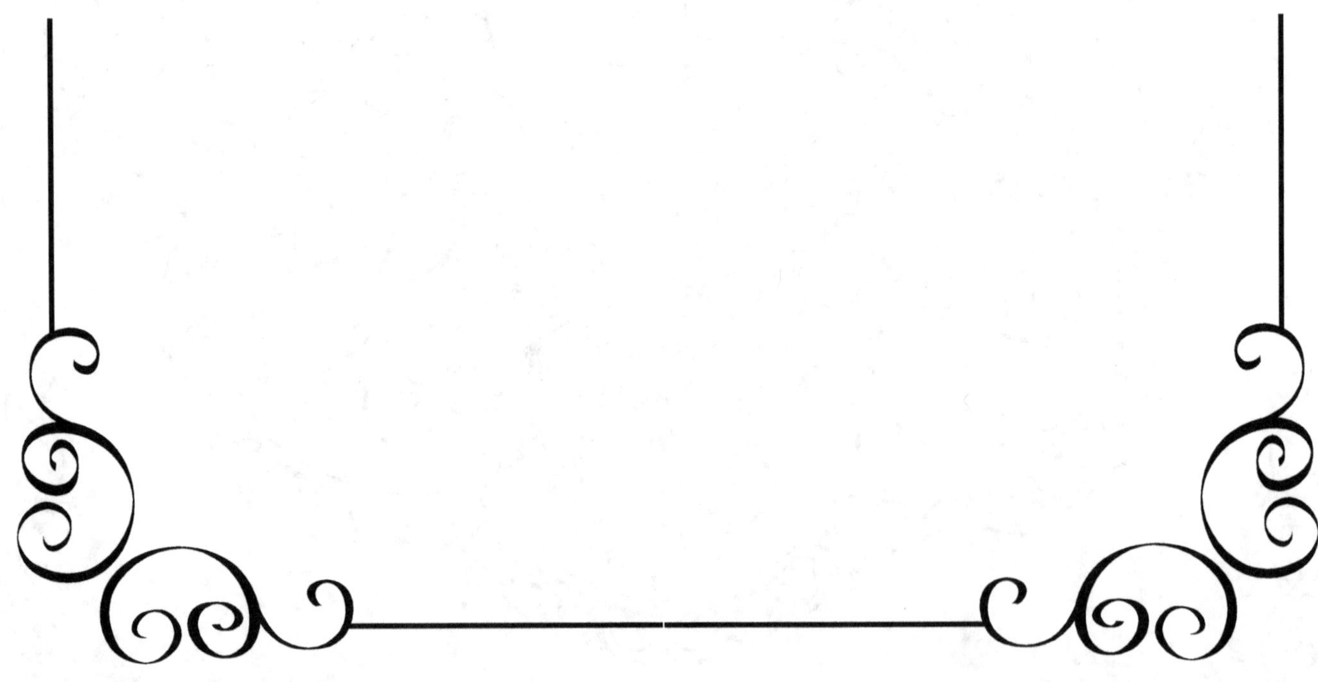

*Exercise:
Choose bright and vibrant colors as you color the
page. With each stroke, visualize your future
becoming brighter and more filled with hope.

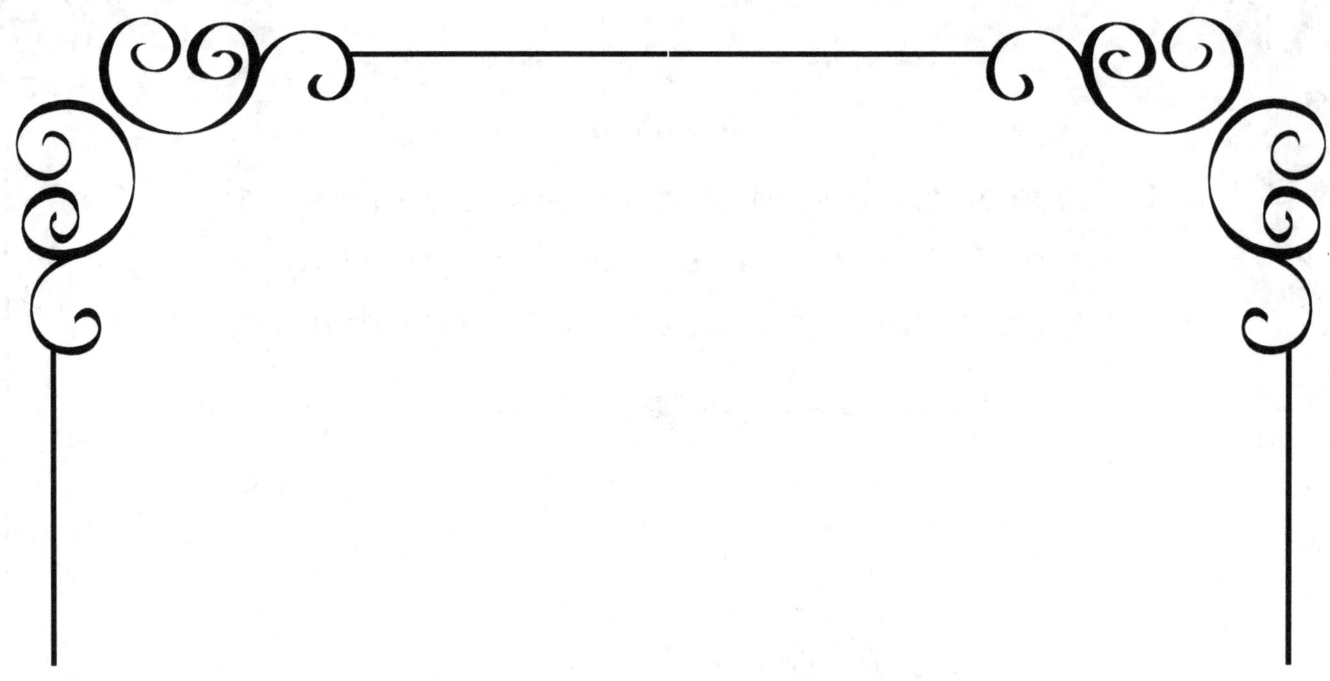

I am stronger
than my addiction.

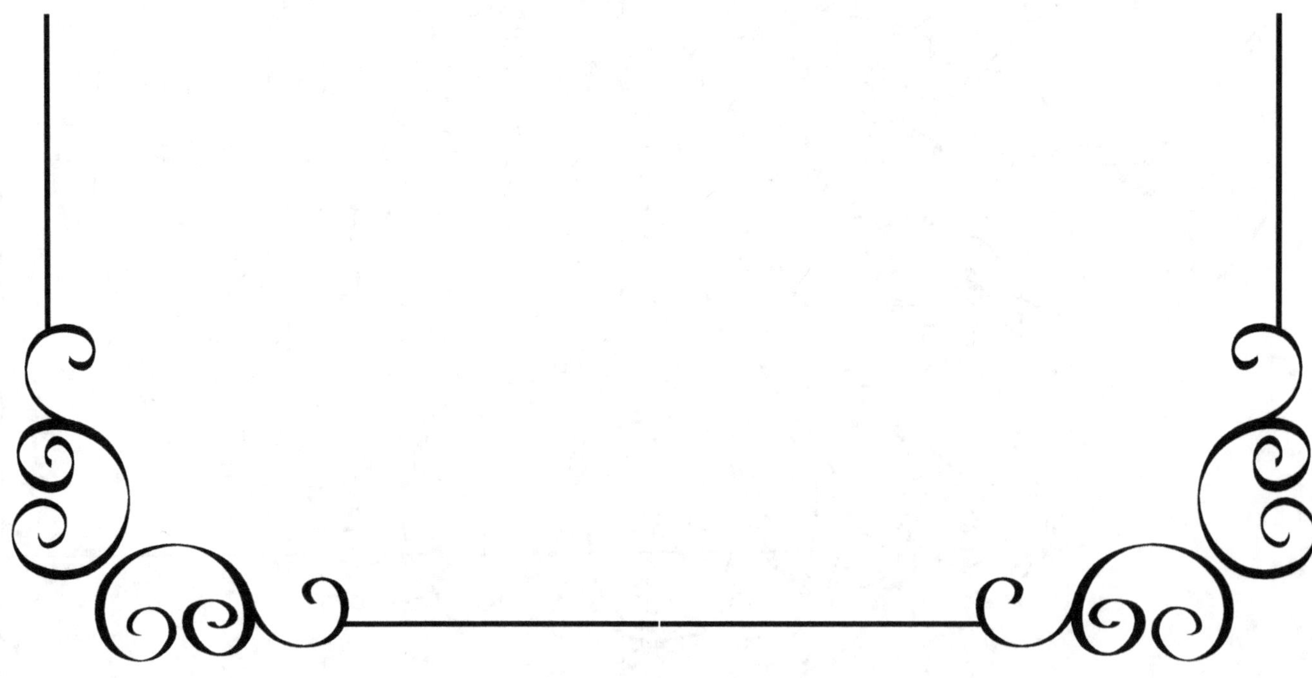

*Exercise:
Use bold and confident lines while coloring. Feel the
strength in your hand as you color, symbolizing
your inner strength to overcome addiction.

I take it one day
at a time,
one step closer
to healing.

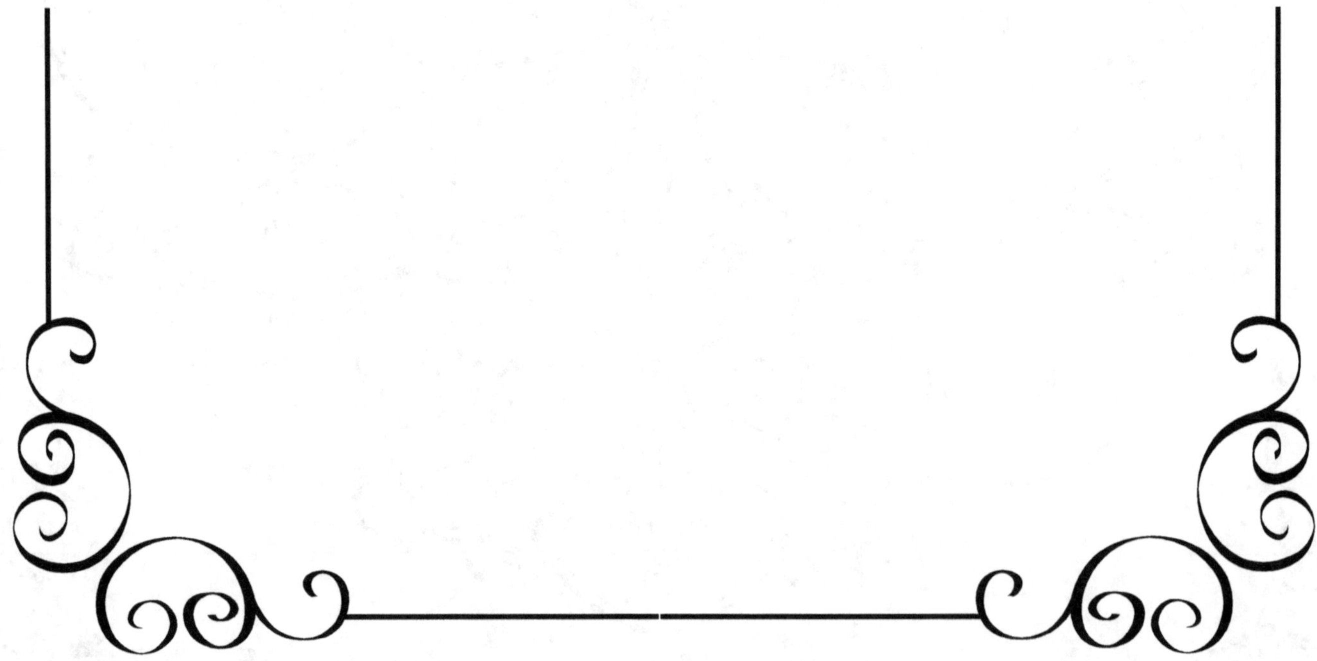

*Exercise:
Practice mindful coloring, focusing on one section
at a time, mirroring your approach to recovery.

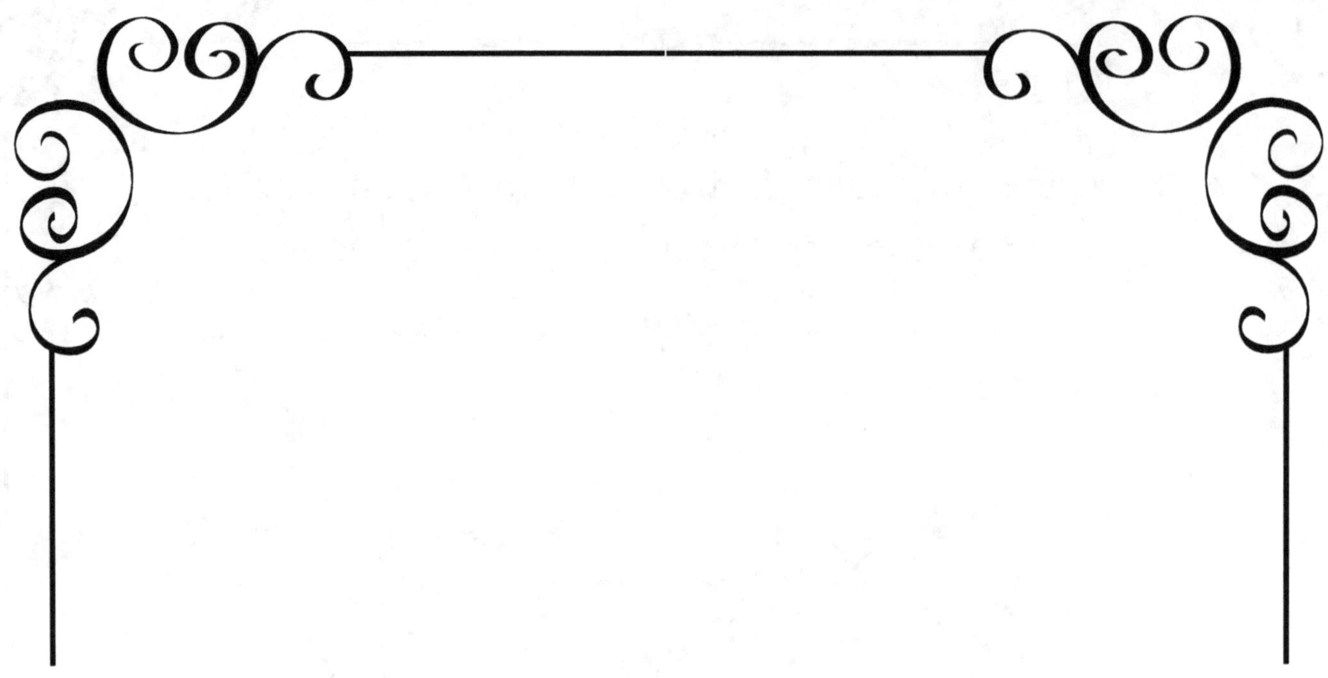

I color my sobriety,
one stroke at a time.

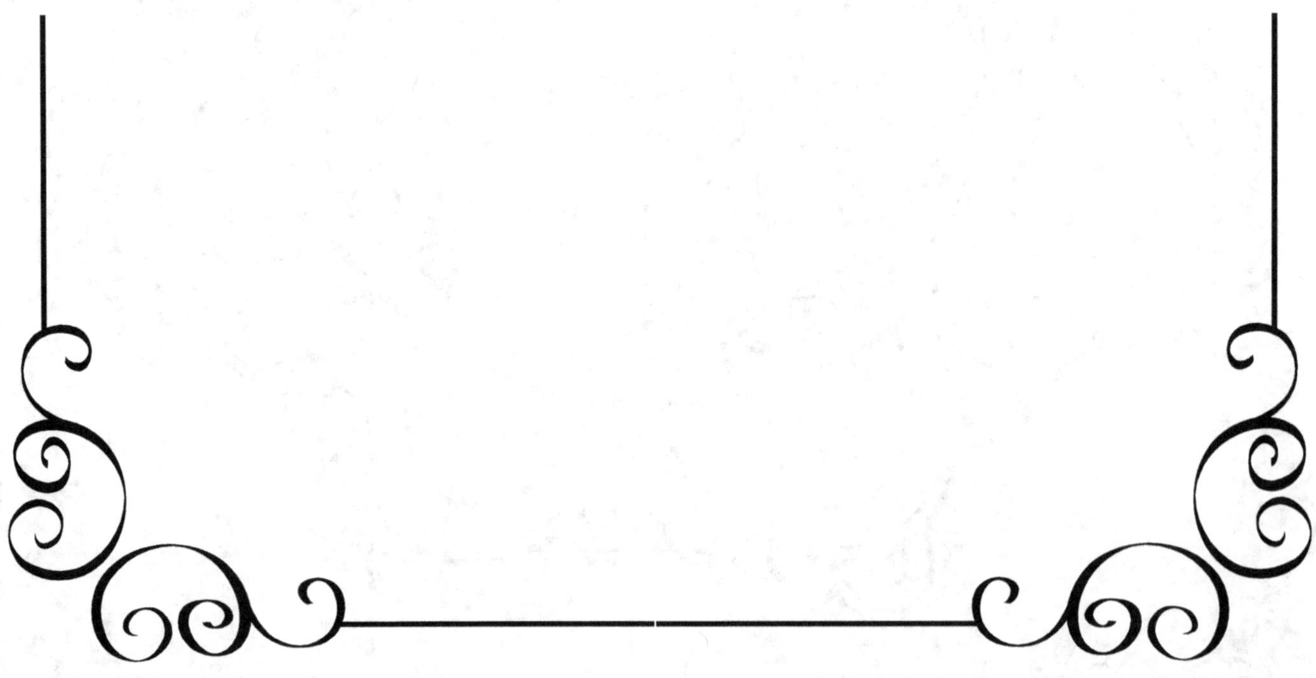

*Exercise:
As you color, focus on the act of coloring itself. With each stroke, remind yourself of your commitment to sobriety and the progress you are making. Each stroke is a small step forward on your journey toward a healthier and alcohol-free life.

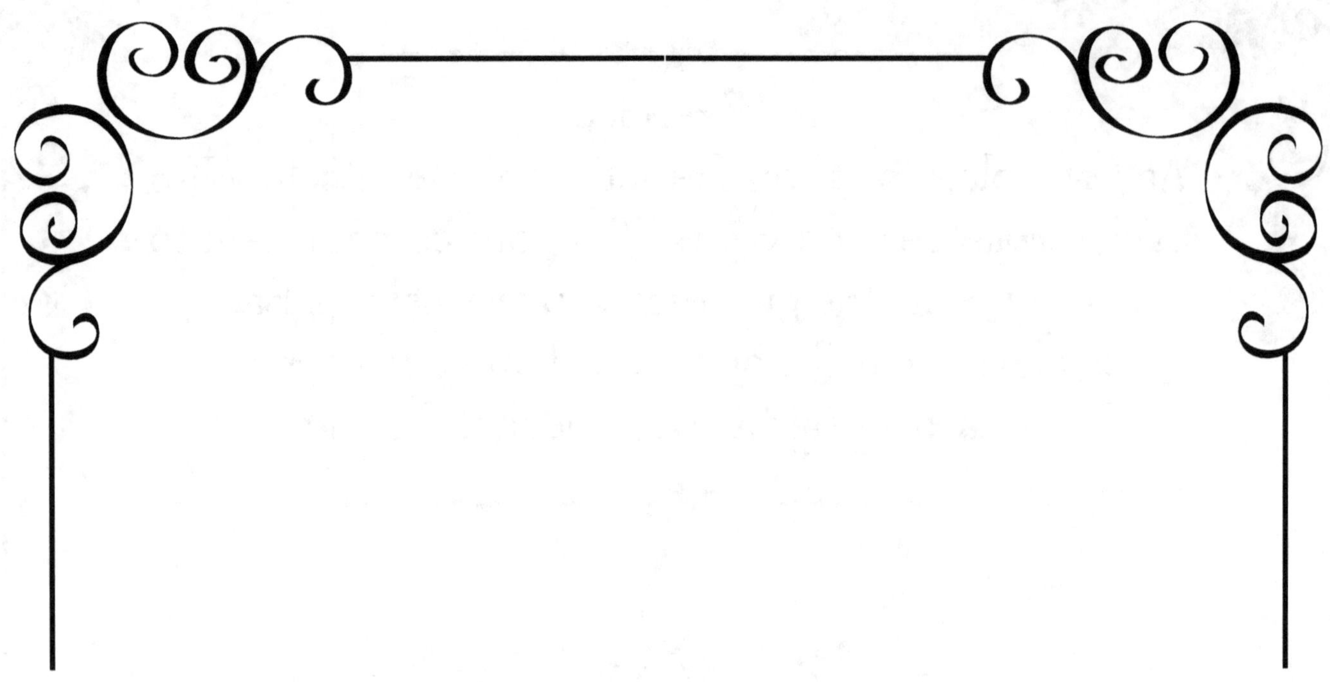

One day at a time,
one step closer to healing.

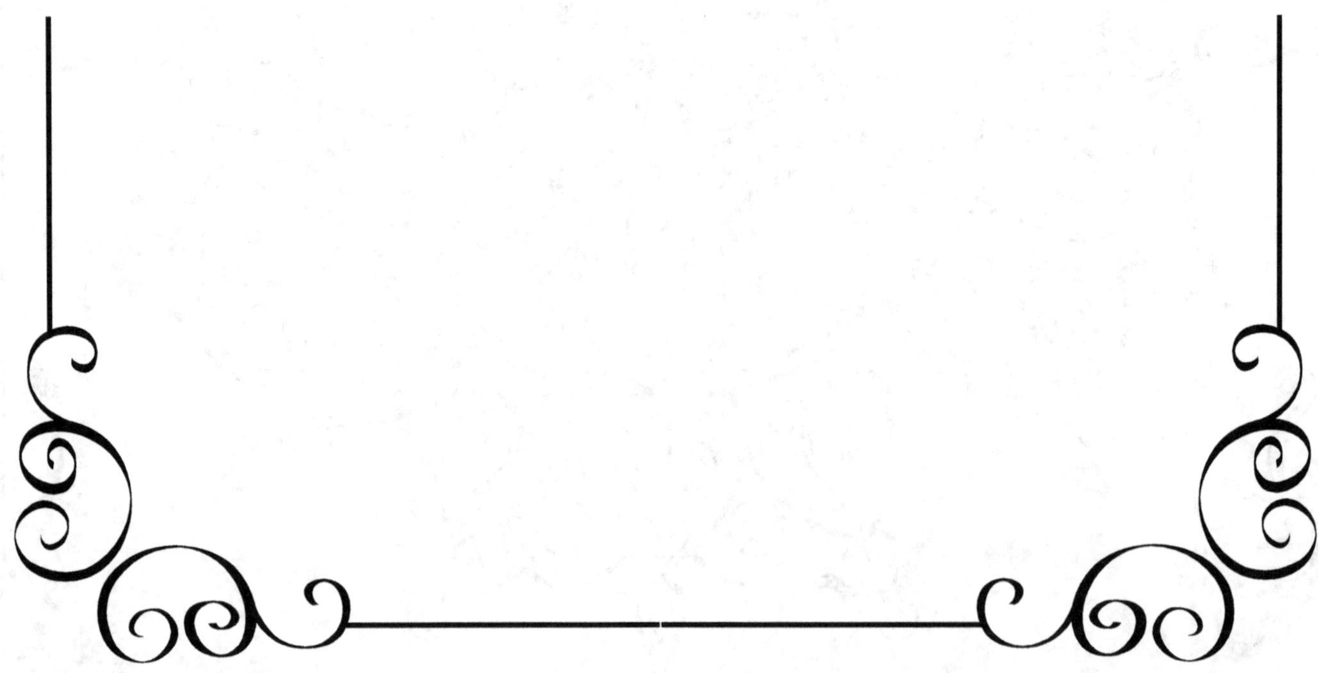

*Exercise:
Color the page one section at a time, taking it slowly and mindfully. This exercise represents the idea of taking one day at a time in your journey to healing.

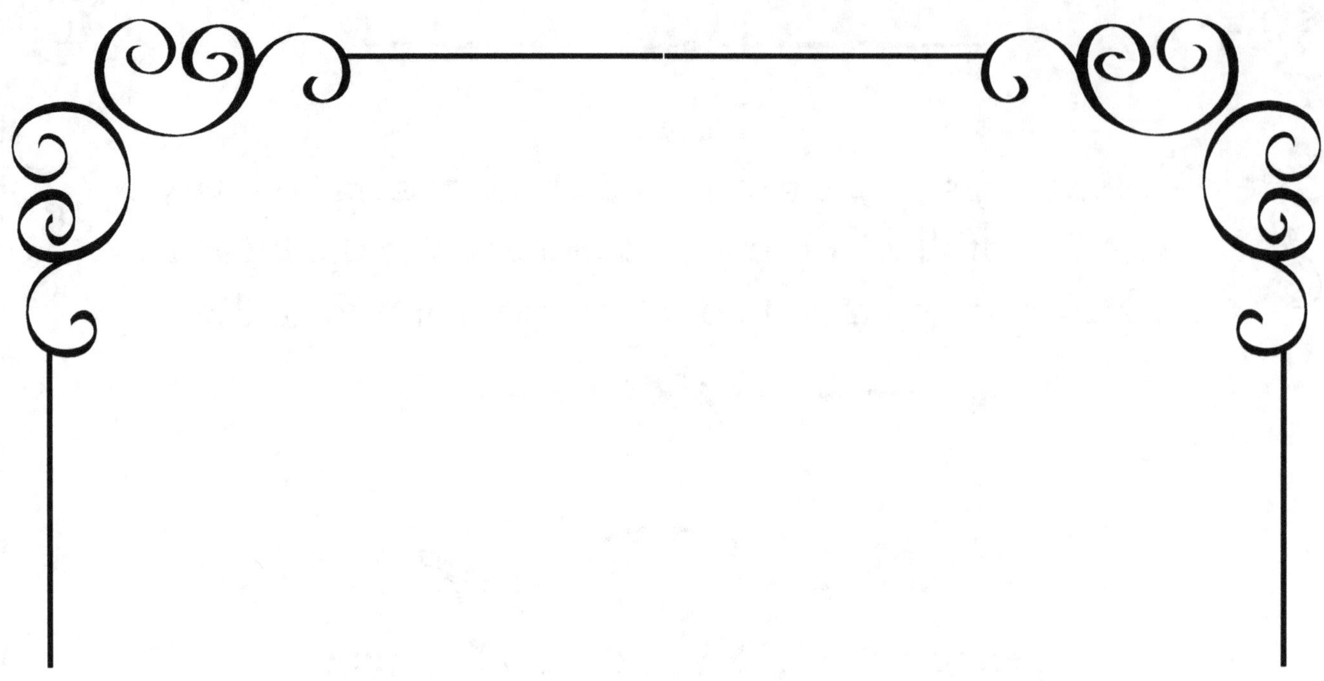

My sober self is my
true self
and I embrace it.

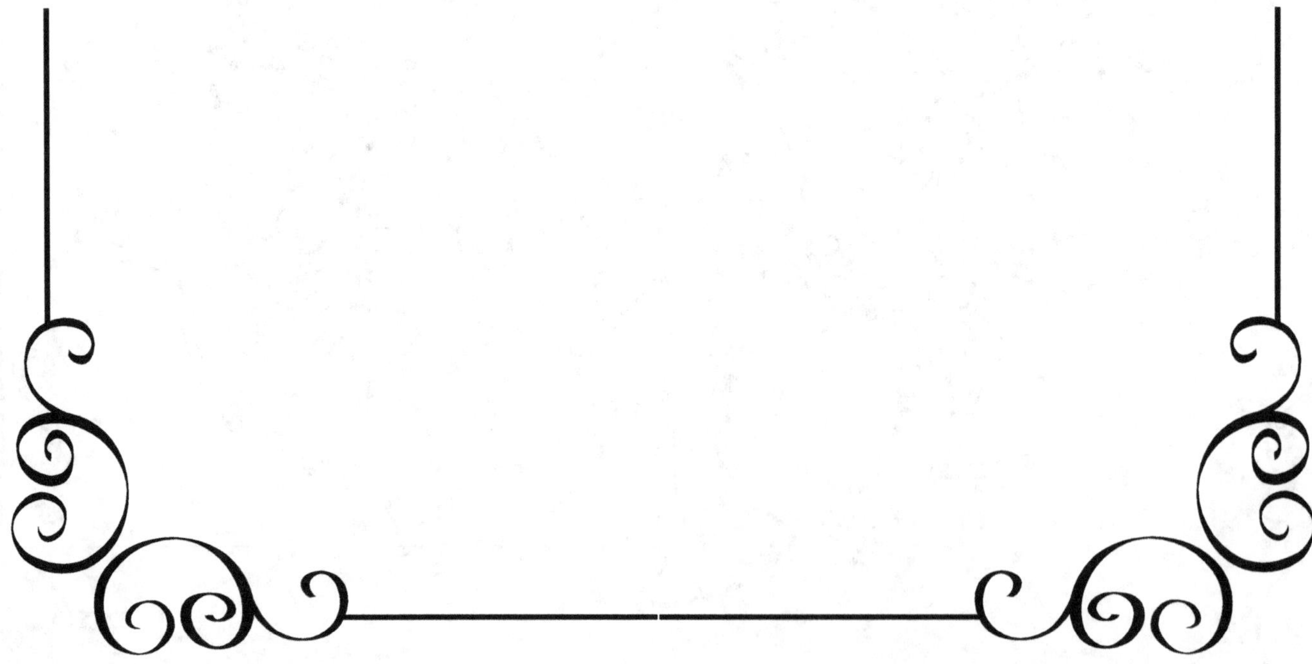

*Exercise:
As you color, visualize your sober self emerging from
the page, embracing you with love and authenticity.

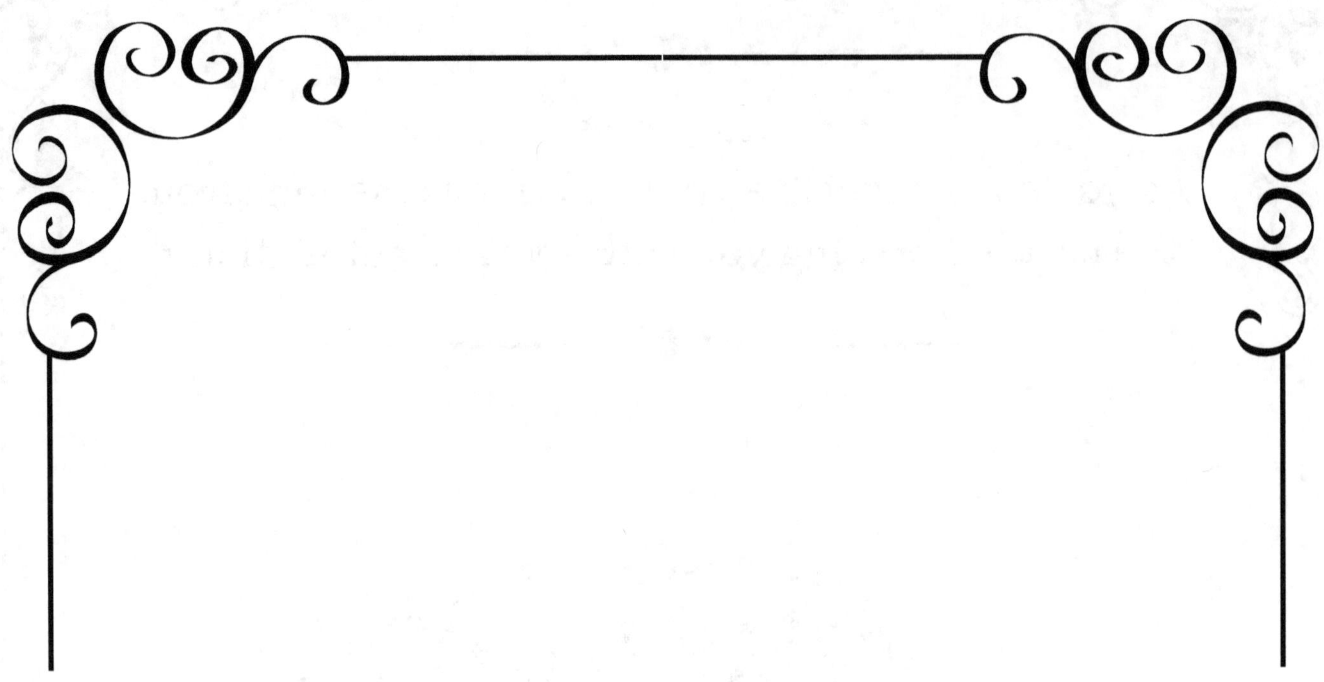

With each sober
moment,
I reclaim my life.

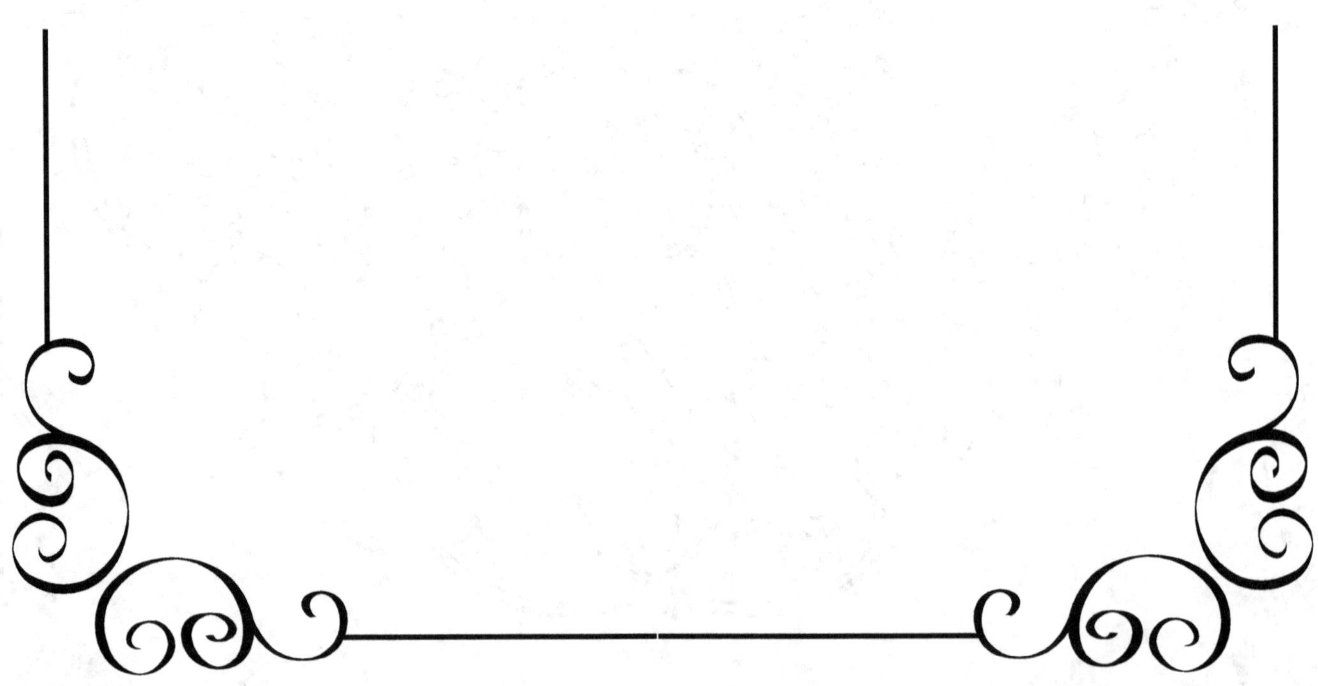

*Exercise:
As you color, see each moment of sobriety as a
piece of a puzzle coming together to form a vibrant,
complete picture of your reclaimed life.

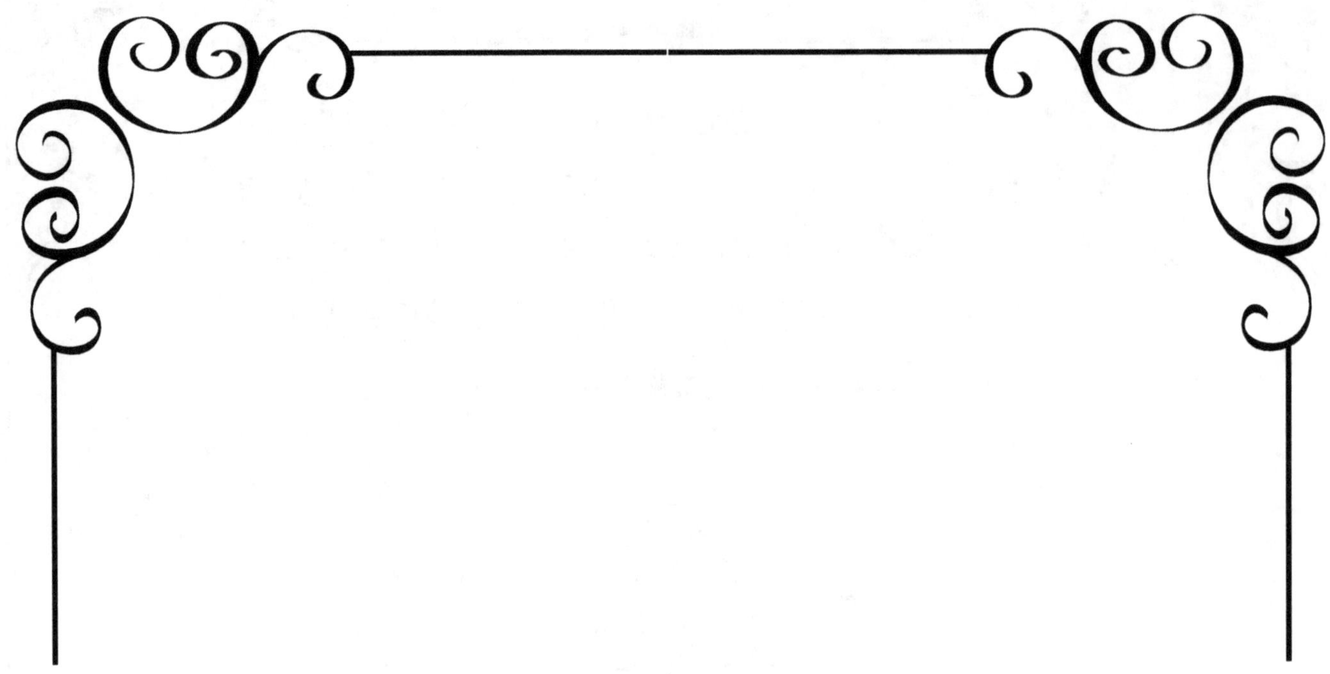

I am worth the
effort.
and happiness.

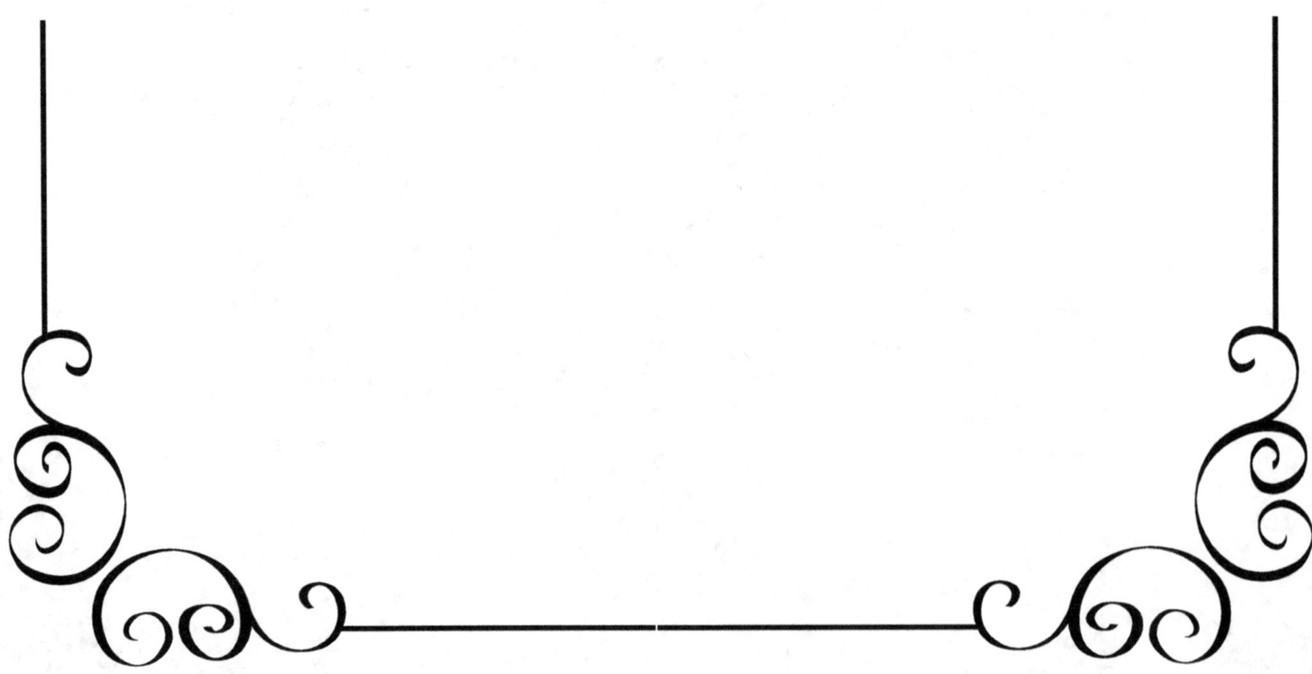

*Exercise:
As you color, focus on the affirmation that you
deserve good health and happiness in your life.

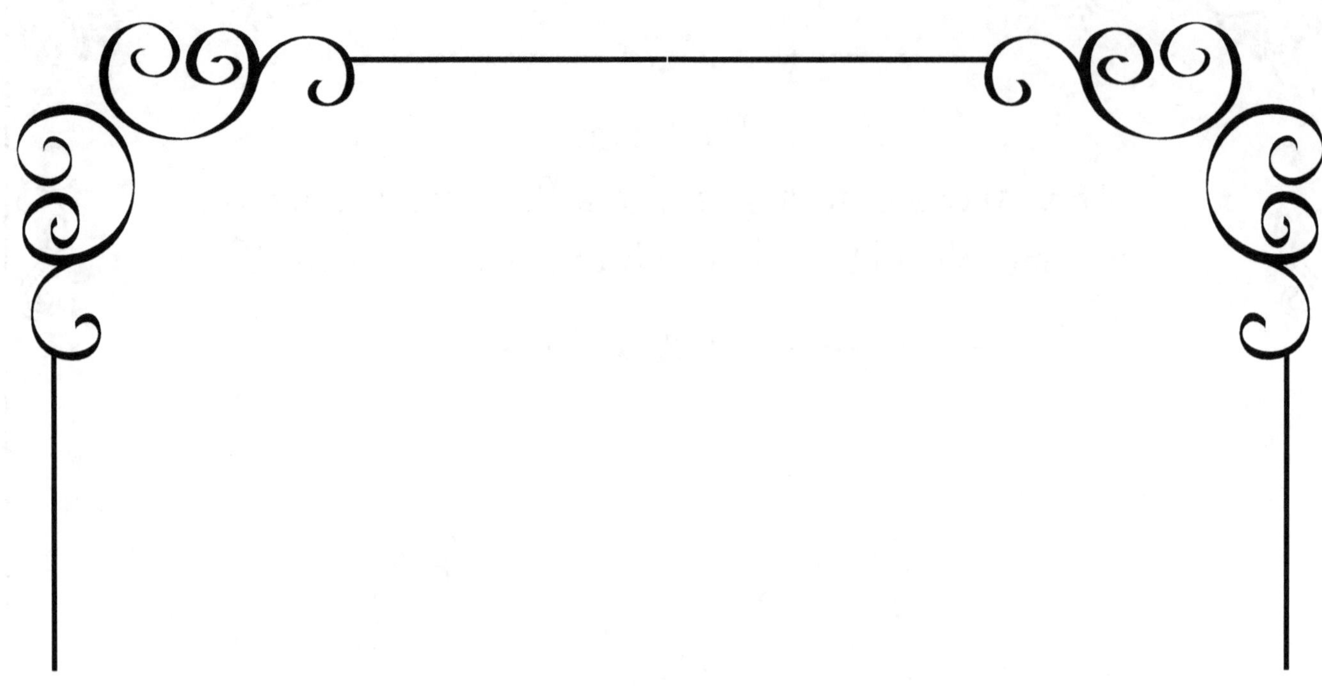

Sobriety is the
greatest gift
I can give myself.

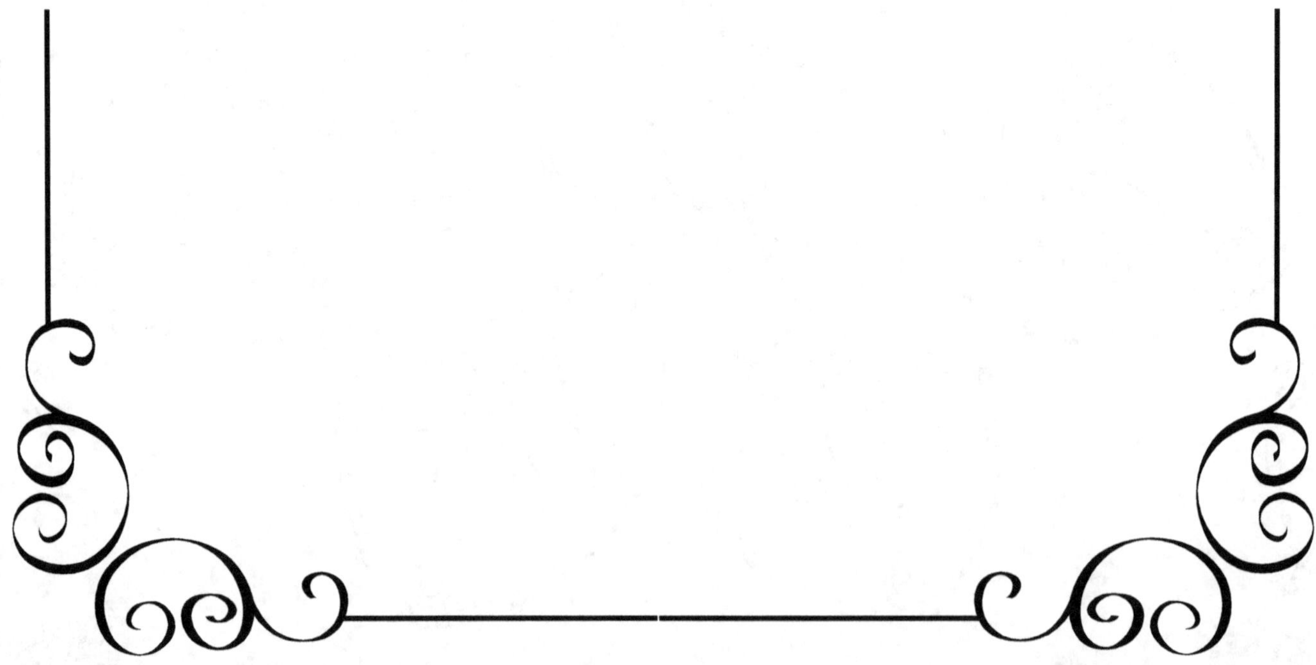

*Exercise:
Imagine the colors on the page forming a beautifully
wrapped gift box. As you color, you're unwrapping
the gift of sobriety for yourself.

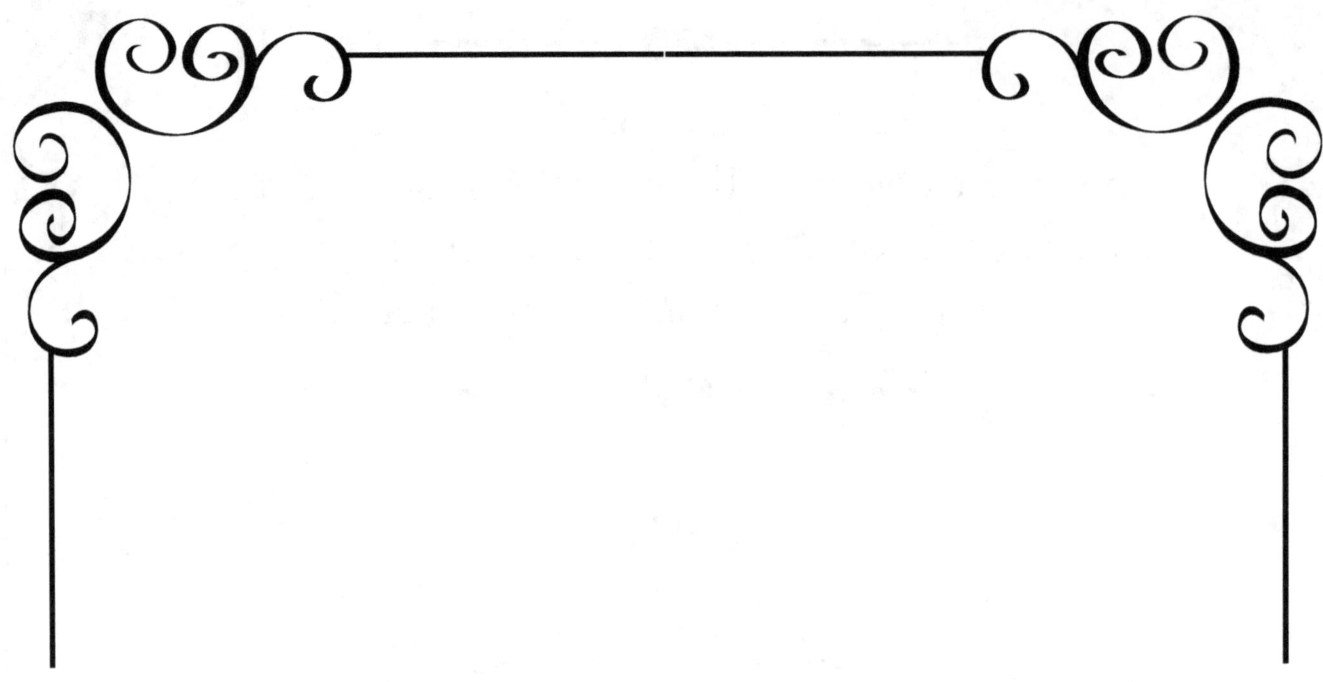

I recognize that
healing
begins from within.

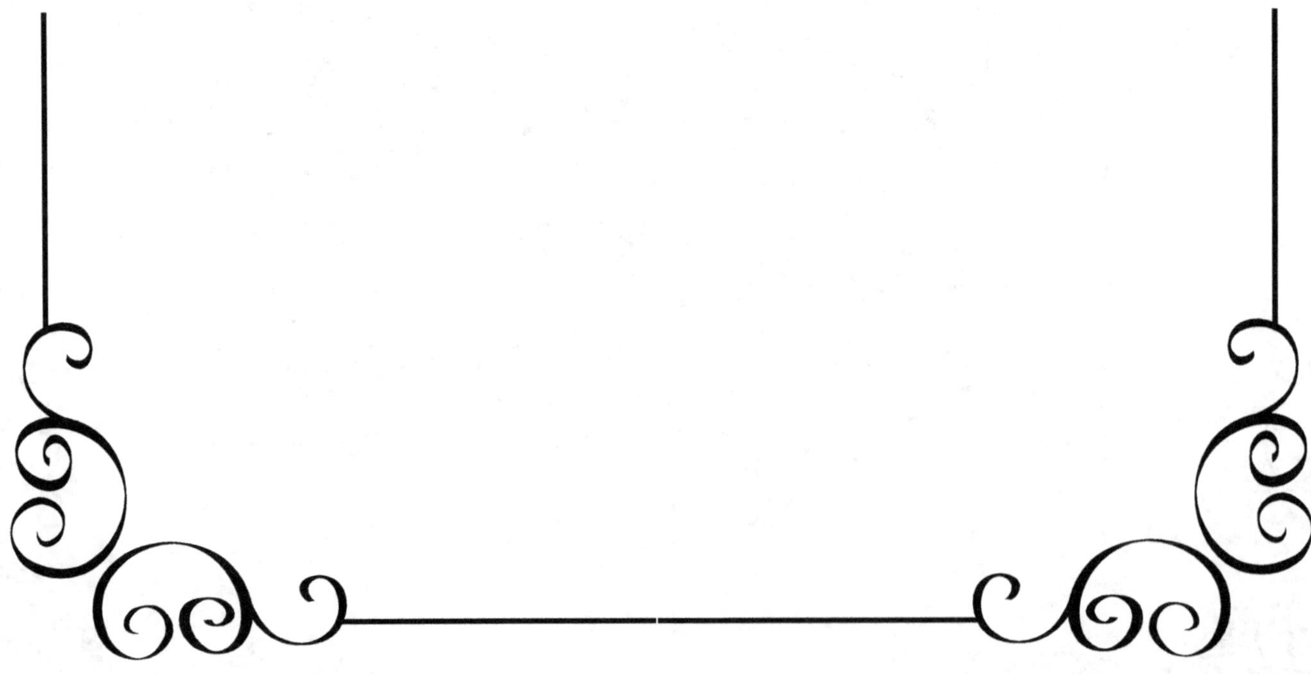

*Exercise:
Begin coloring from the center of the mandala,
symbolizing the start of your inner healing journey.
Let the colors radiate outward as your healing spreads.

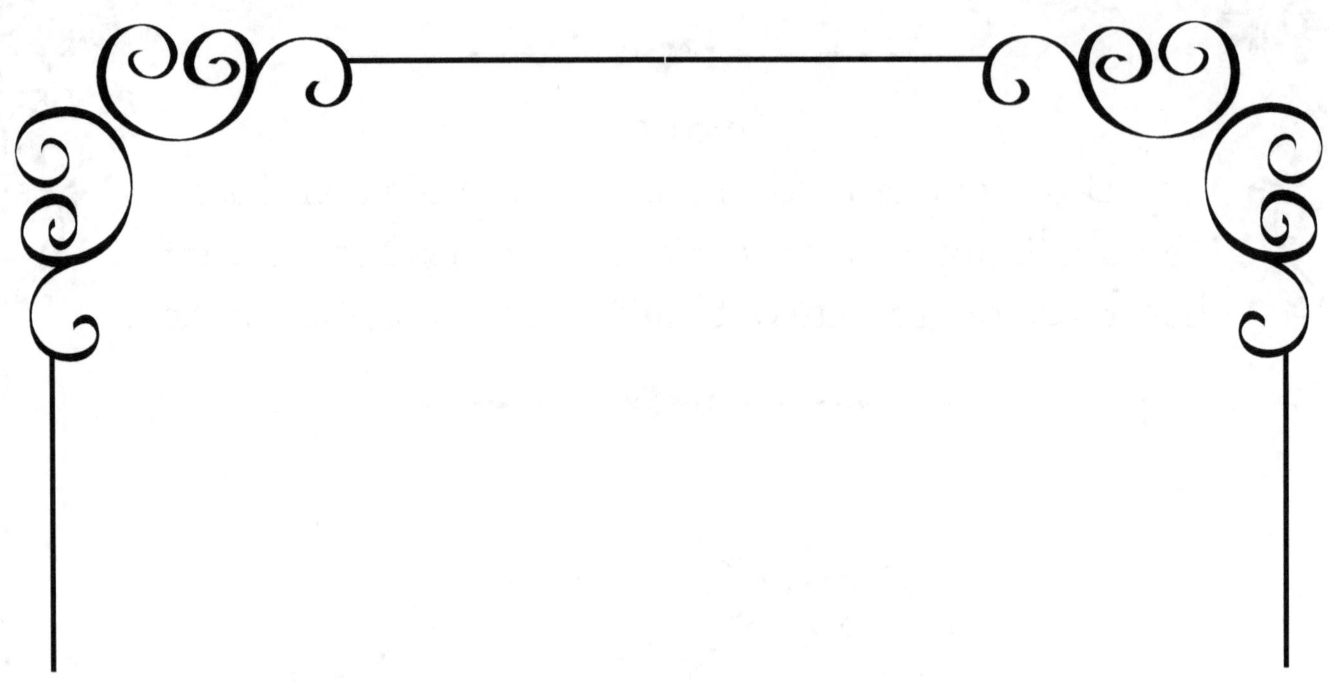

I have the power
to rewrite my story.

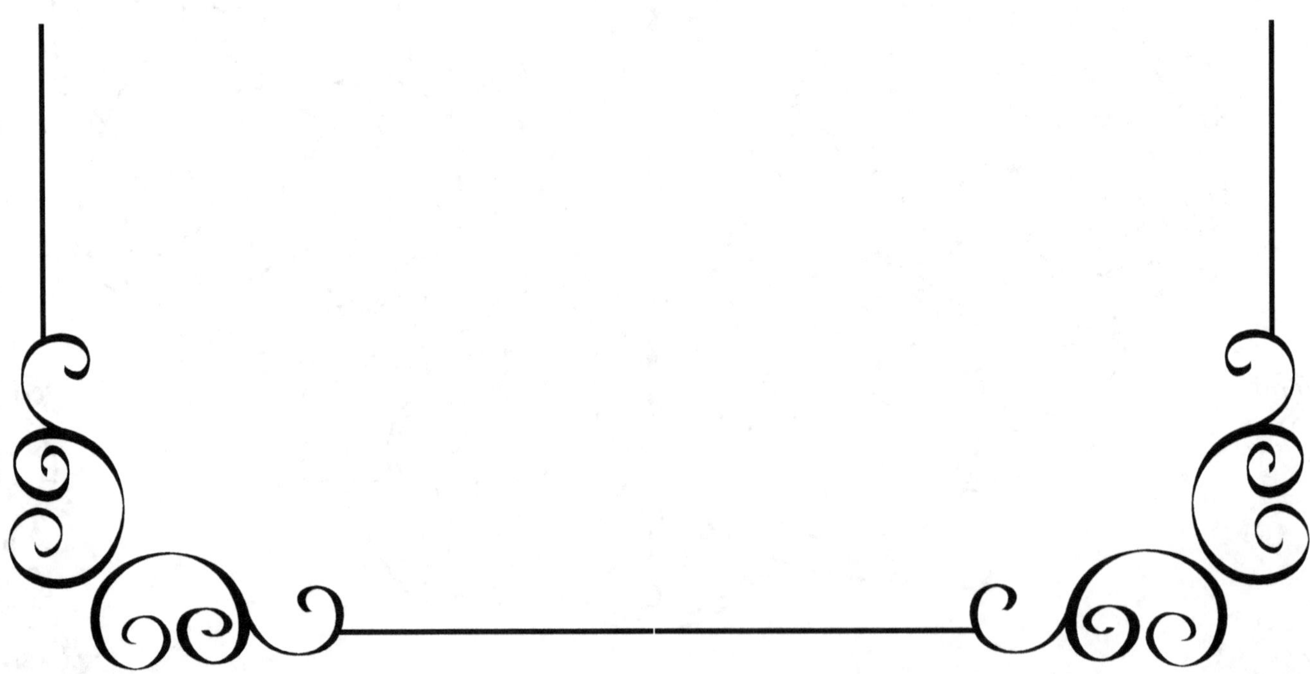

*Exercise:
As you color, see the page as a blank canvas for your new story. Each color choice is a brushstroke that contributes to the masterpiece of your rewritten life.

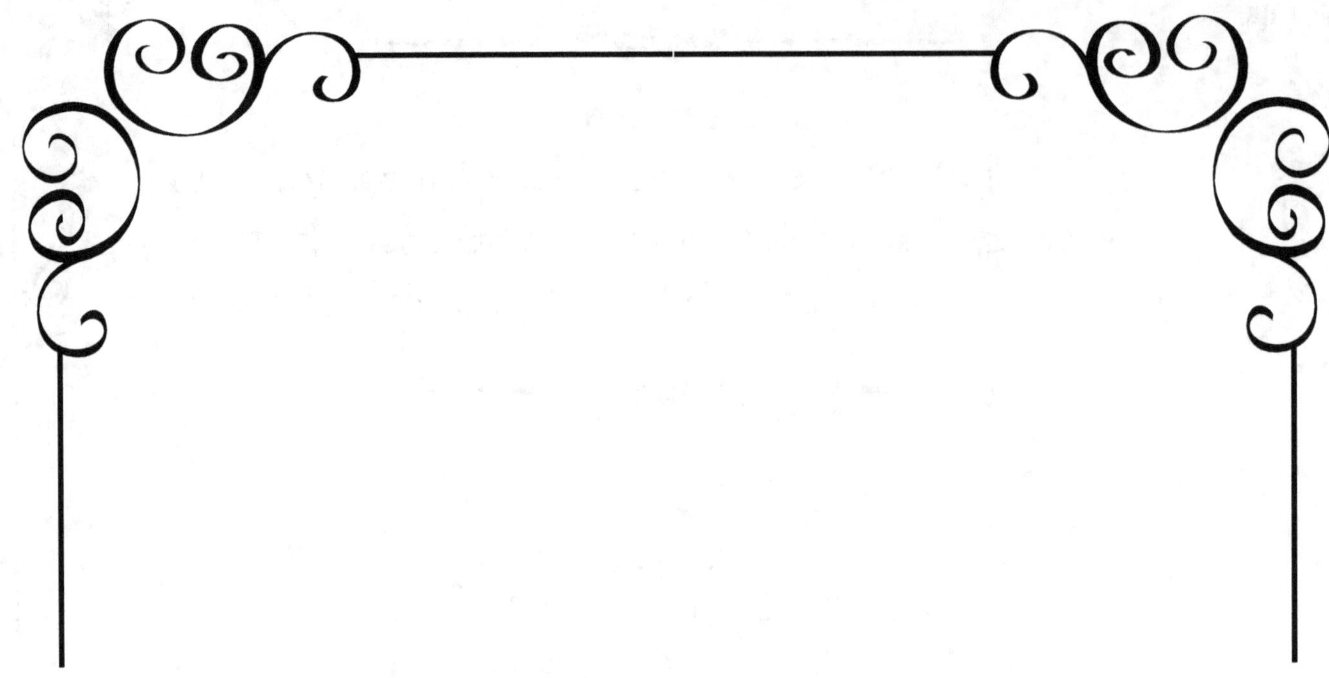

I uncover inner peace
with every stroke.

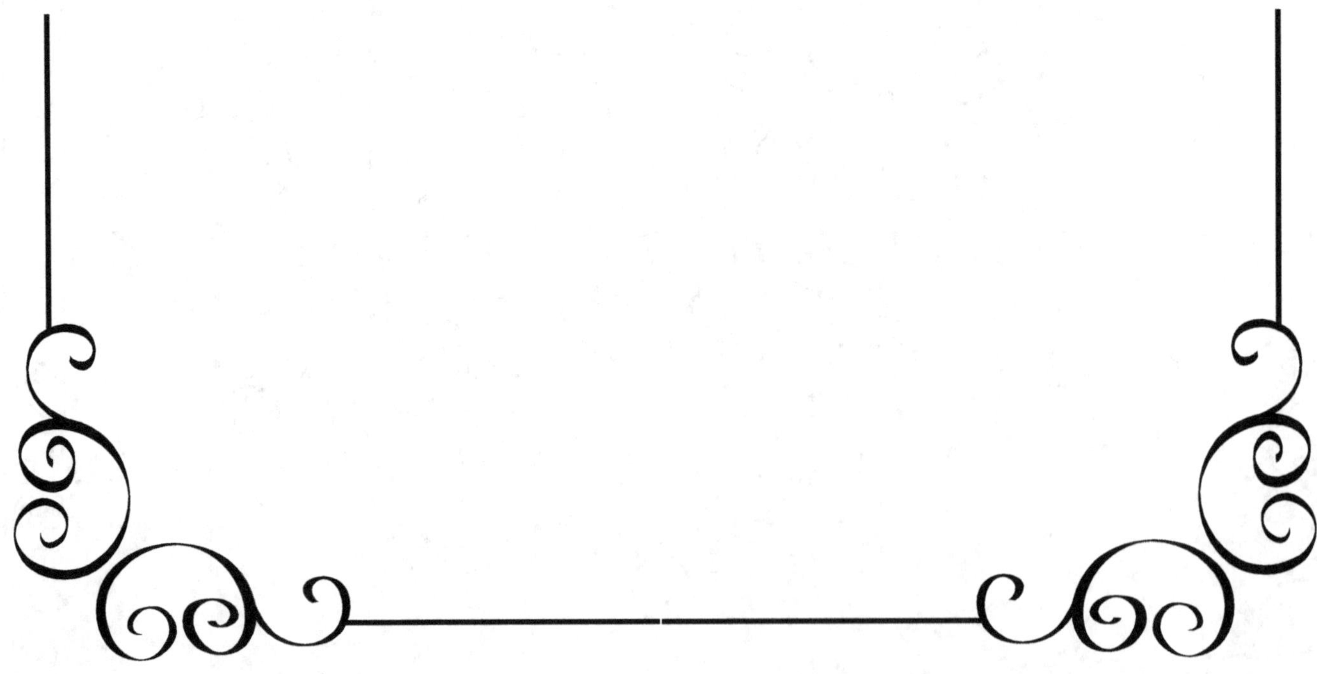

*Exercise:
Imagine inner peace as a calming color that spreads
across the page as you color.

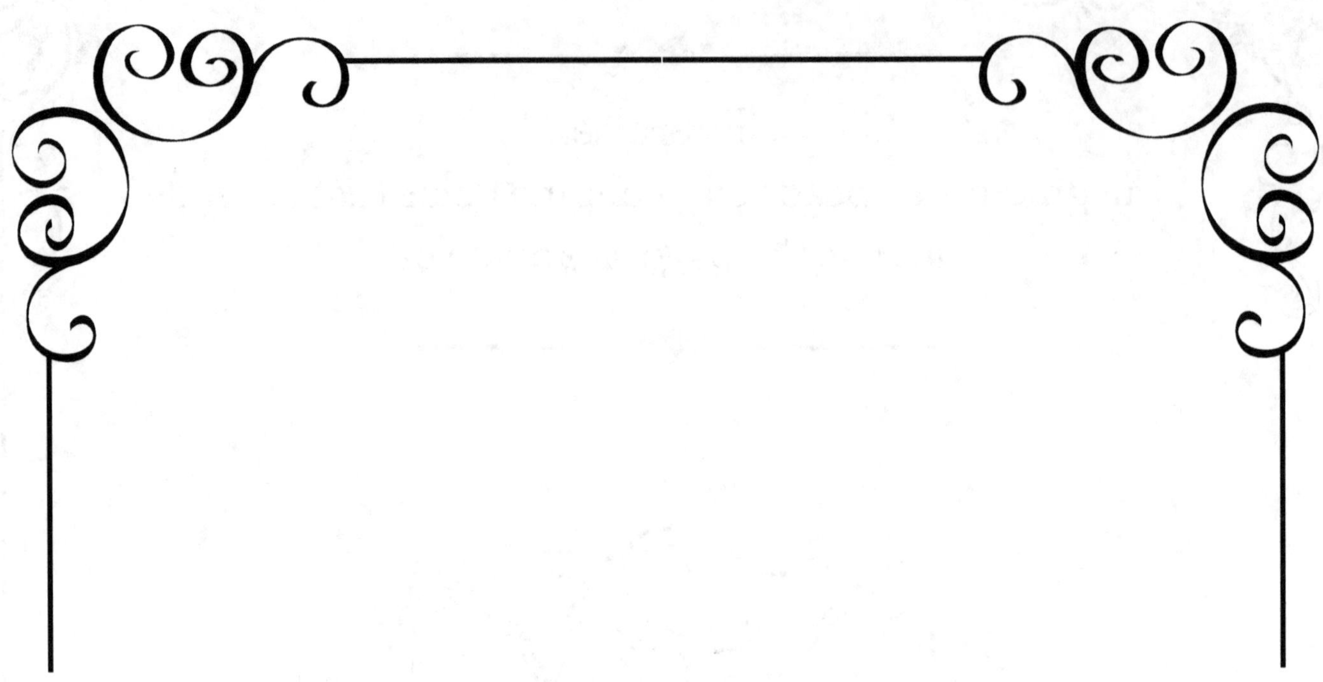

I paint my brighter
tomorrow
with colors of recovery.

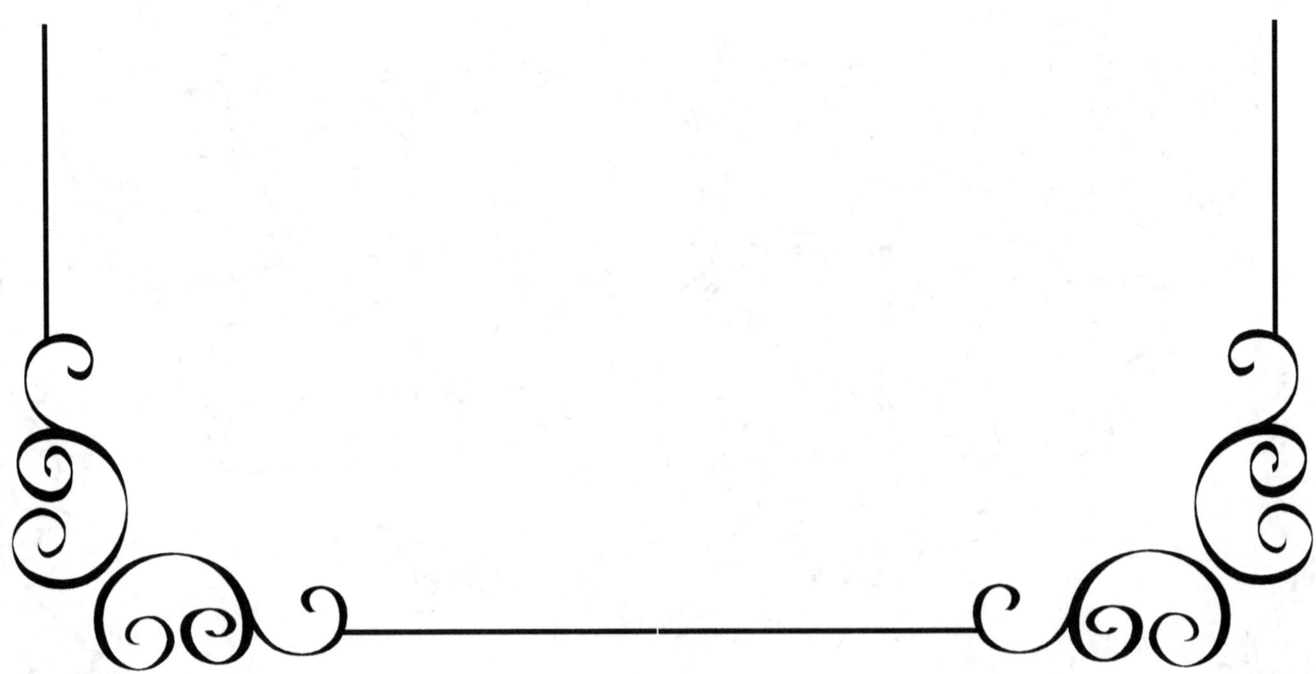

*Exercise:
Picture the page as a canvas where you paint a
brighter future with your chosen colors.

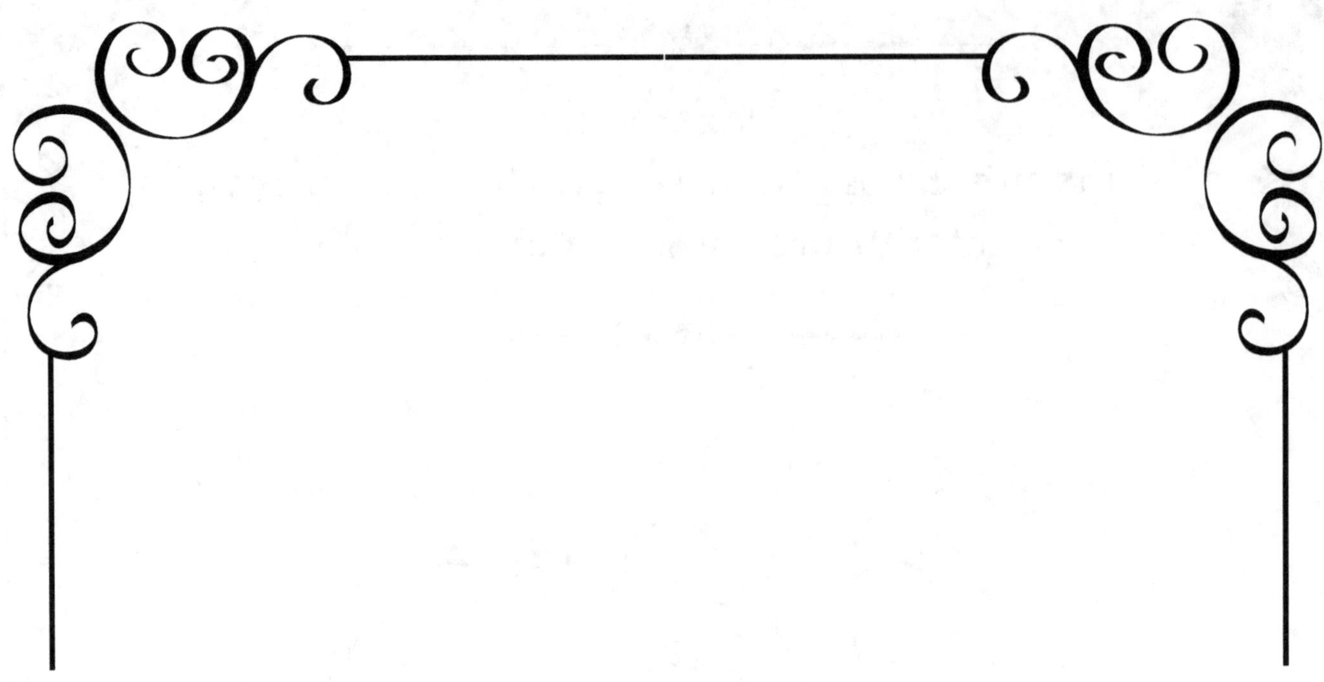

I express my inner
transformation
through colors.

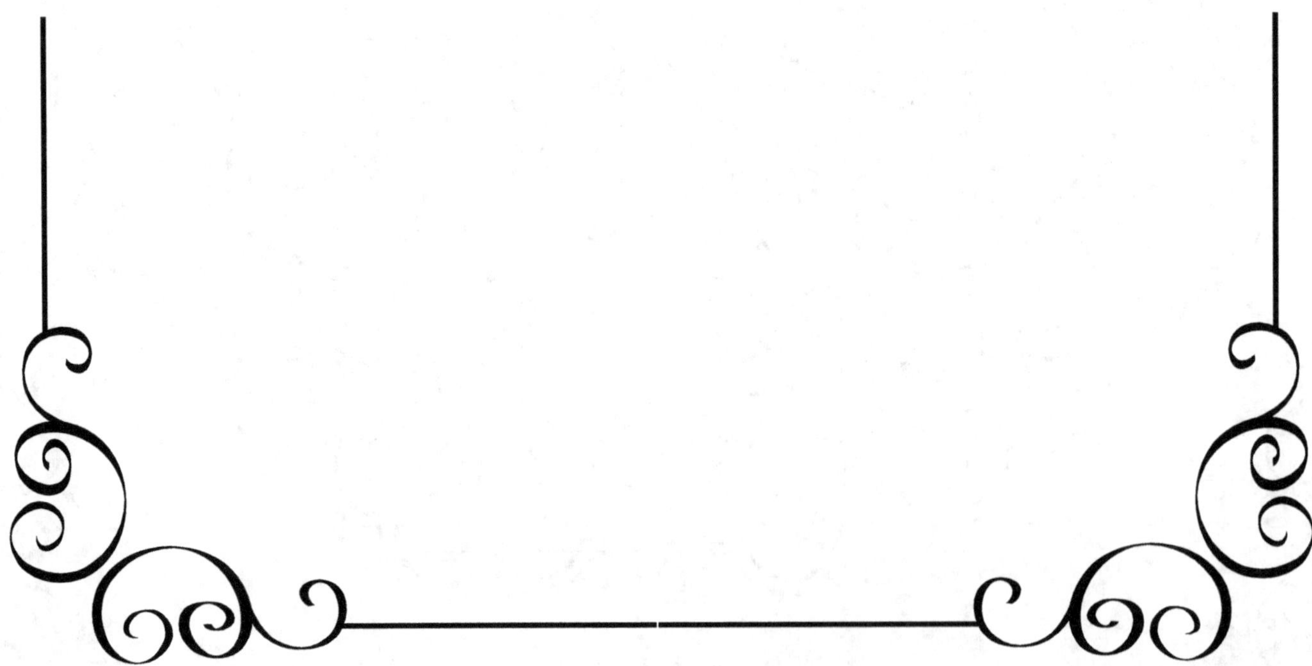

*Exercise:
Use colors to symbolize the different facets of your
inner transformation, letting them shine on the page.

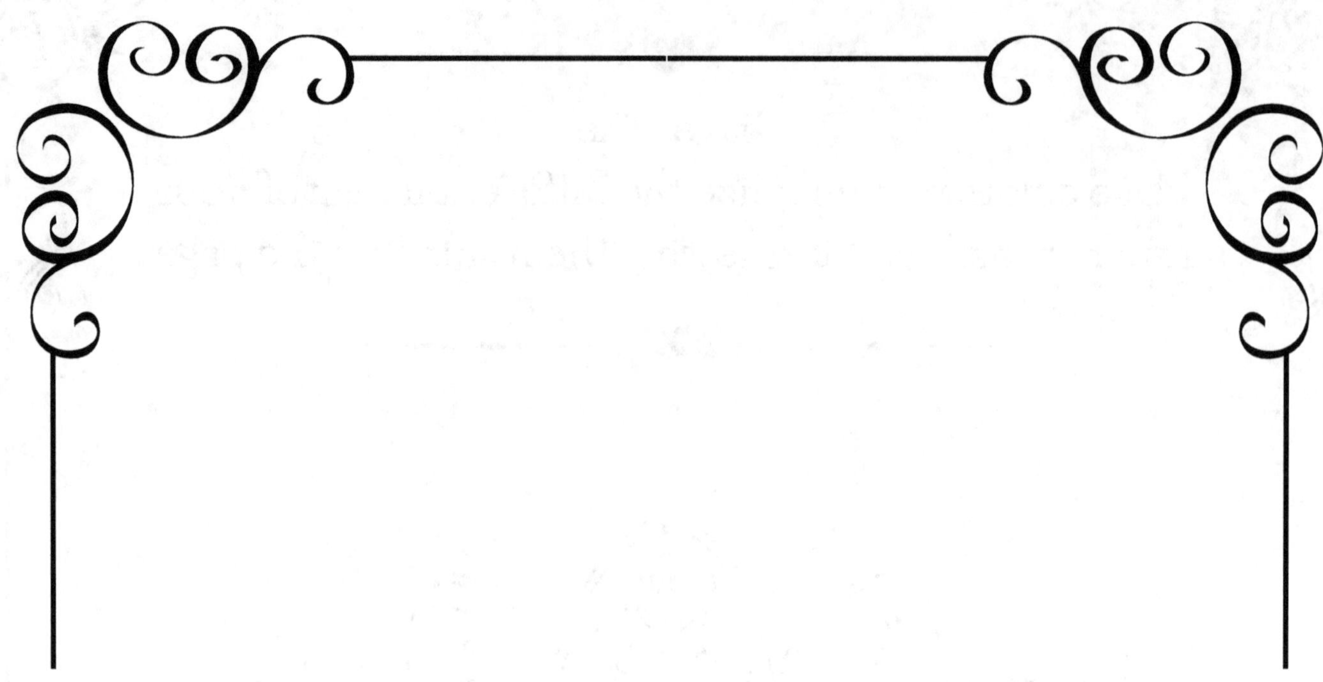

I hold the palette of
hope
for my journey.

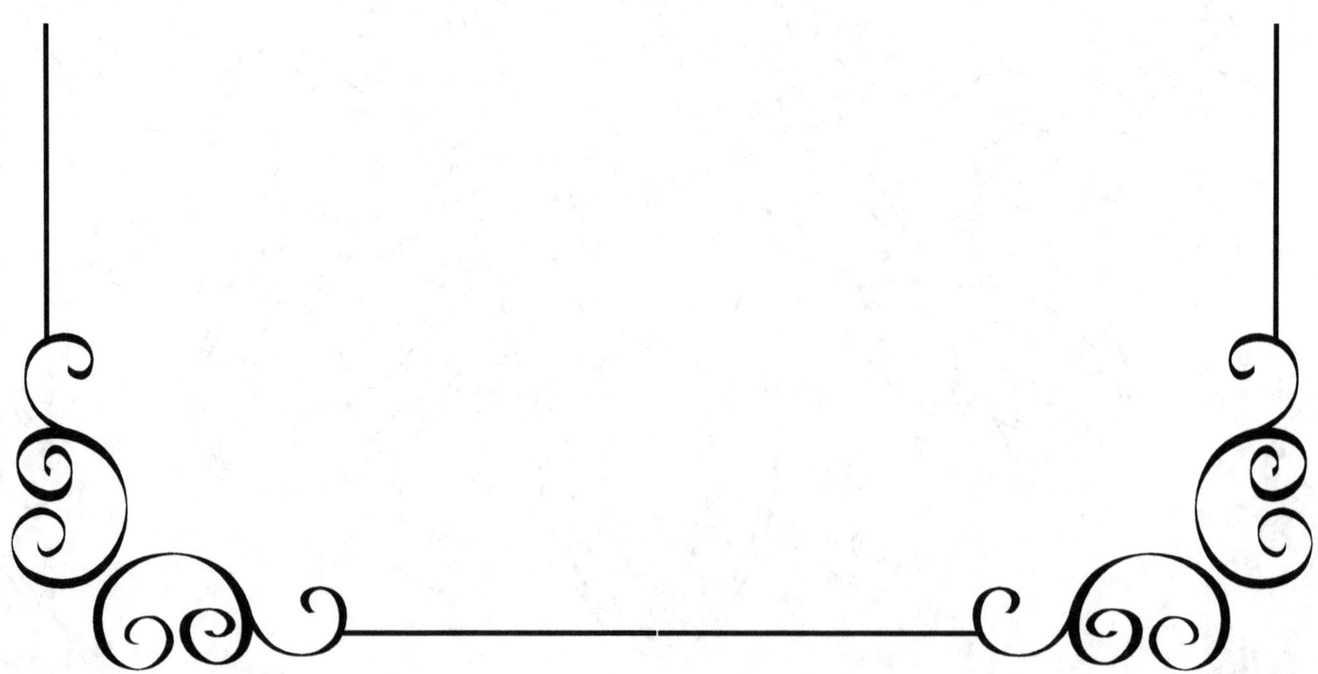

*Exercise:
Envision your palette filled with vibrant colors of
hope, which you use to breathe life into your page.

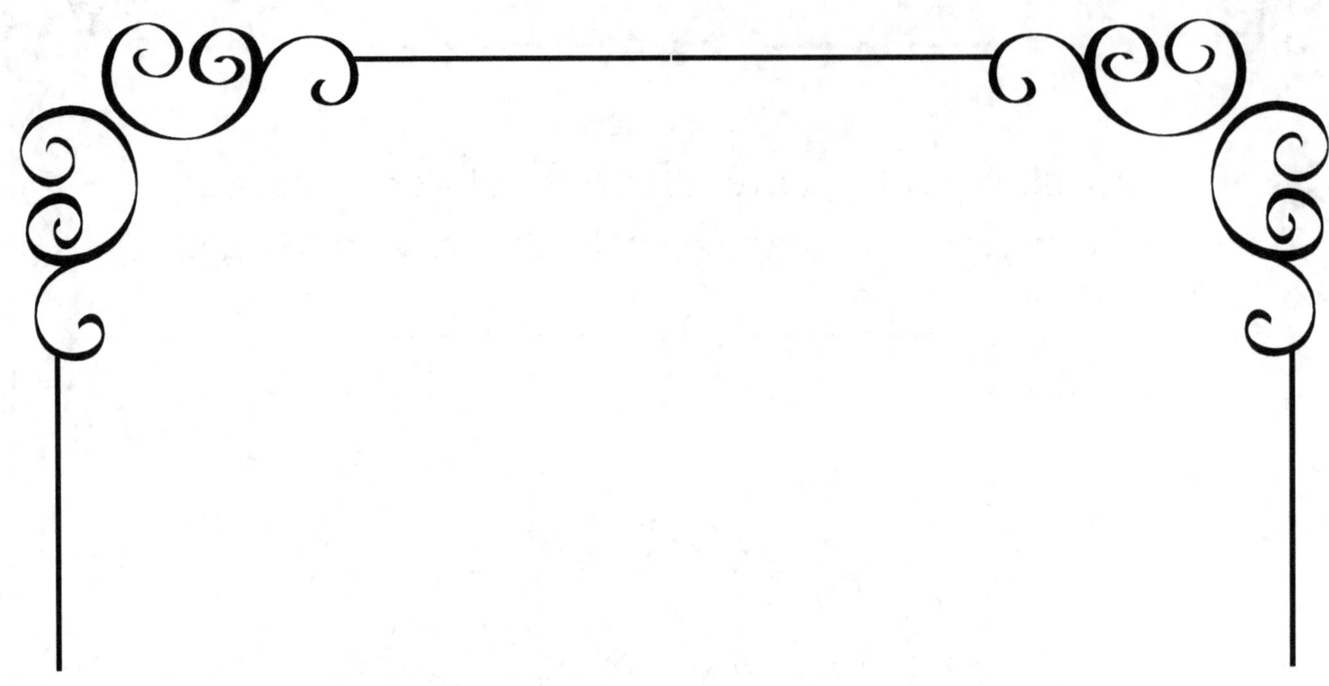

I blend my colors,
symbolizing my
blended future.

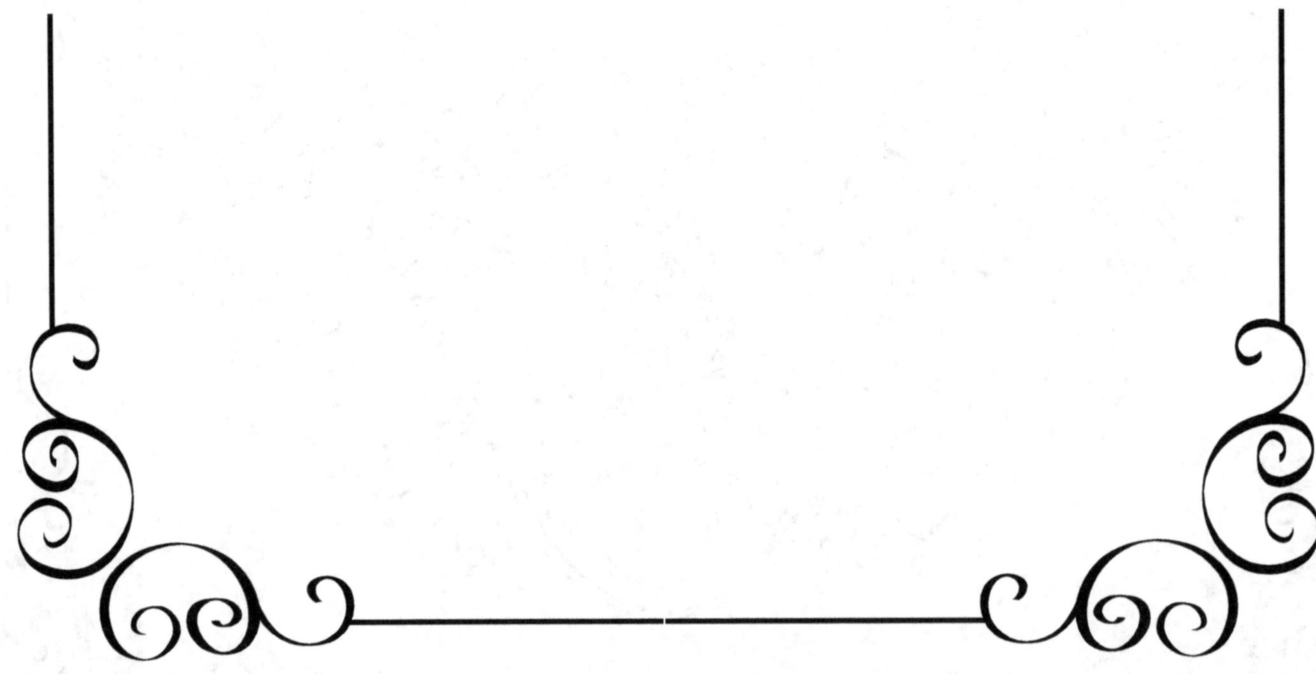

*Exercise:
Experiment with blending colors on the page,
symbolizing the blending of your future in sobriety.

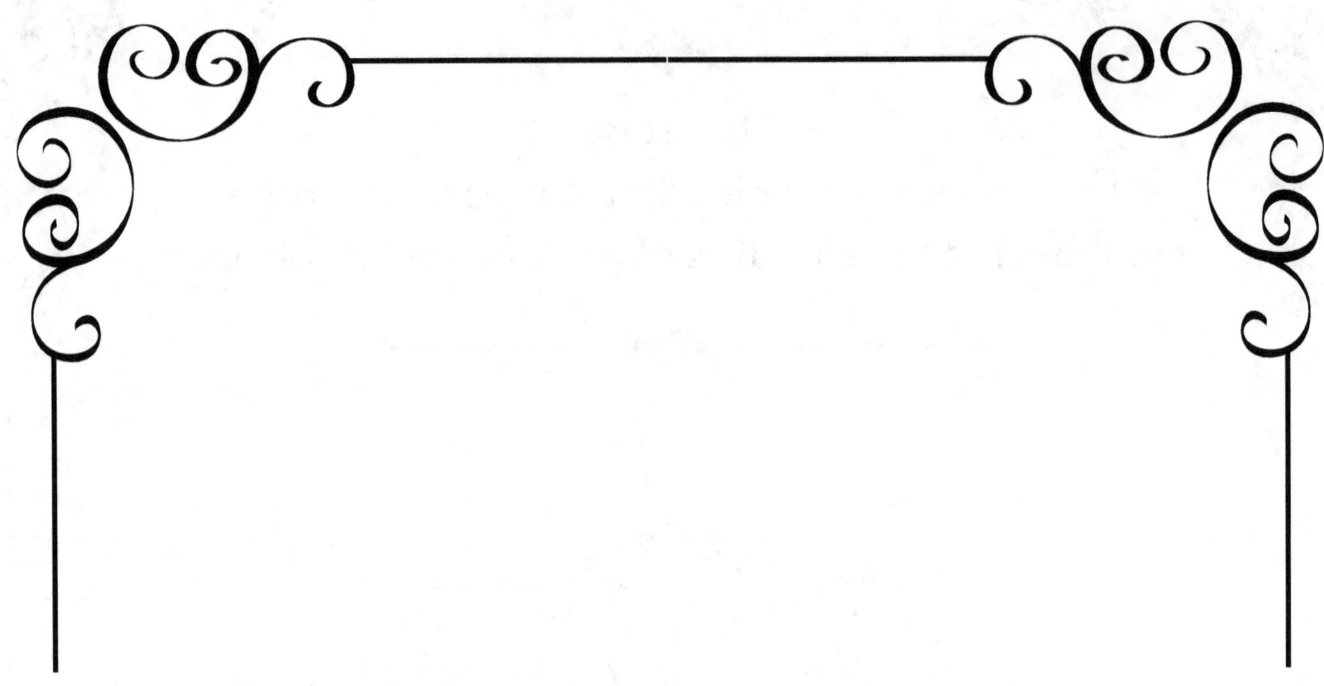

I acknowledge
my inner changes
with every hue.

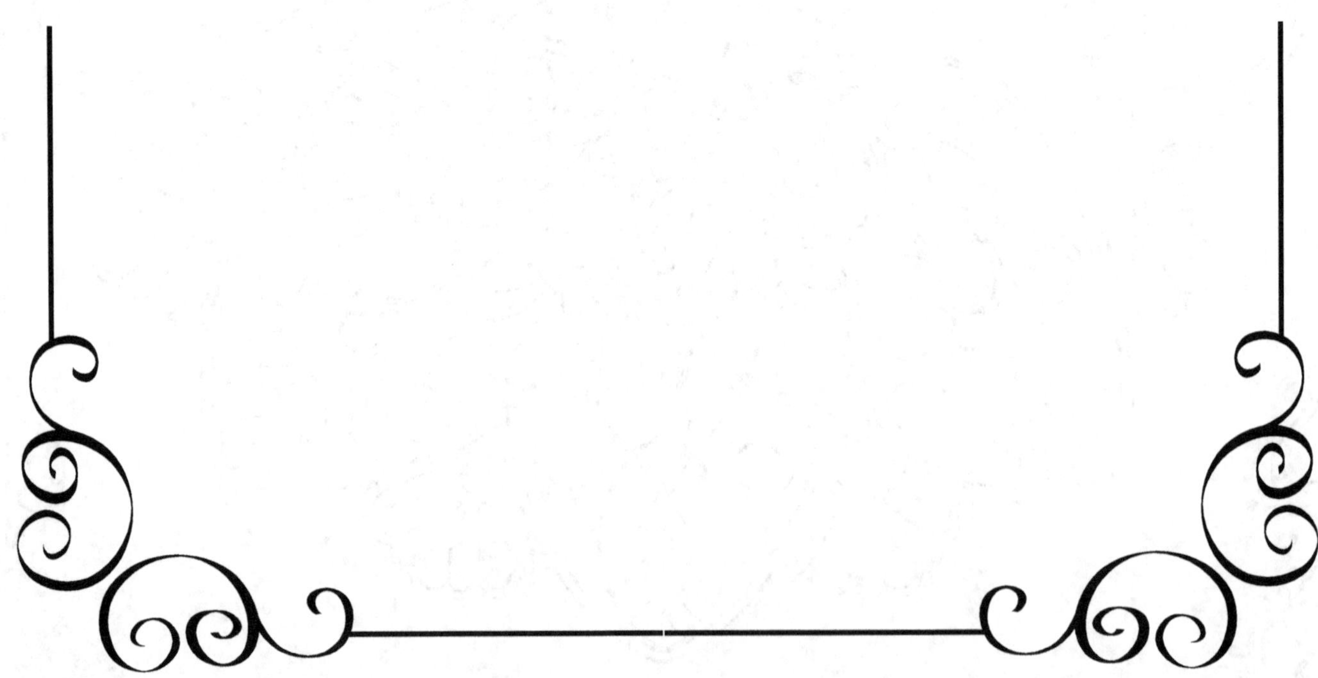

*Exercise:
Use colors to symbolize your inner changes, with each hue representing a different aspect of your transformation.

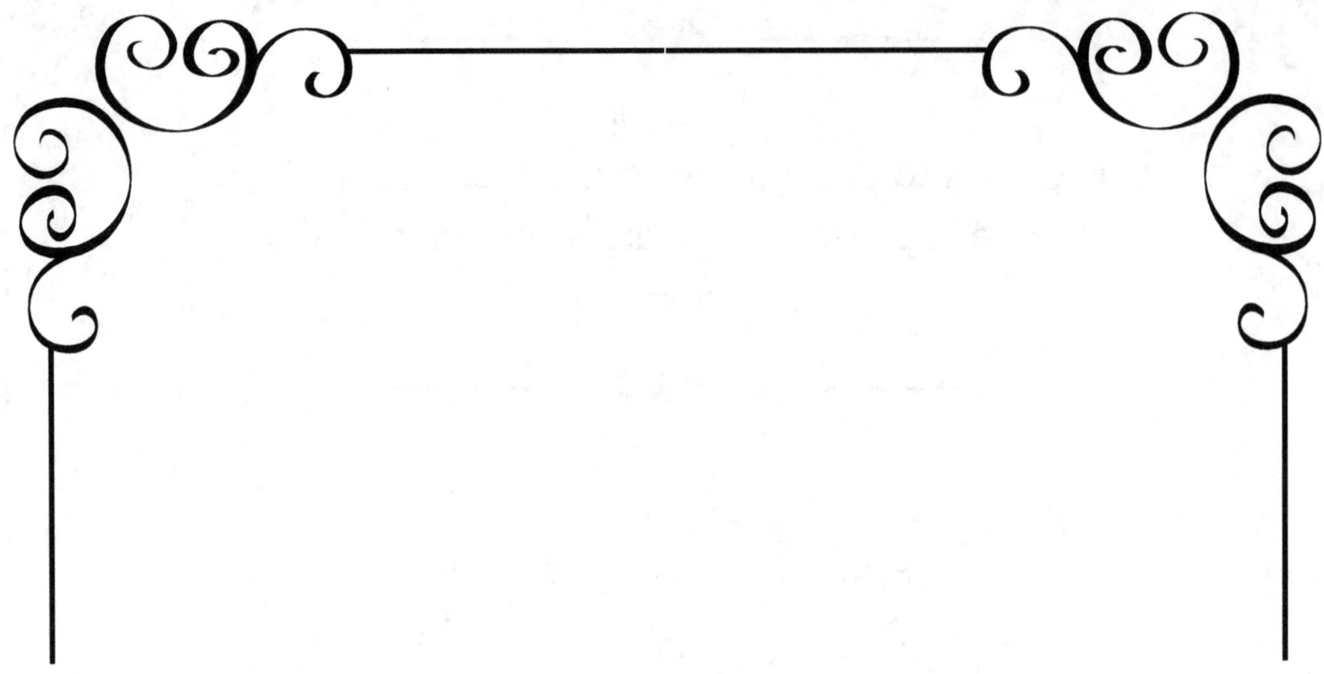

I see sobriety as
a canvas
for my inner champion.

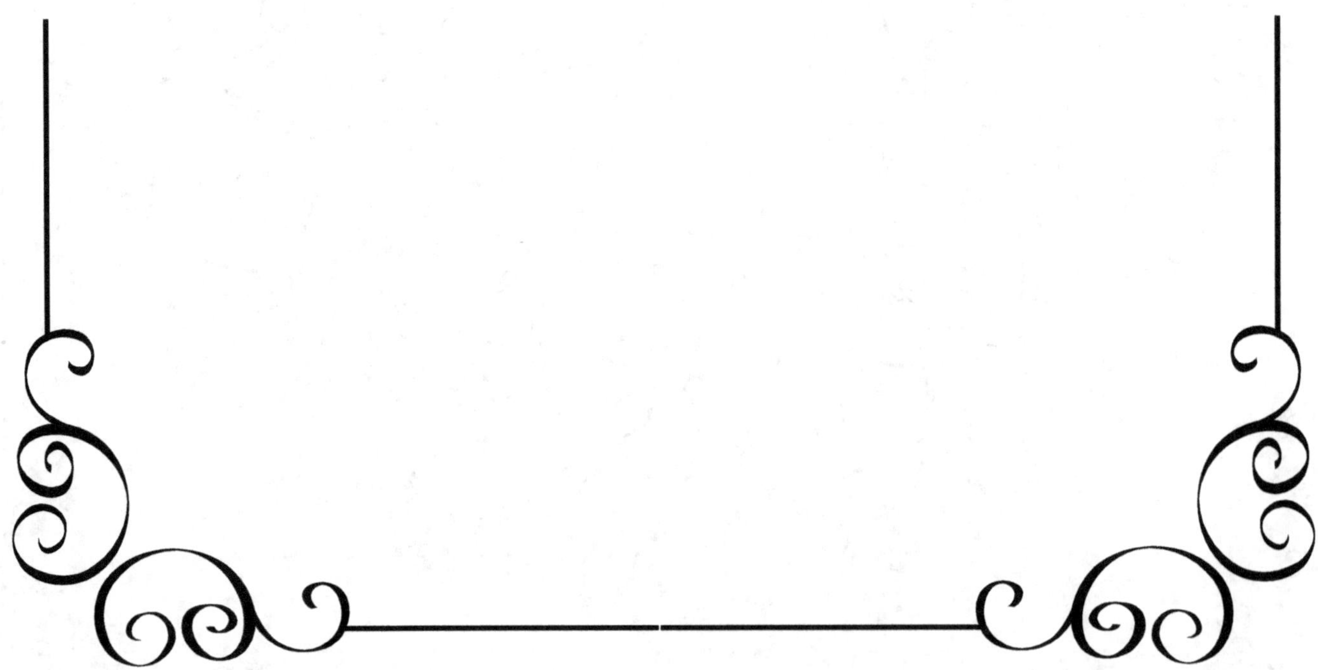

*Exercise:
Embrace your inner champion as you color, using
colors to depict your victories.

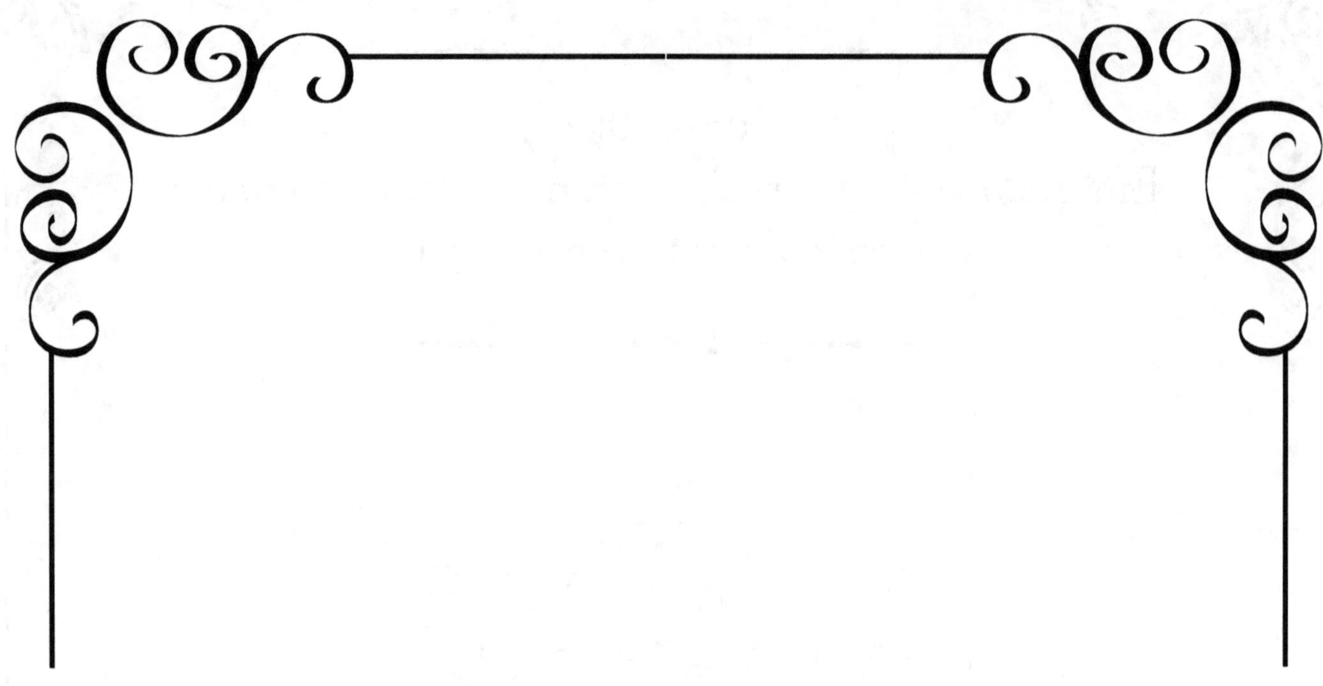

I am a testament
to my commitment
to recovery.

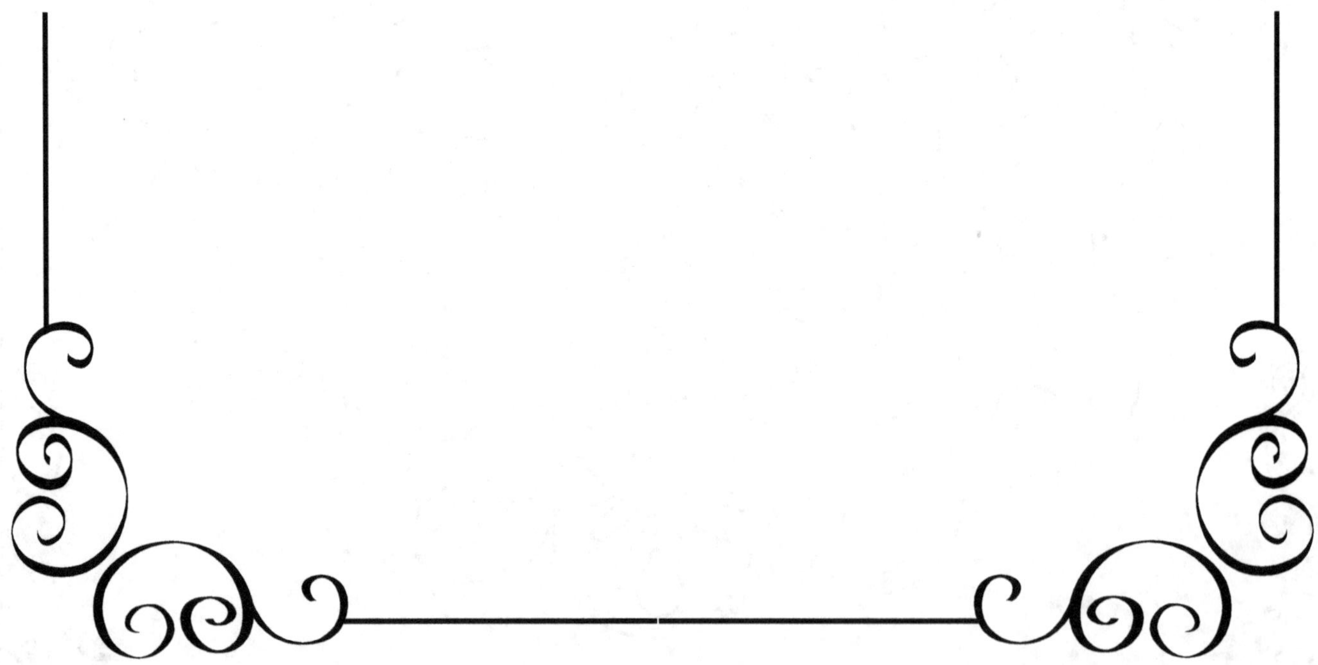

*Exercise:
Recognize that each coloring stroke is a testament to
your dedication and progress on your recovery journey.

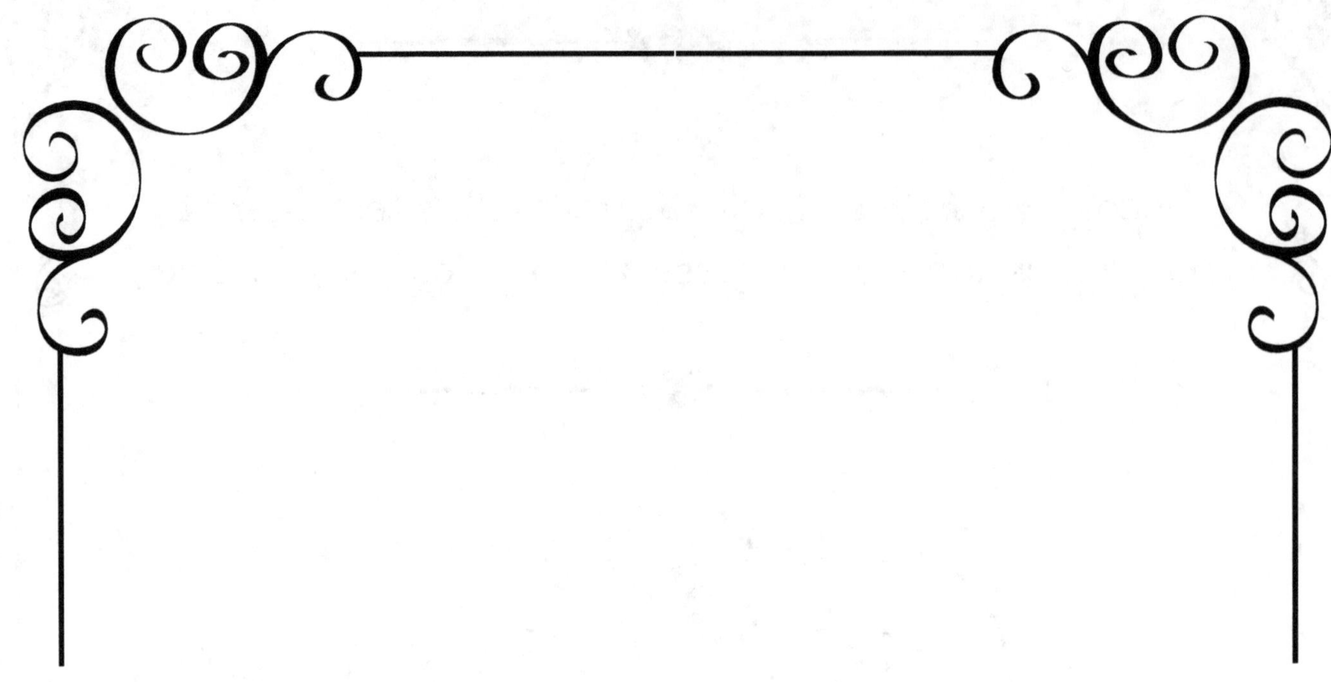

I embrace my
inner artist
as I color.

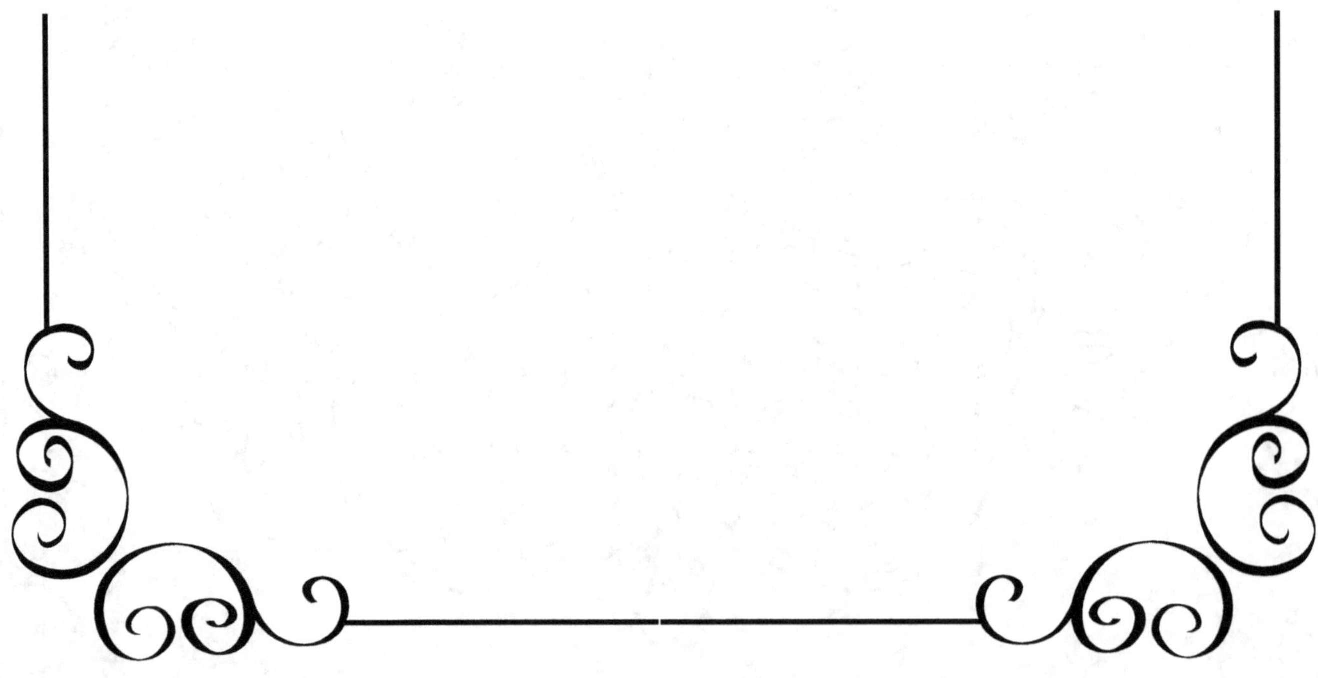

*Exercise:
Let your inner artist shine through as you color,
expressing yourself and your journey on the page.

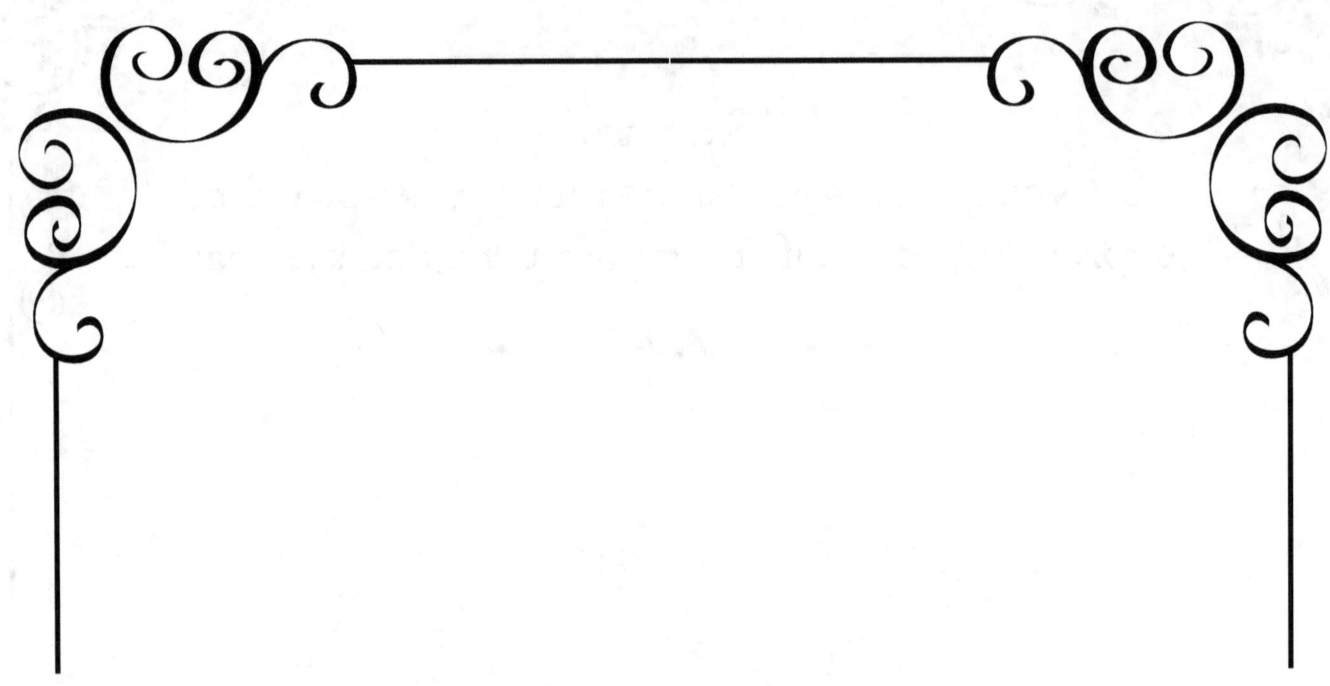

I paint my true self
with every hue.

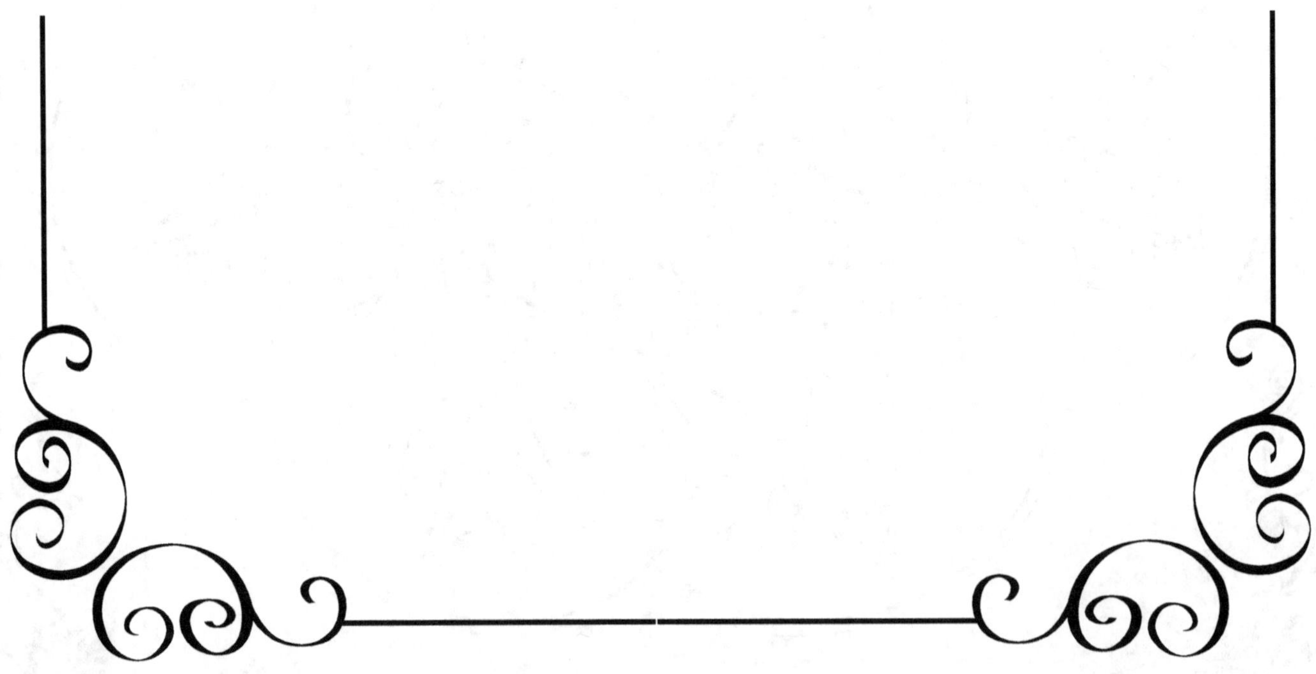

*Exercise:
Allow the colors you choose to represent the
discovery of your authentic self.

I am the
architect
of my sober
sanctuary.

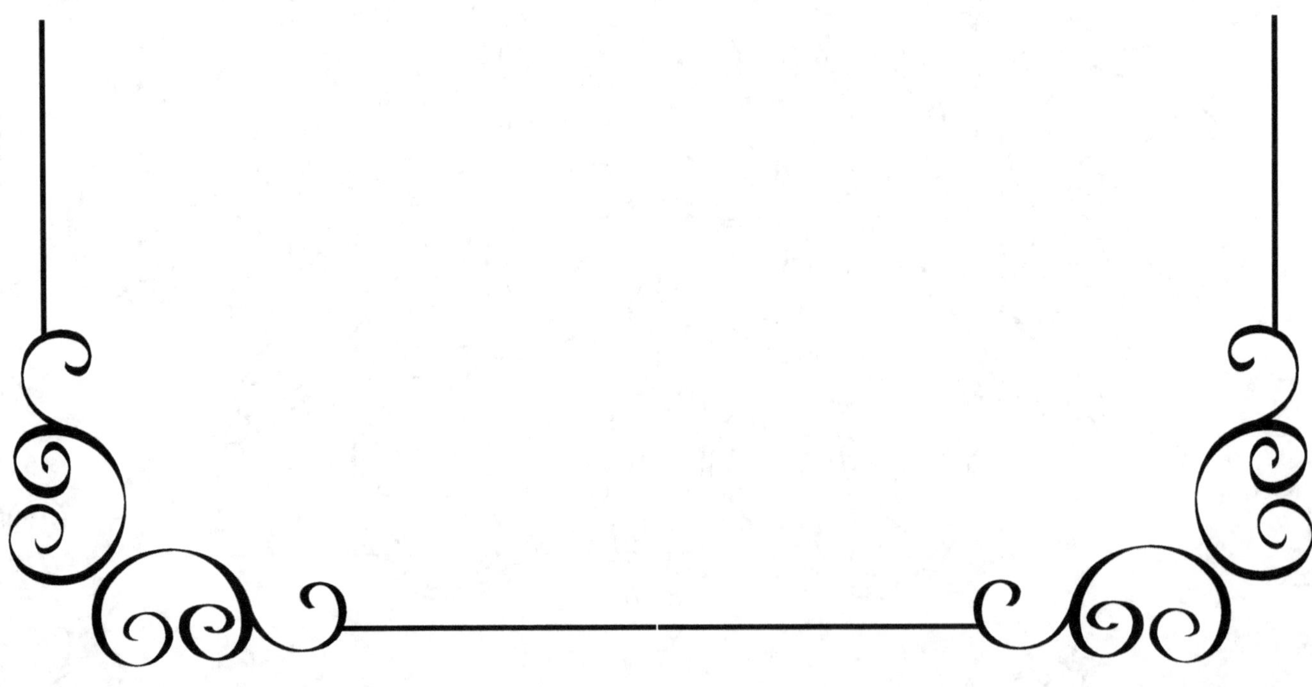

*Exercise:
As you color, imagine constructing a sanctuary of sobriety, brick by brick, with each color choice.

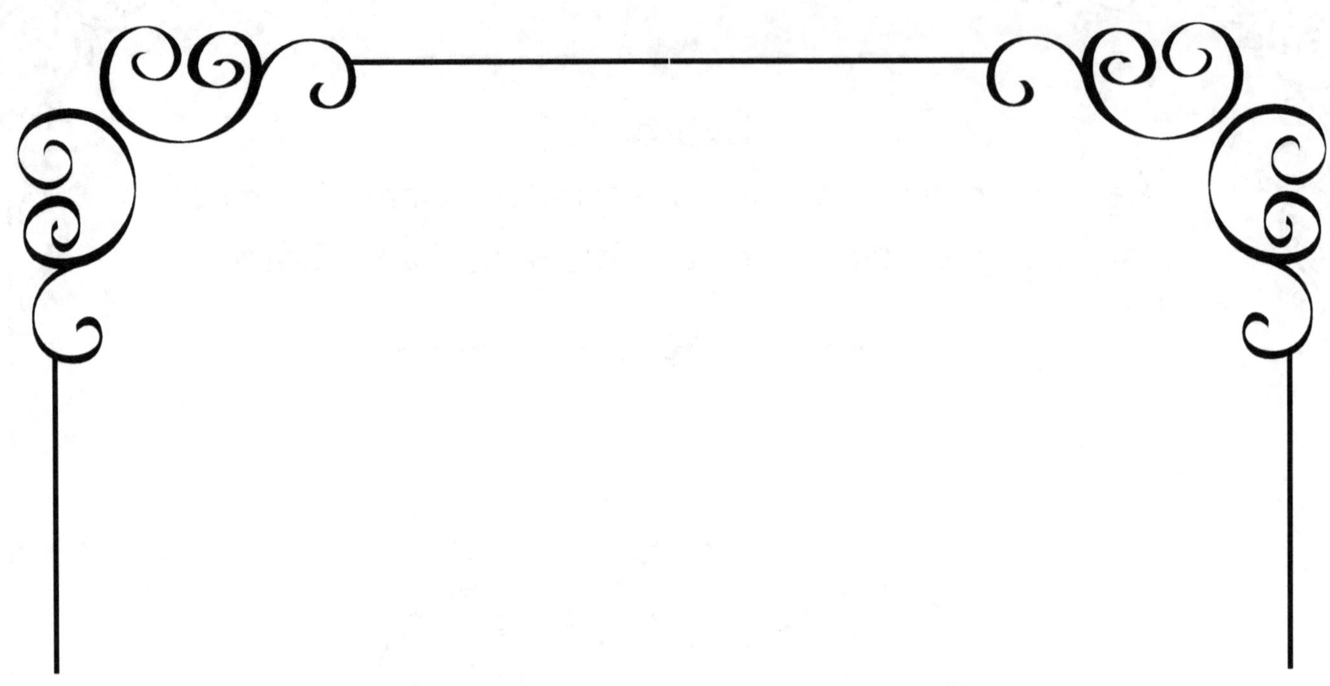

I visualize my sobriety
as a beacon of hope.

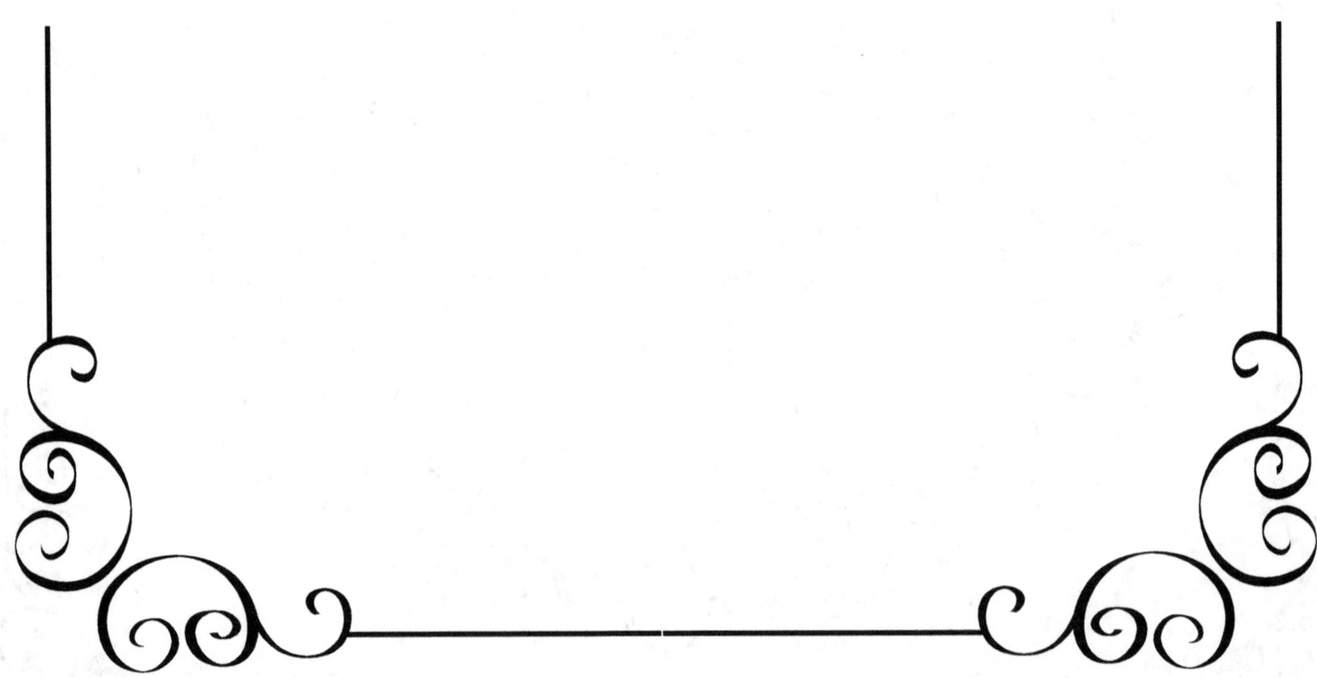

*Exercise:
See your sobriety as a shining lighthouse guiding
you through challenging times as you color.

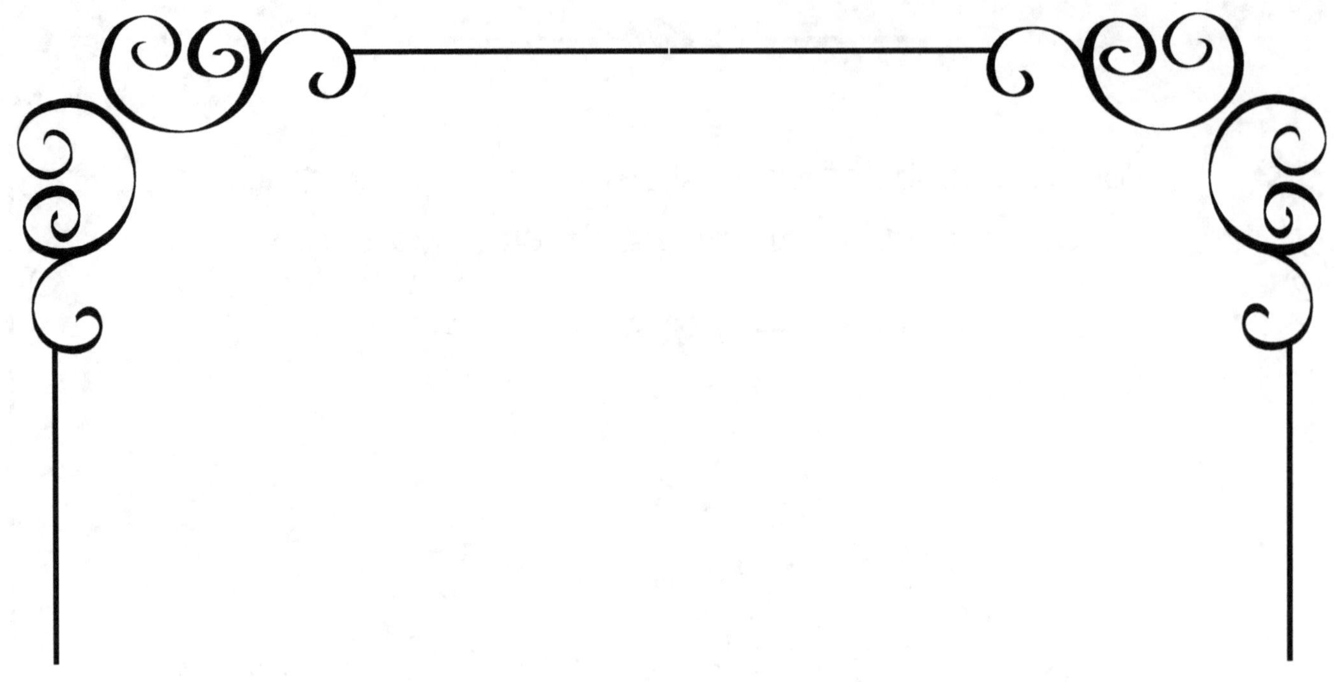

I color my way
through life's
ups and downs.

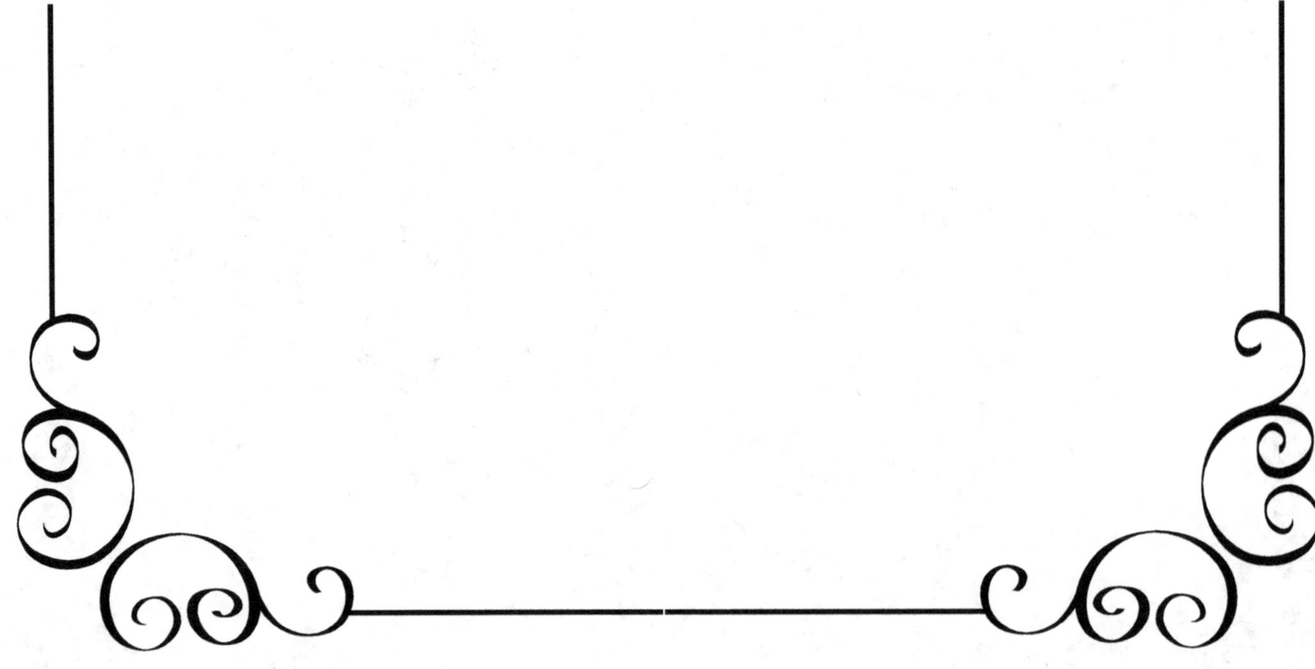

*Exercise:
Use the act of coloring as a meditative practice,
helping you navigate the highs and lows of life.

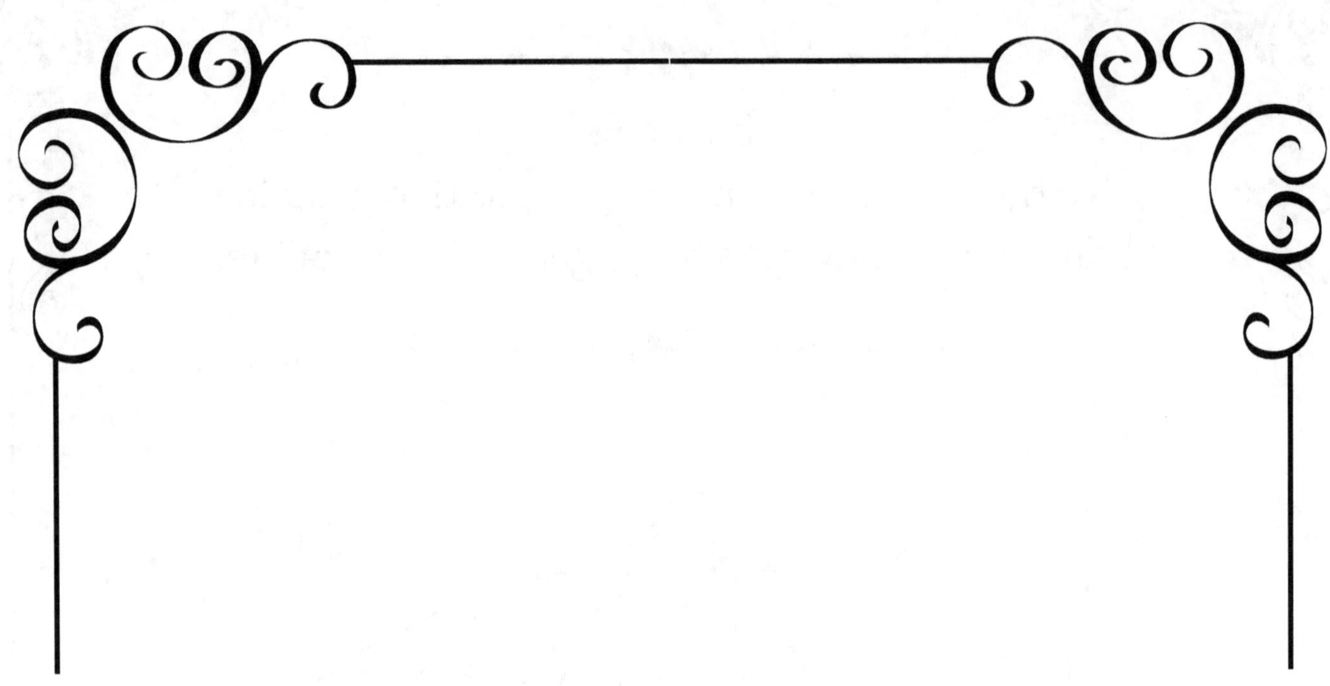

I find strength in the
intricate
details of my journey.

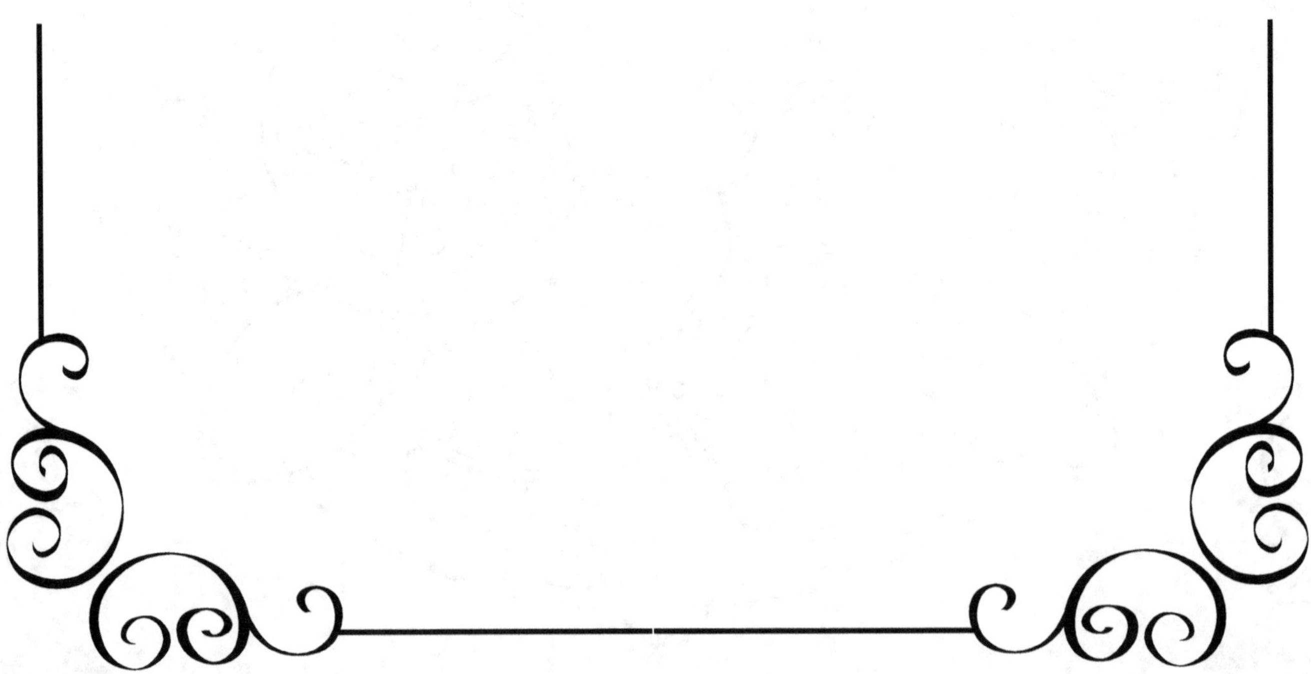

*Exercise:
Select detailed areas to color, symbolizing the strength
you gain from the nuances of your experiences.

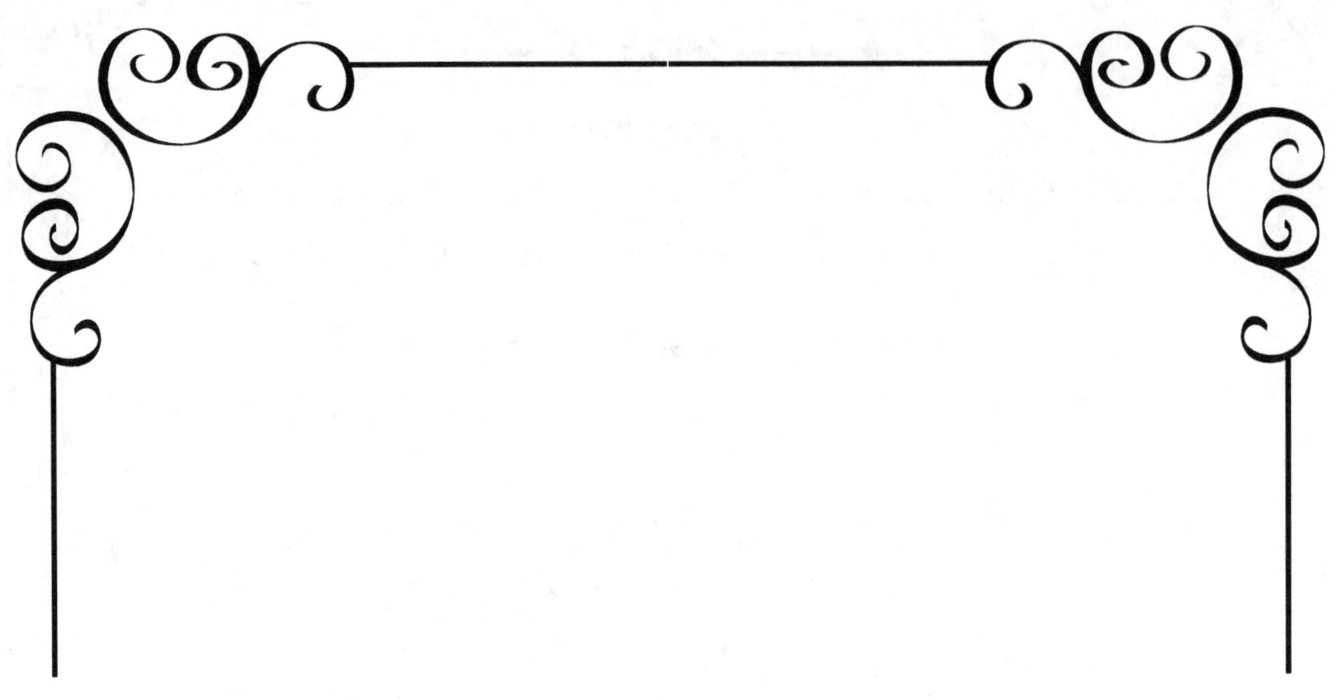

I visualize my
challenges
transforming into
stepping stones.

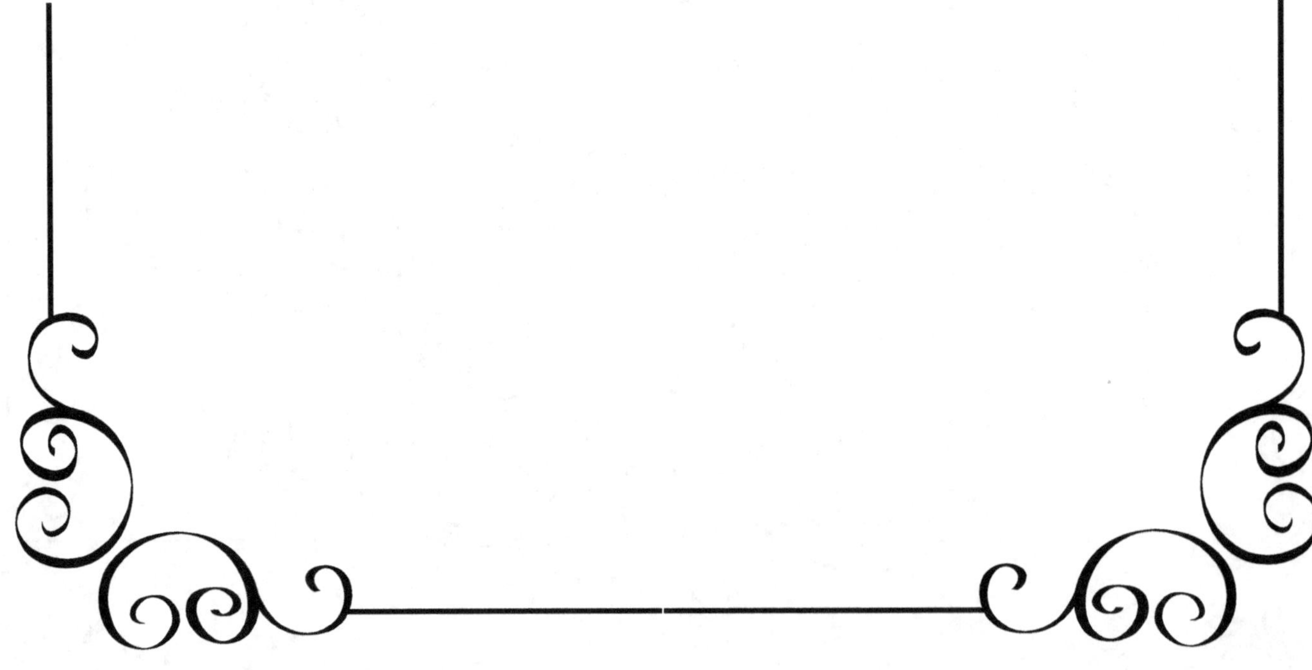

*Exercise:
Imagine each coloring stroke as a stepping stone,
leading you forward and helping you overcome
challenges.

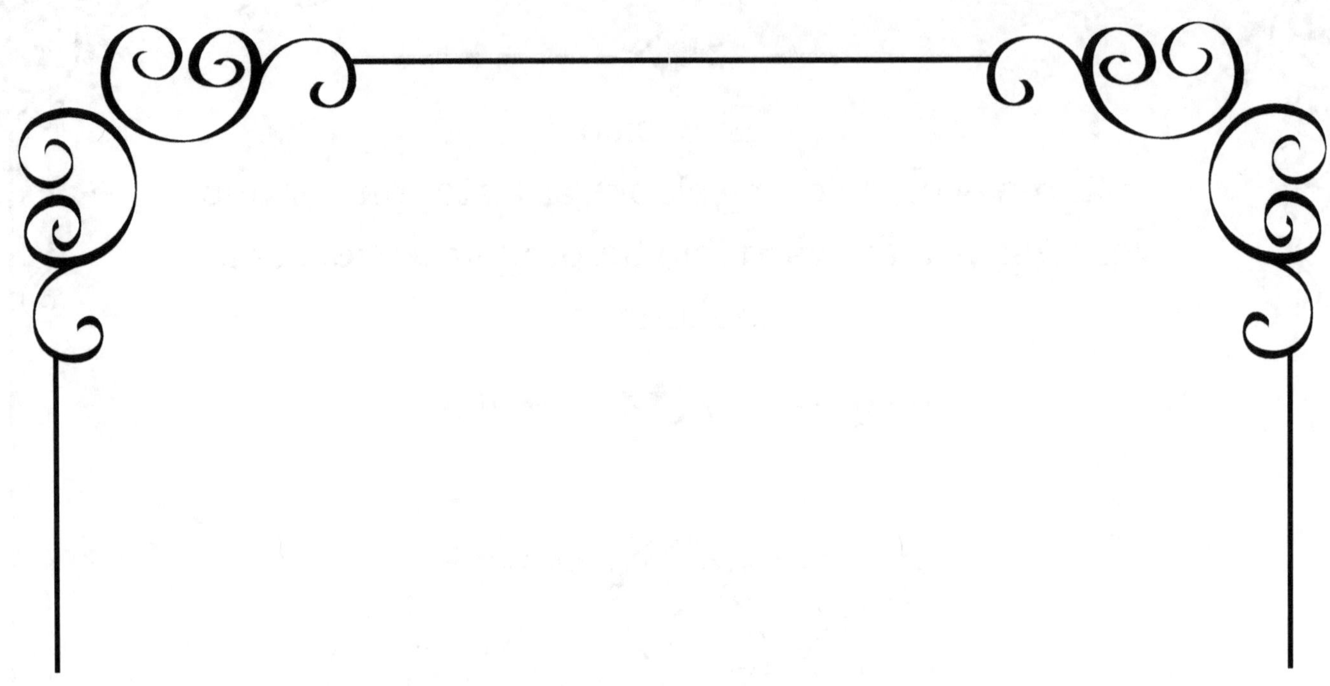

I find serenity in the
rhythmic strokes
of coloring.

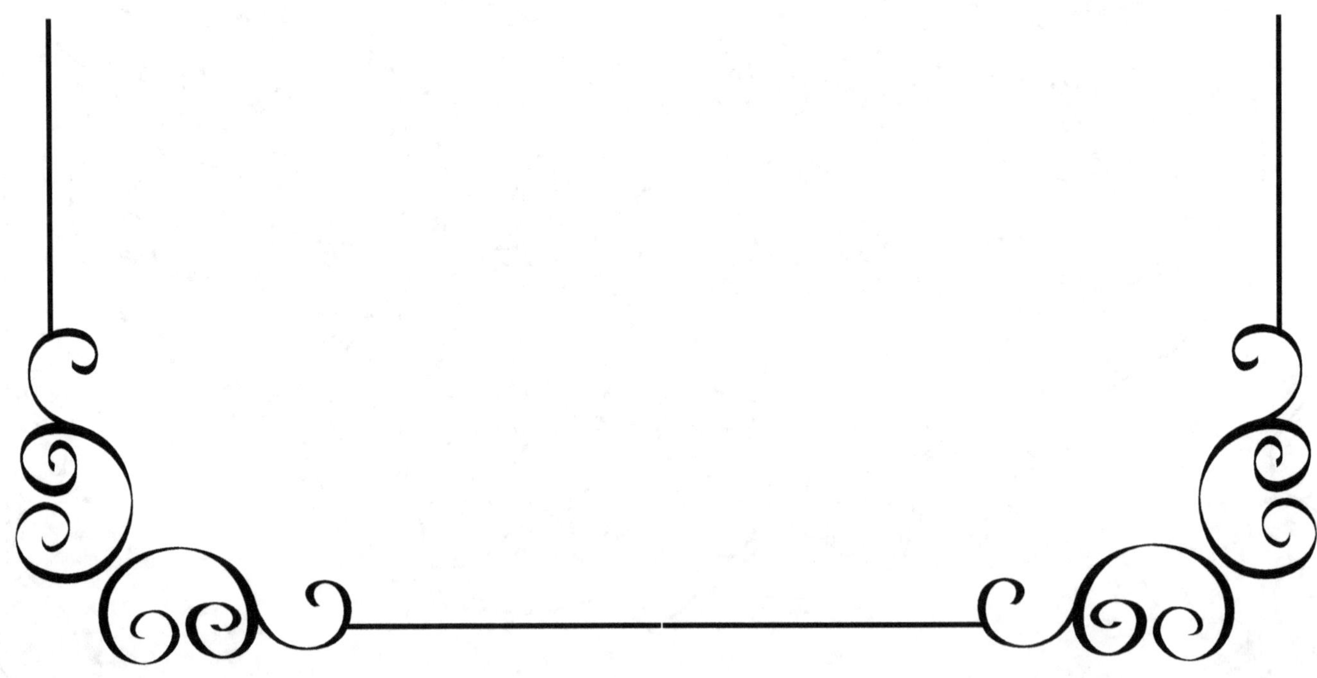

*Exercise:
Embrace the calming rhythm of coloring as a source of
serenity, allowing your mind to relax and find peace.

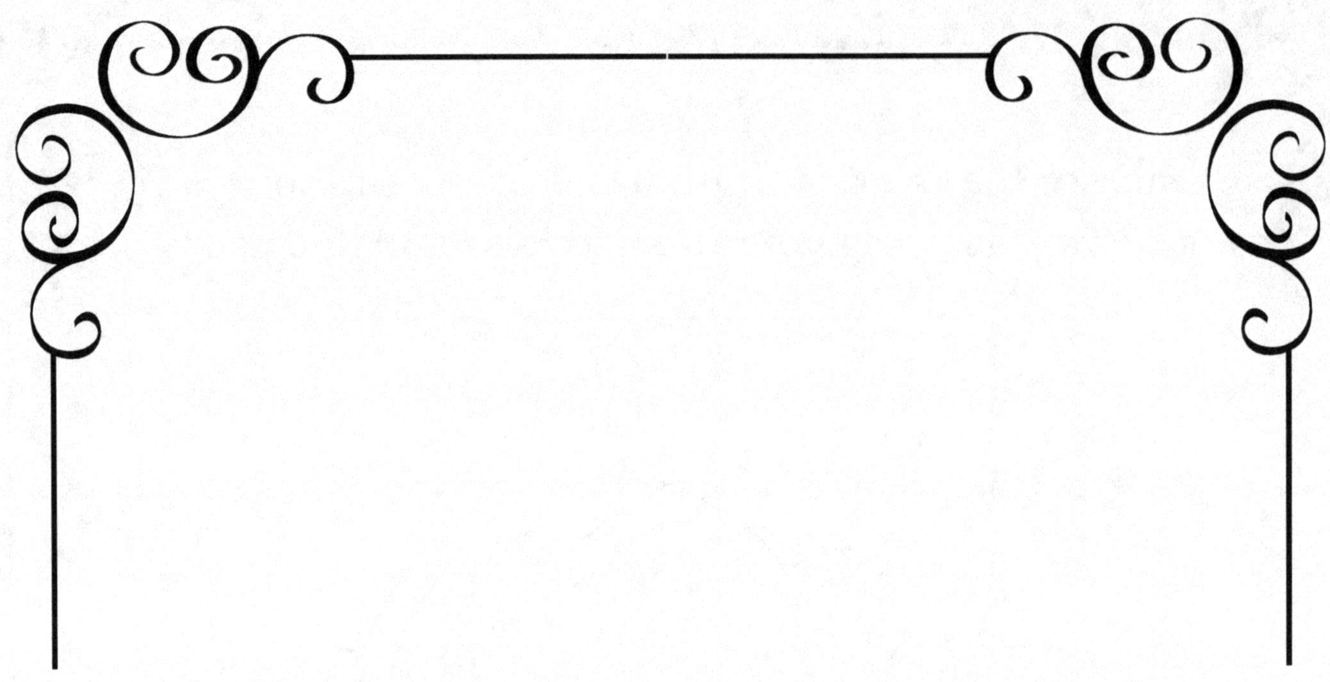

I am the author of
my own healing story.

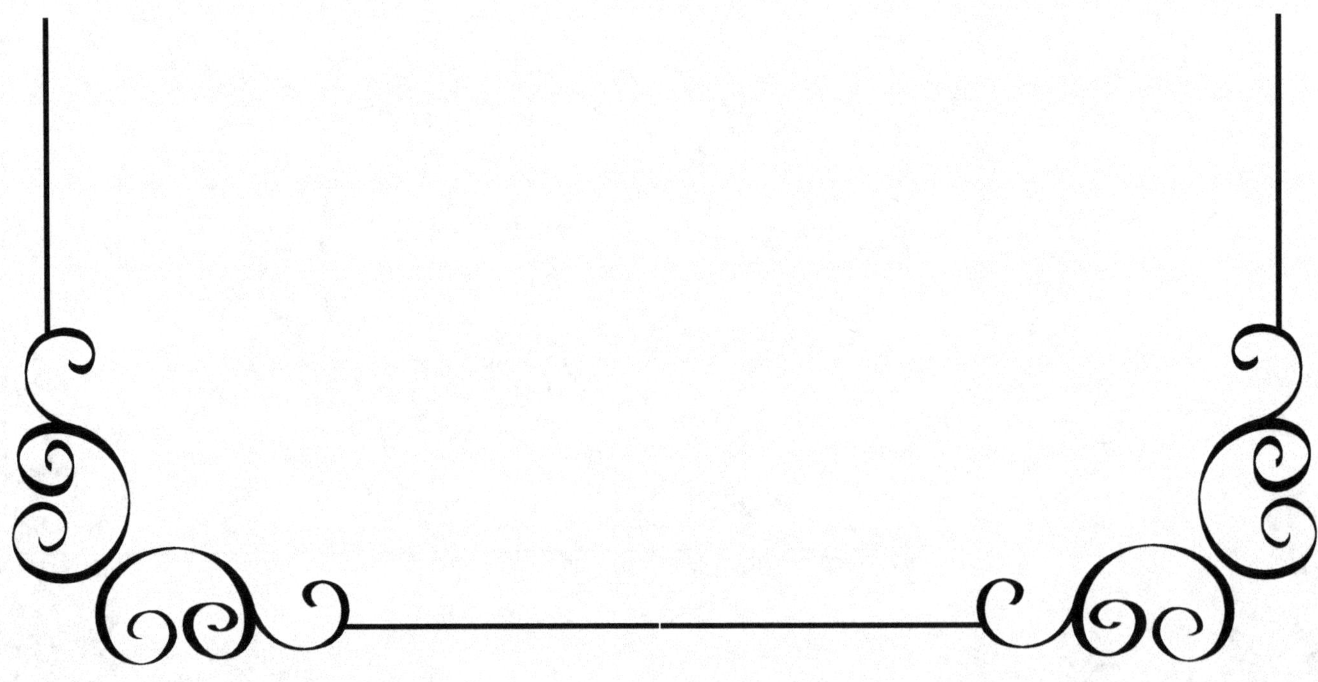

*Exercise:
See your coloring page as a storybook, with each color
representing a chapter of your healing journey.

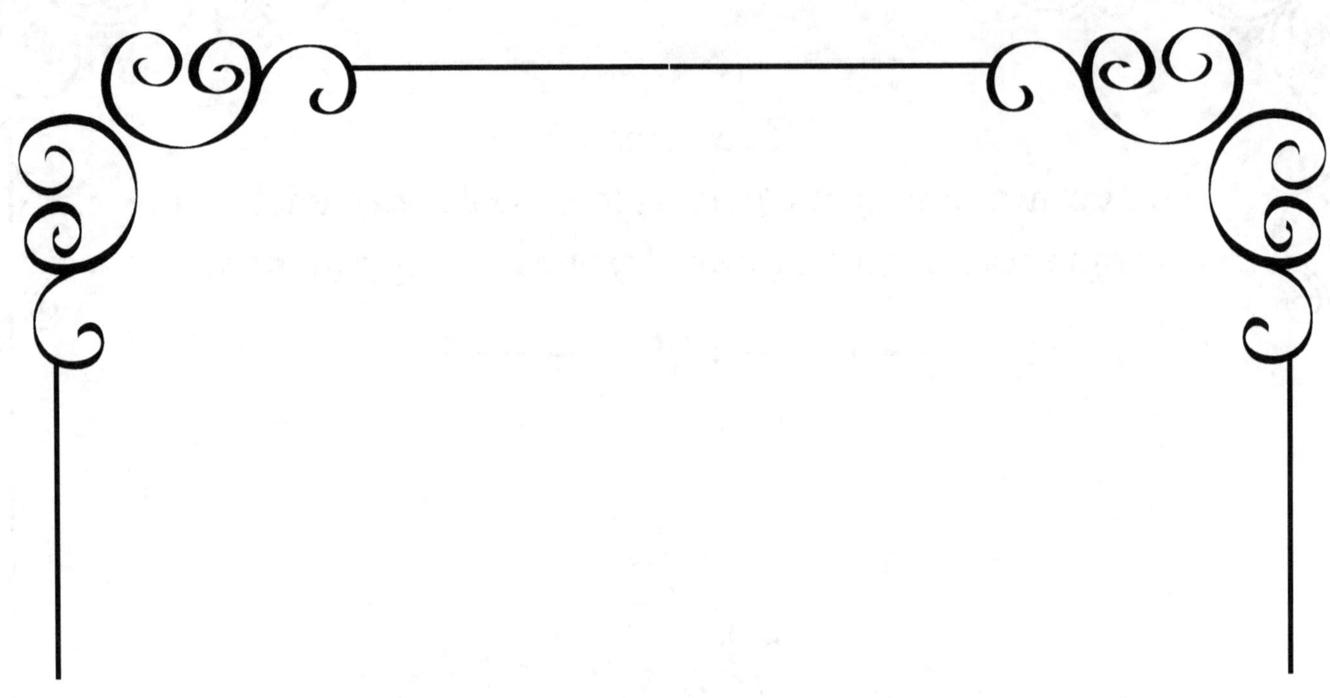

I color through the
darkest days,
knowing dawn
will break.

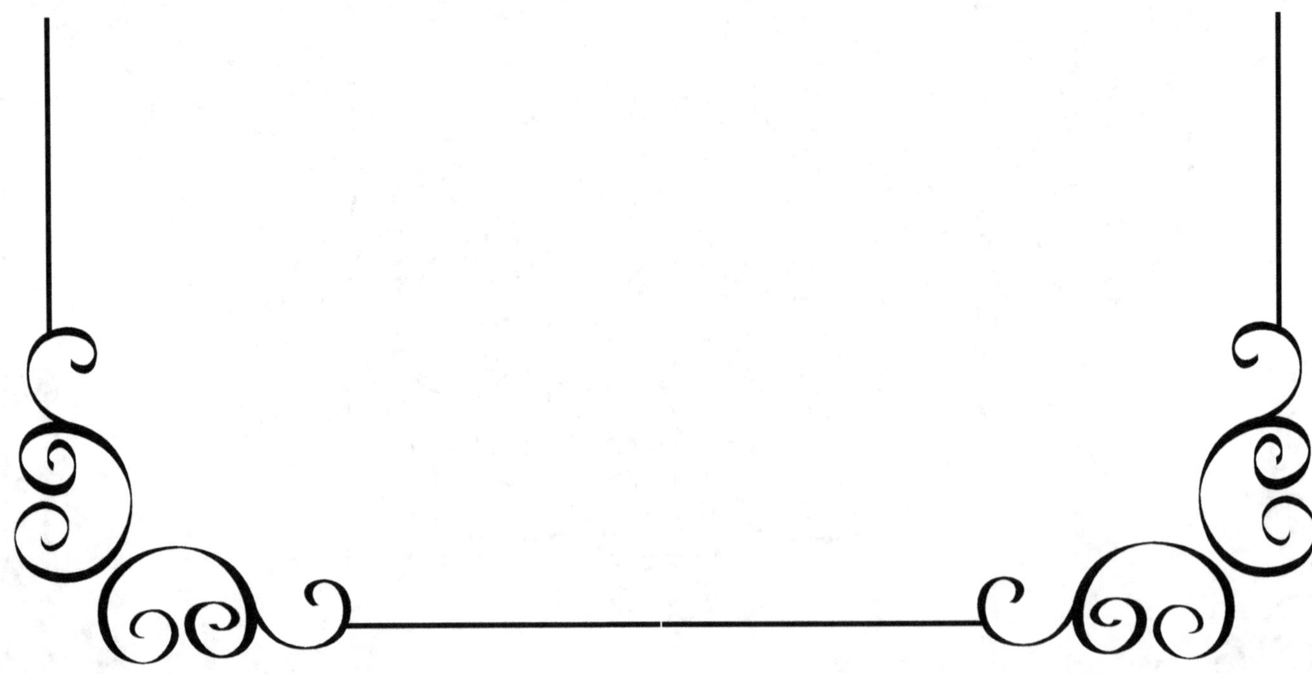

*Exercise:
During difficult moments, use darker colors and
visualize a sunrise on the horizon, symbolizing hope.

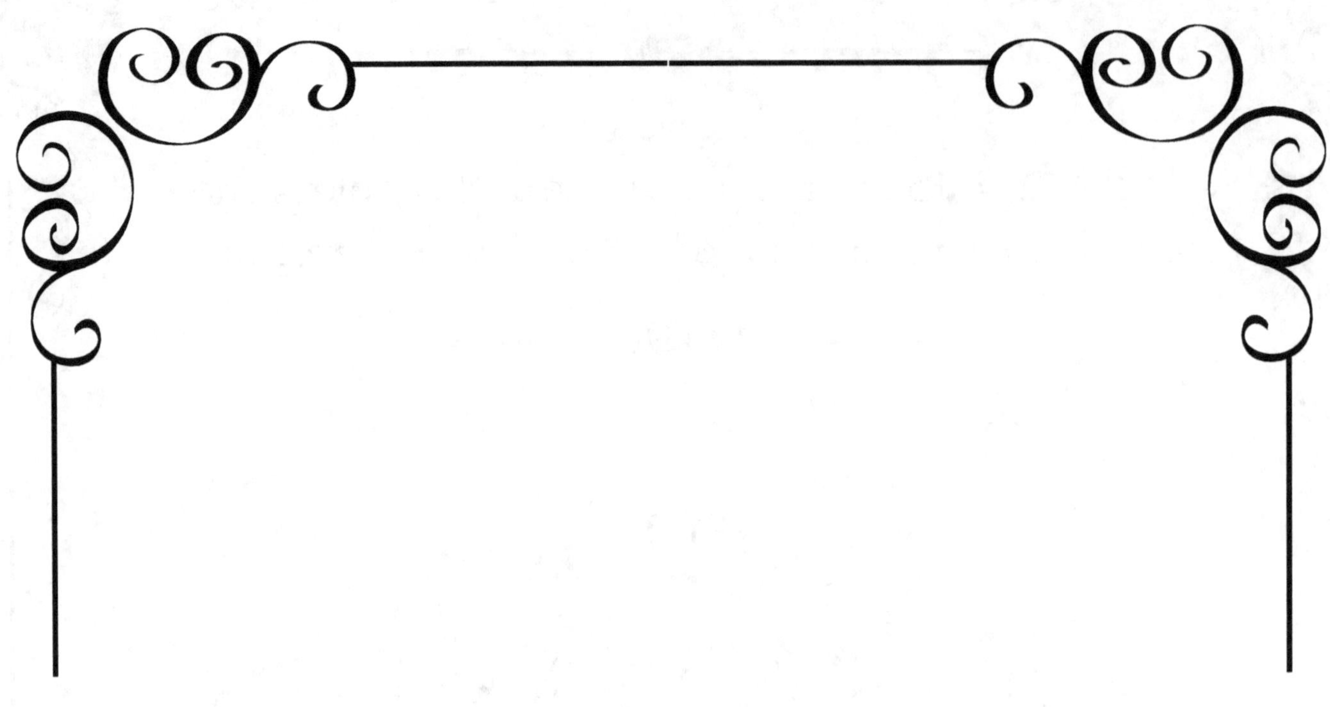

I am a warrior
painting my
battles
with courage.

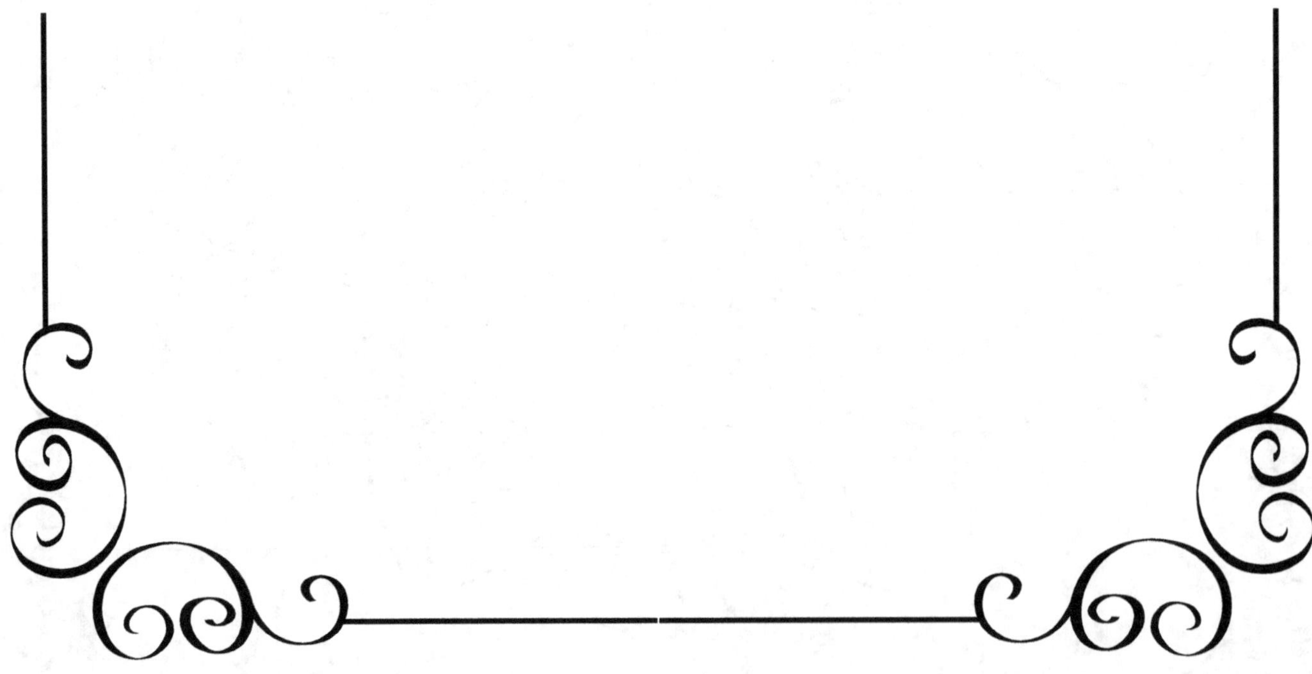

*Exercise:
Use bold, confident strokes as you color, channeling
your inner warrior and resilience.

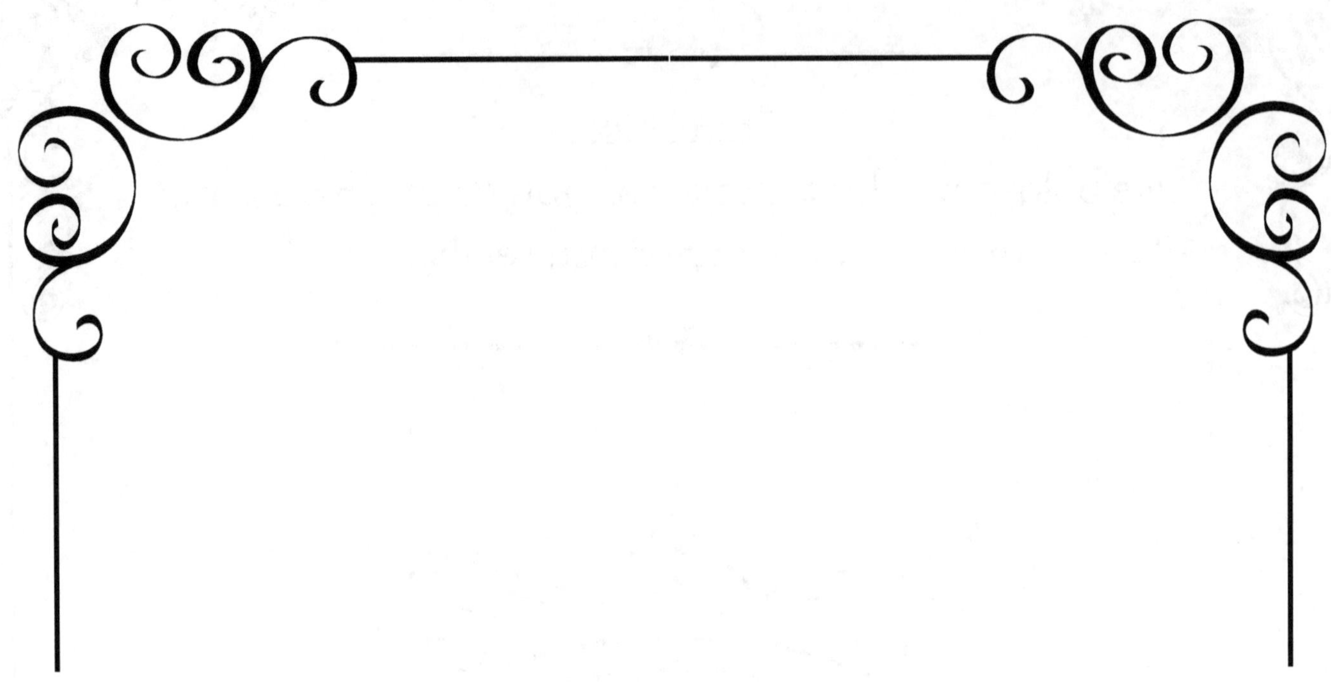

I visualize my
recovery
as a blossoming flower.

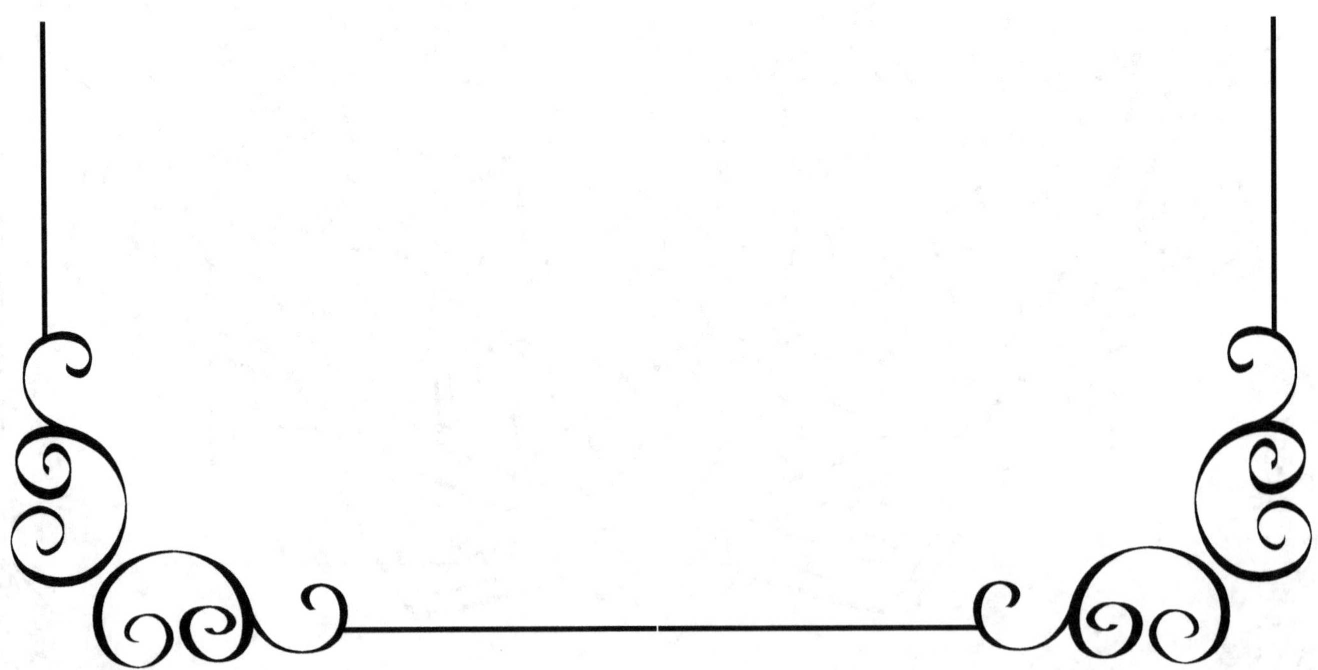

*Exercise:
Imagine each color stroke as a petal unfurling,
symbolizing the growth and renewal of your recovery.

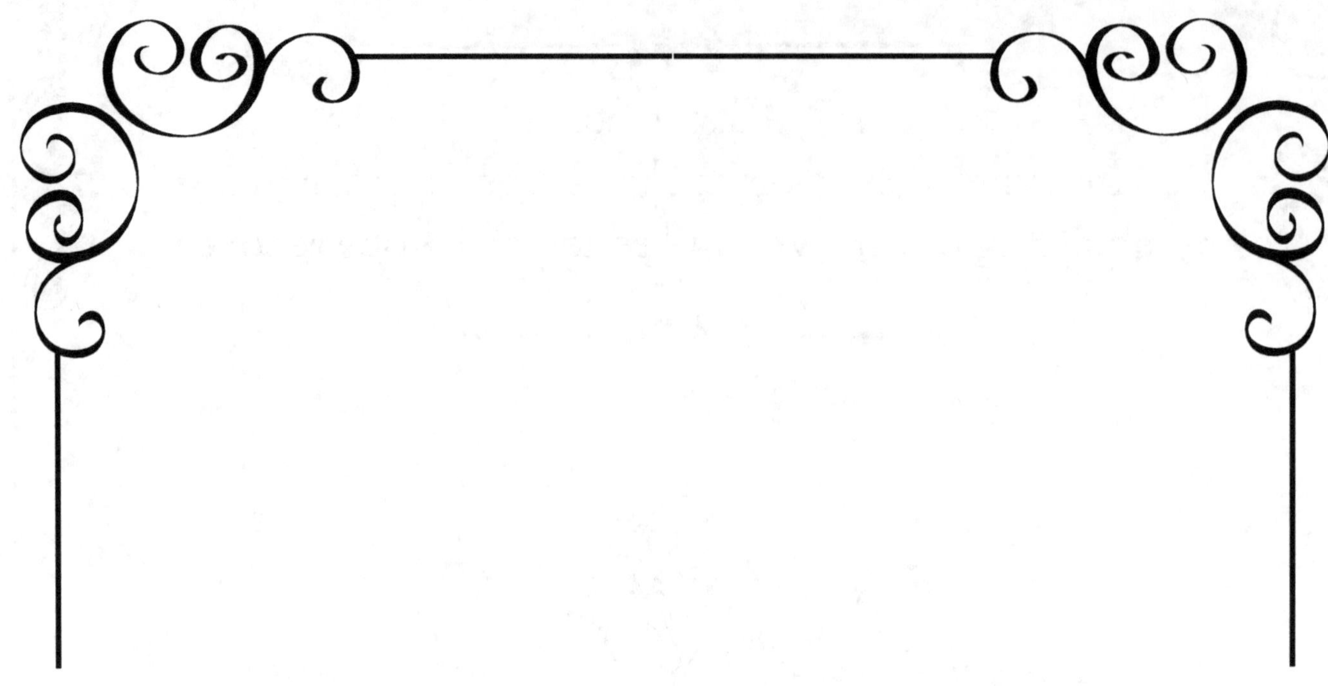

I find solace in the
stillness of coloring,
a sanctuary for
my mind.

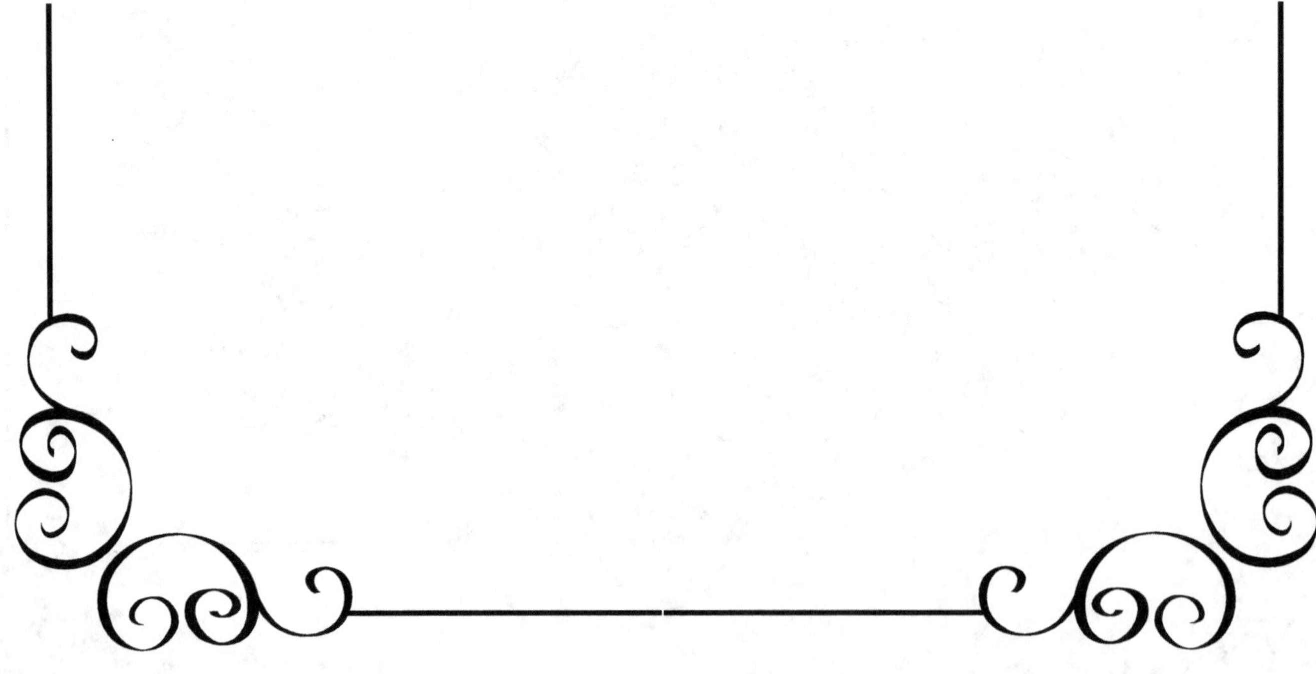

*Exercise:
As you color, visualize your body as a canvas, and with each
stroke, paint it with the nourishing choices that promote
health and vitality, fostering a sense of well-being.

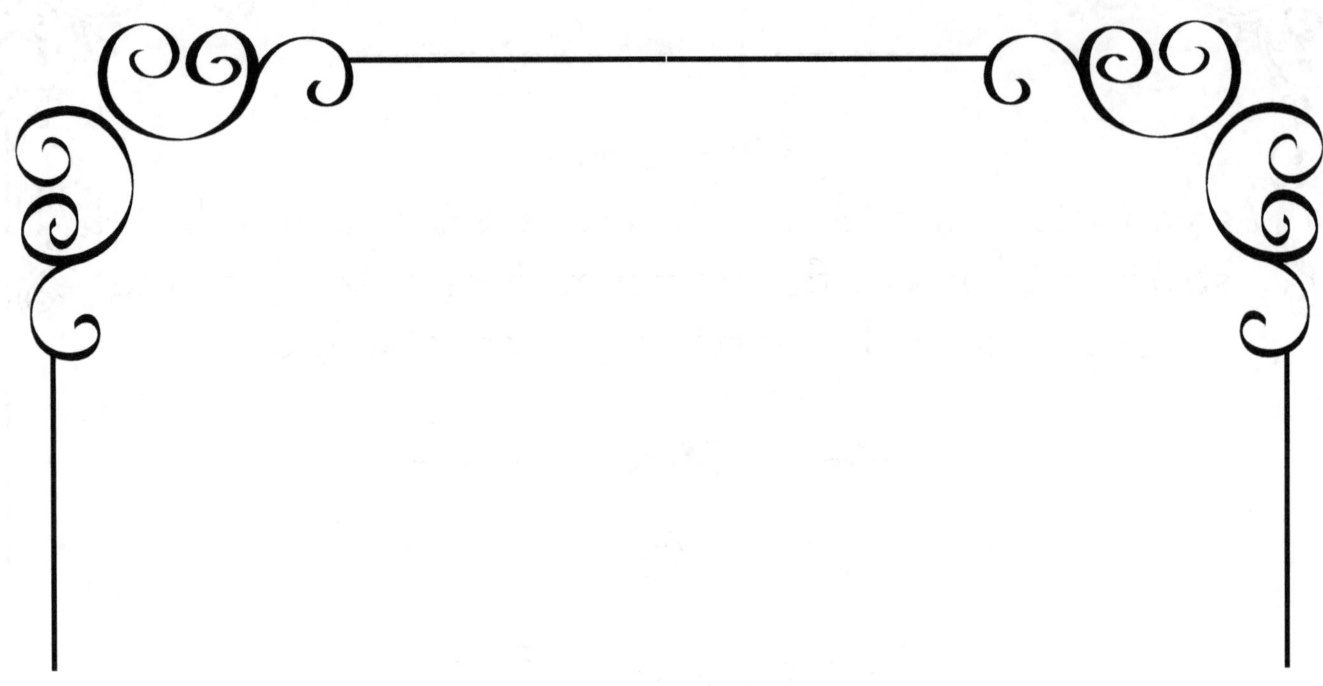

I see the colors of
hope even on the
grayest days.

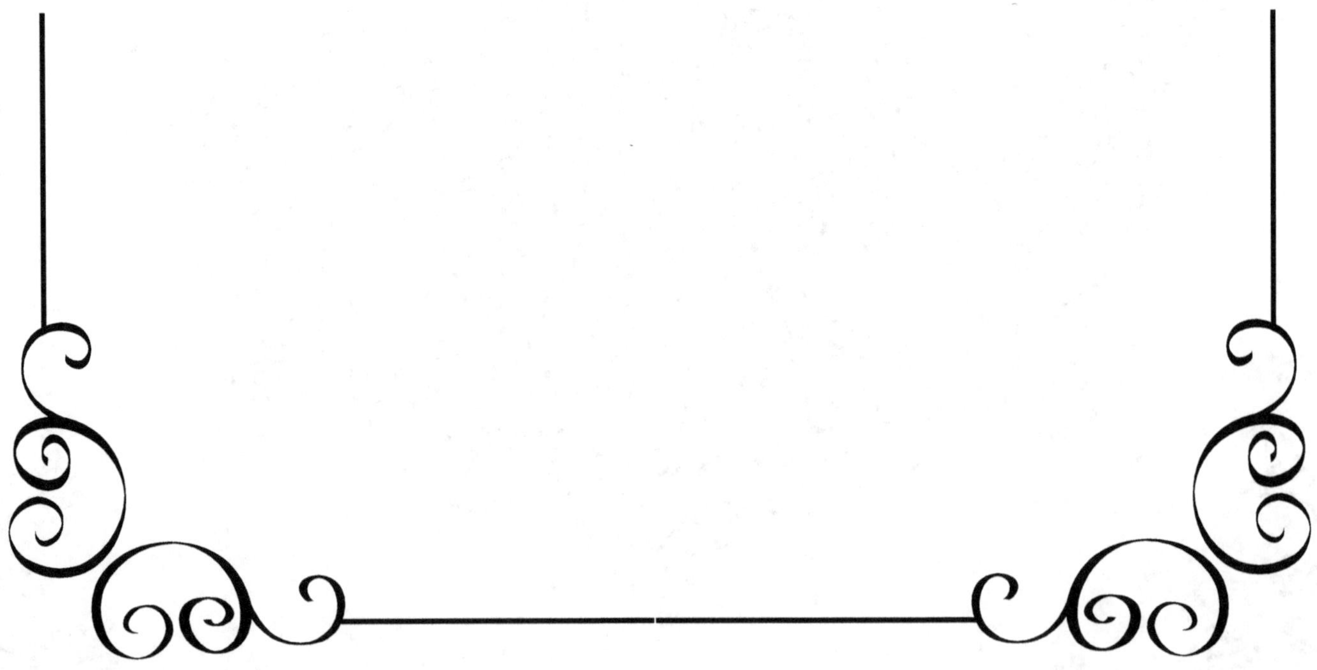

*Exercise:
Use bright and vibrant colors on gray days, reminding
yourself that hope can shine through any darkness.

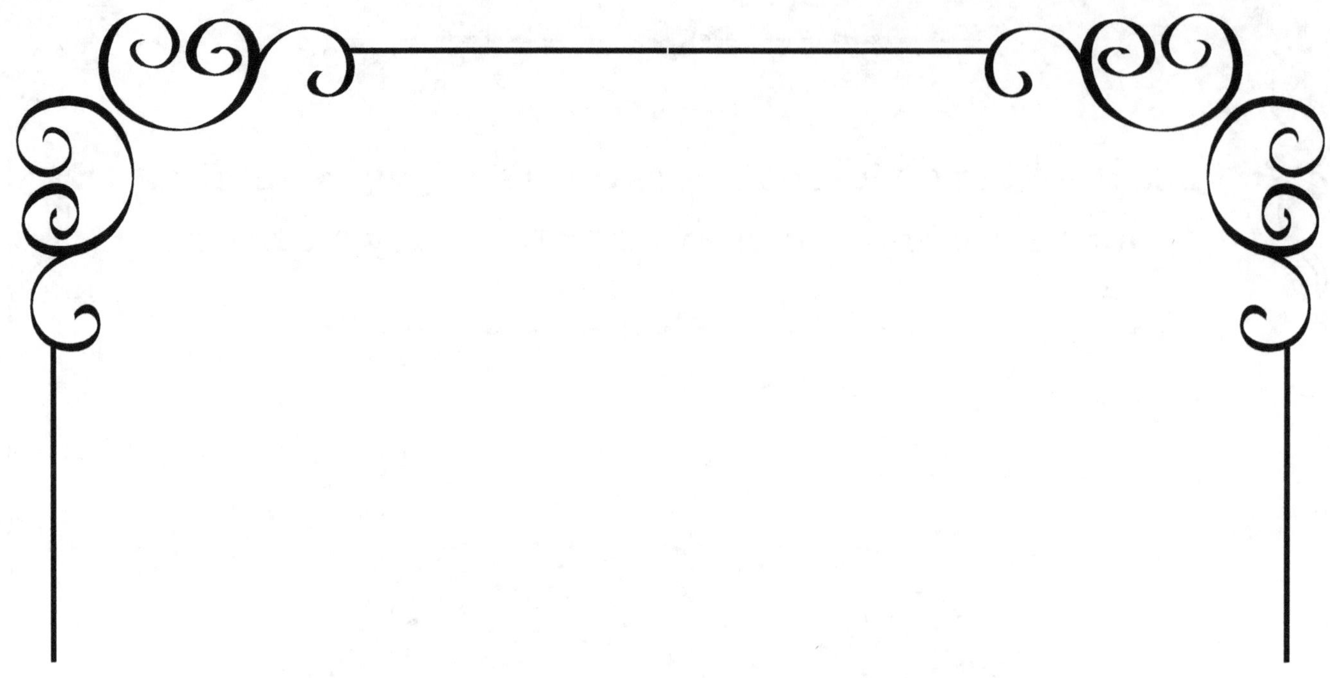

I visualize my journey
as a mountain climb,
each stroke a step higher.

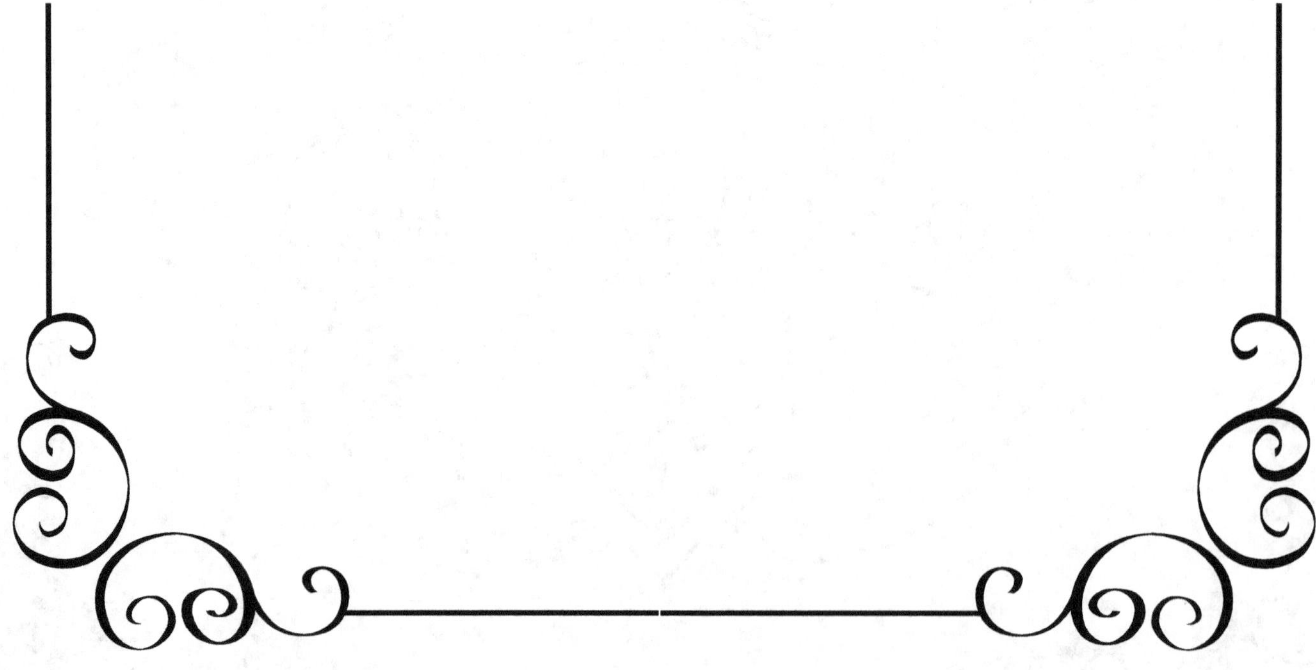

*Exercise:
See each coloring stroke as a foothold on your
ascent, climbing towards the peak of your recovery.

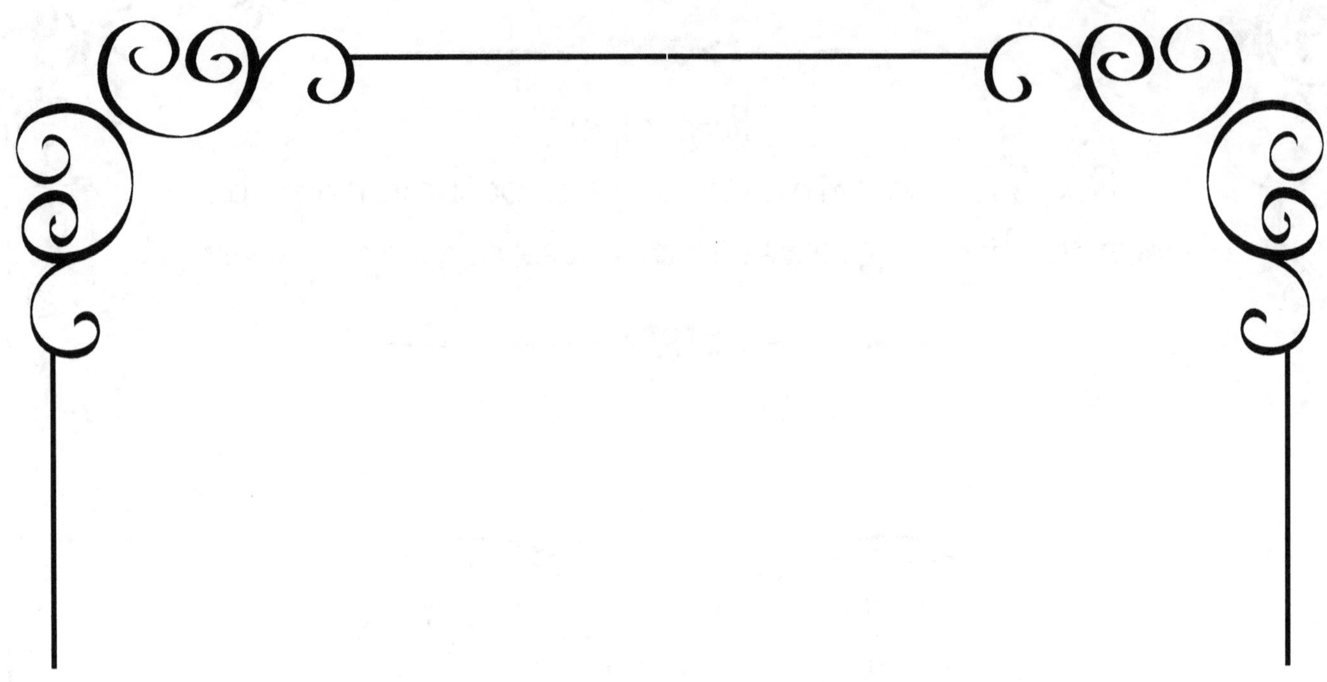

I create art as a form
of self-care and healing.

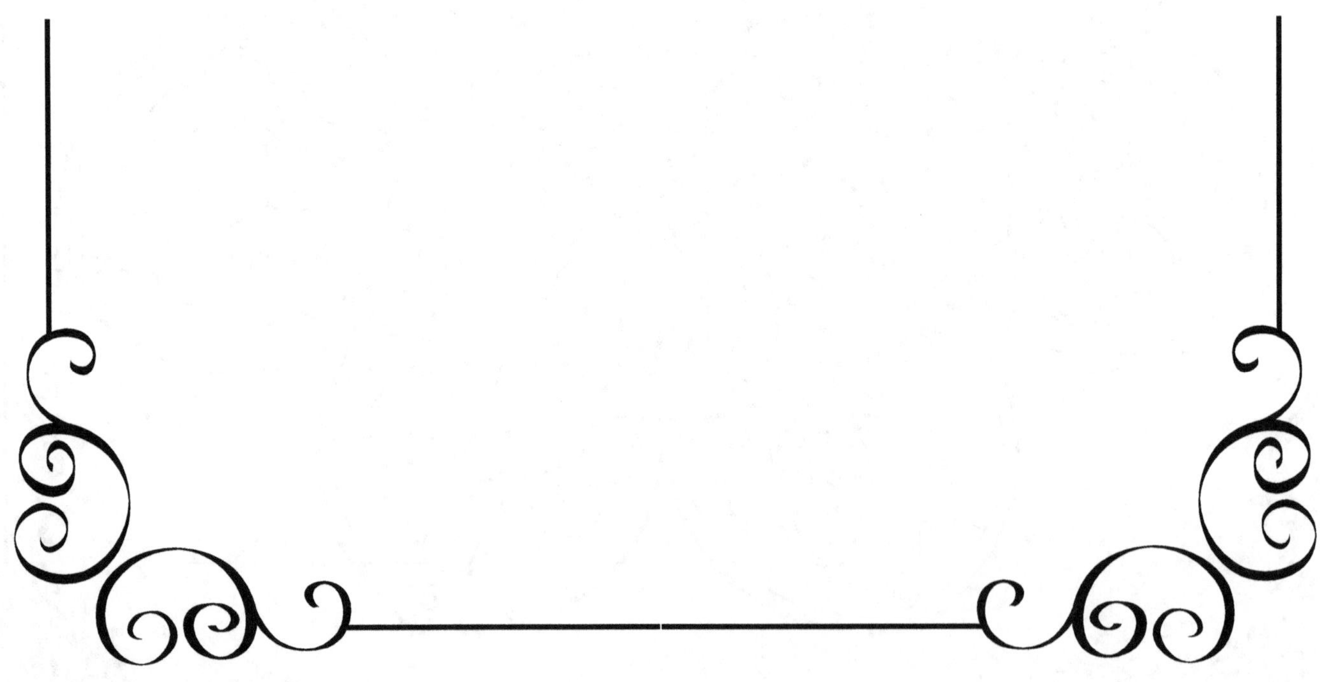

*Exercise:
Use coloring as a form of self-care, recognizing its healing power in your recovery journey.

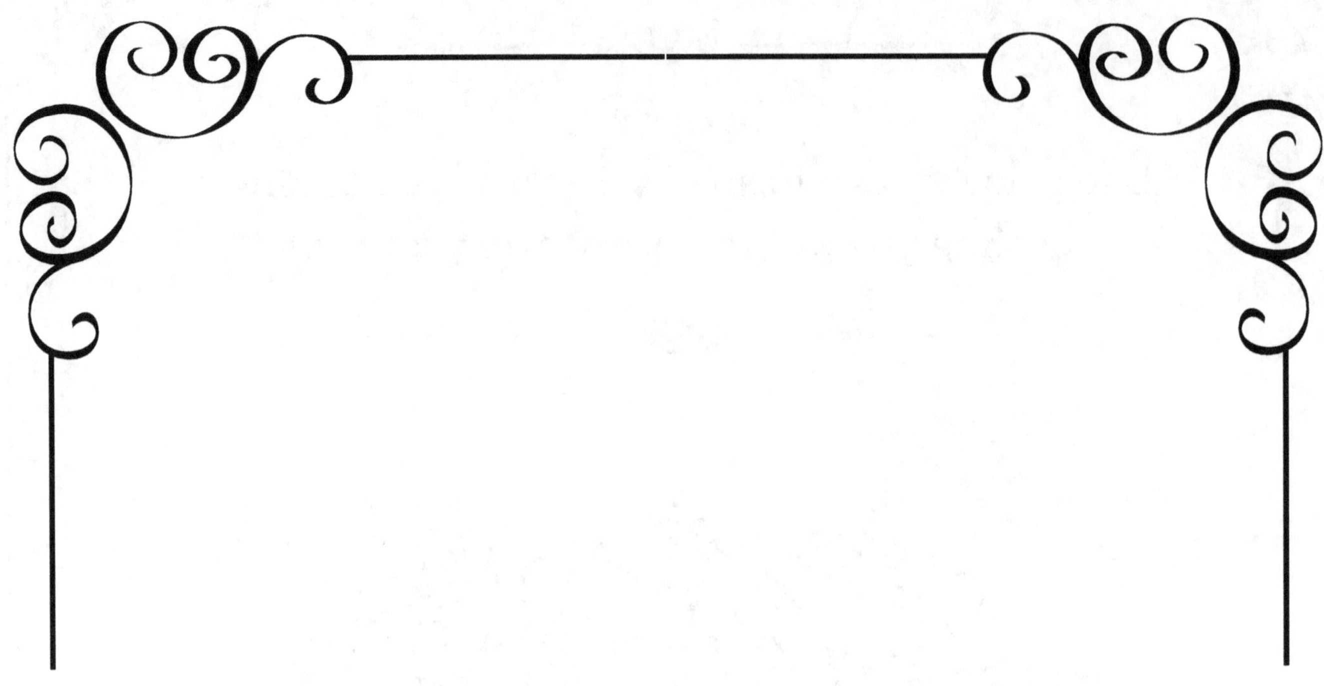

With sobriety, every day
is a chance to create
a better version of myself.

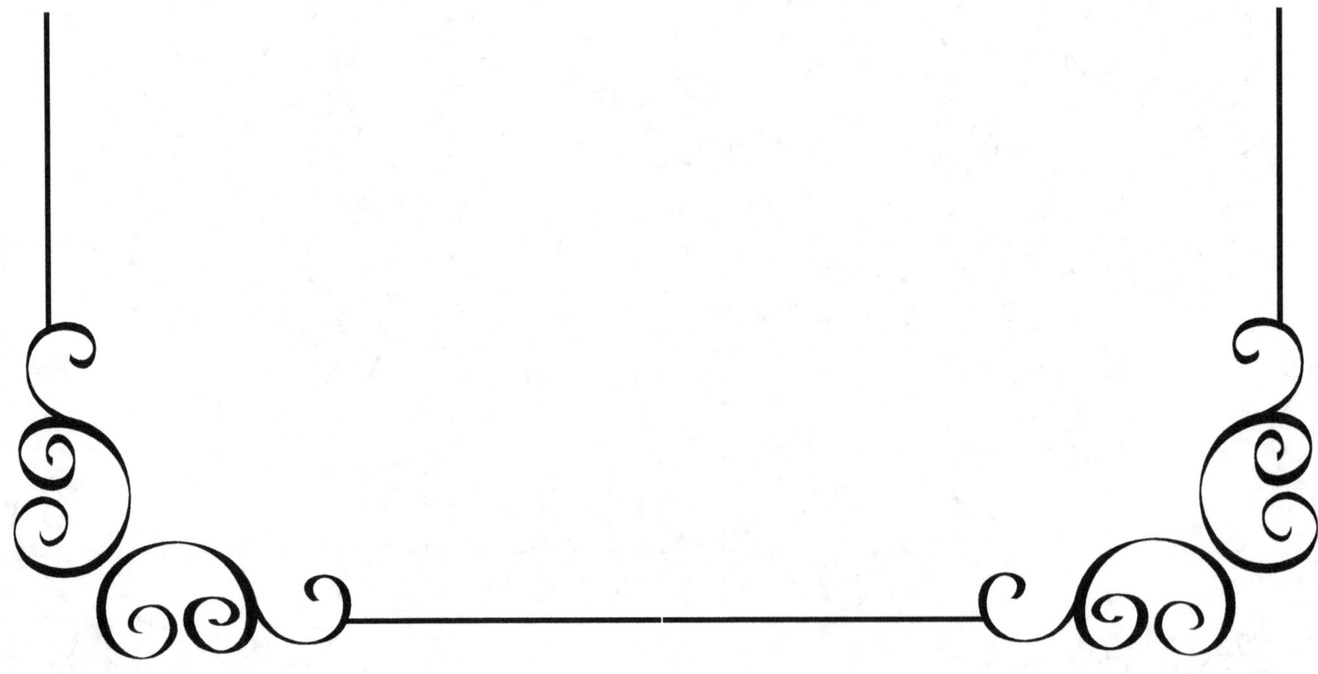

*Exercise:
While coloring, imagine each stroke as a step toward
becoming a better version of yourself in sobriety.

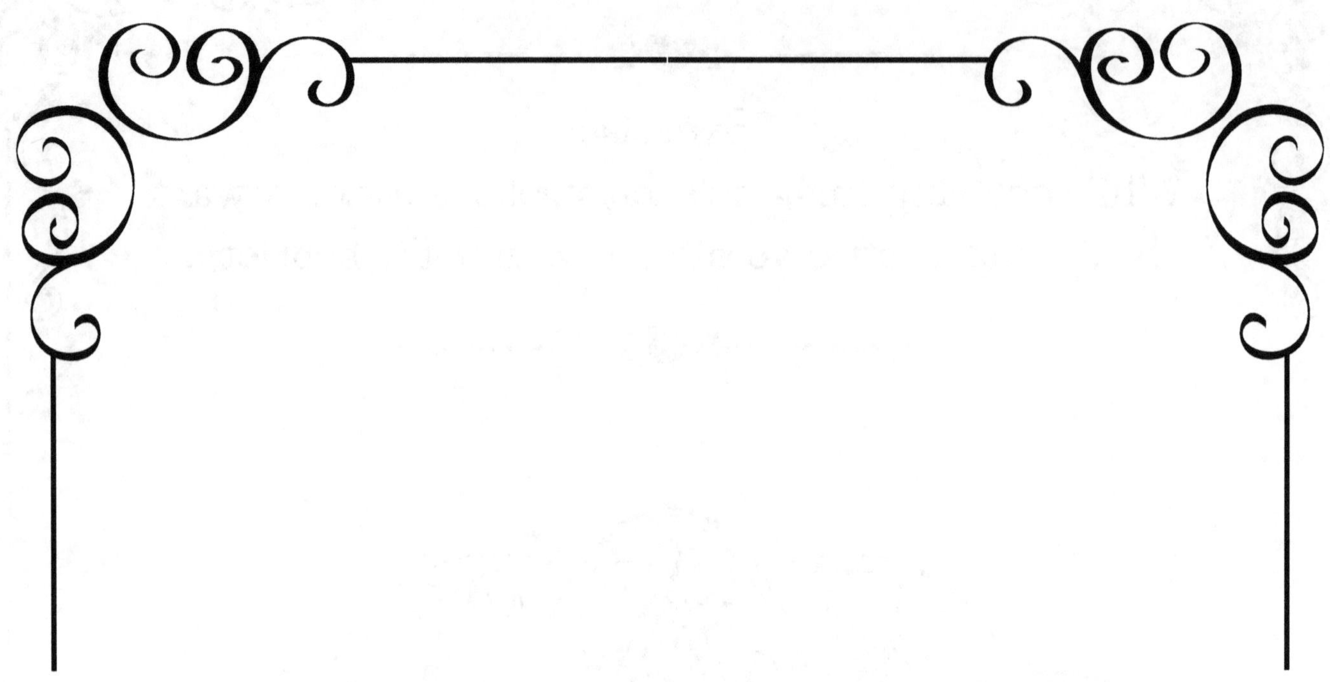

I find peace in the
process,
not just the destination.

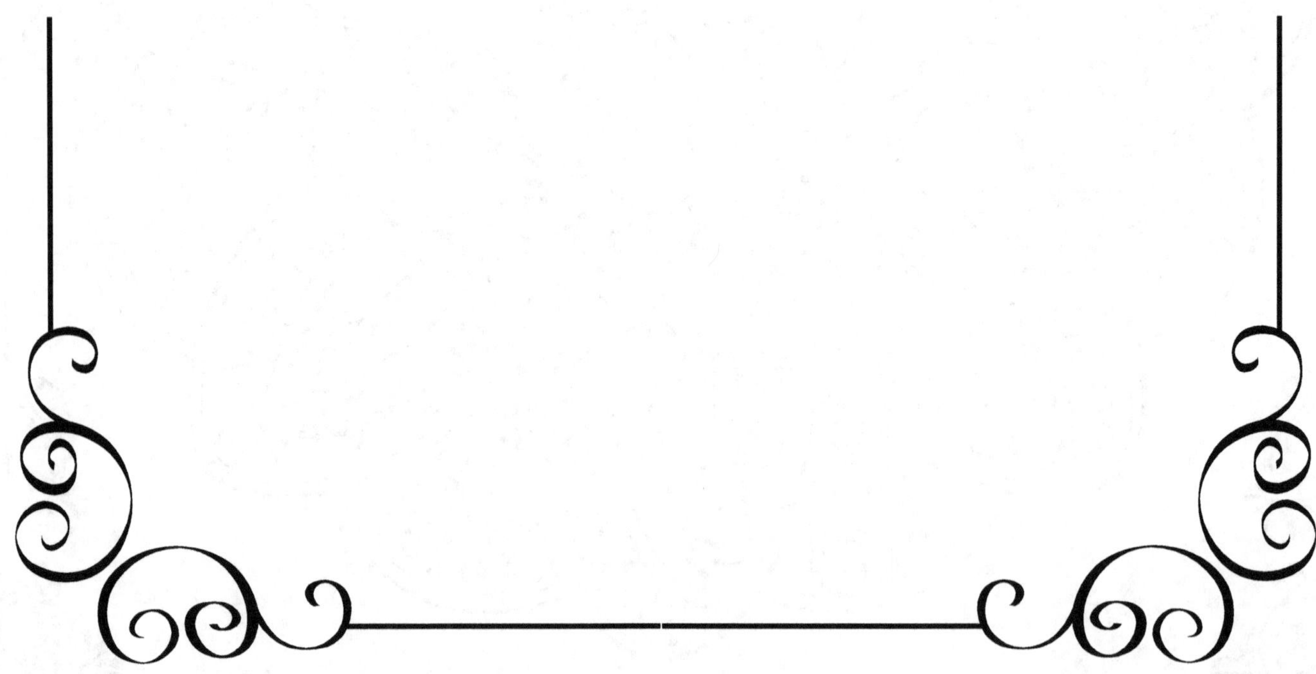

*Exercise:
Embrace the process of coloring, finding peace in
the act itself, rather than solely focusing on the
finished page.

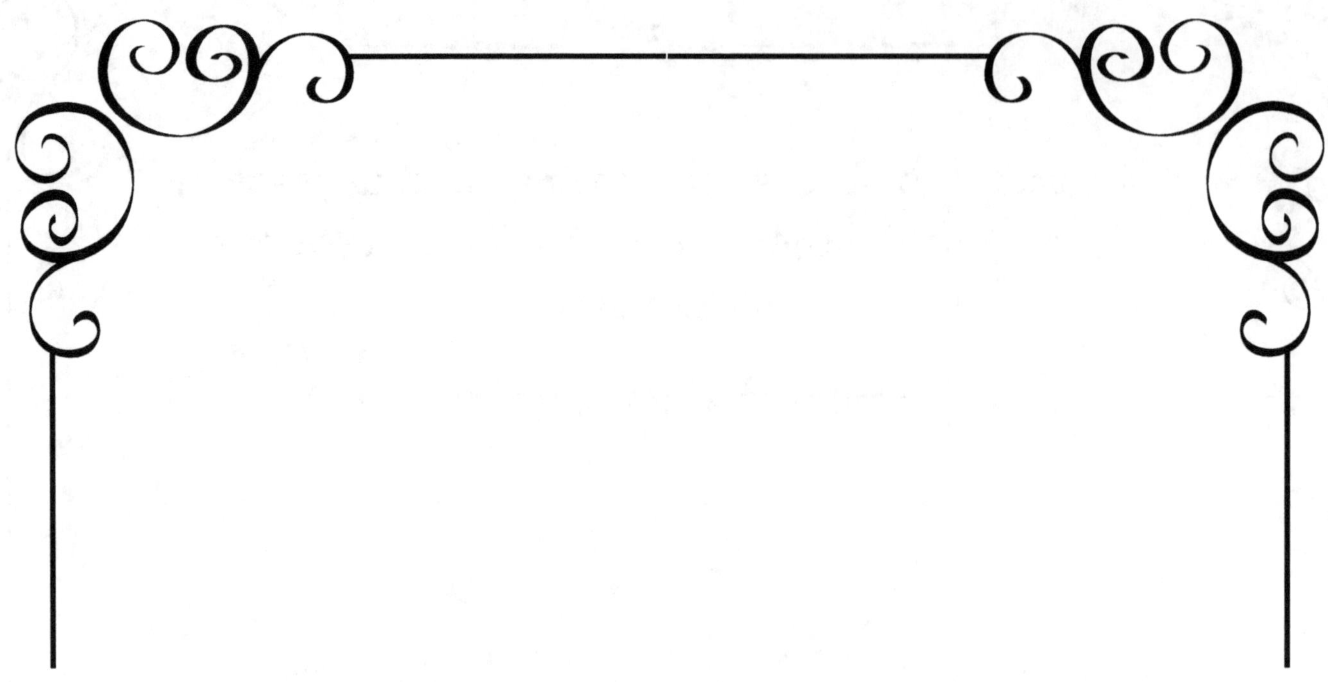

I am the architect of
my inner sanctuary,
where sobriety resides.

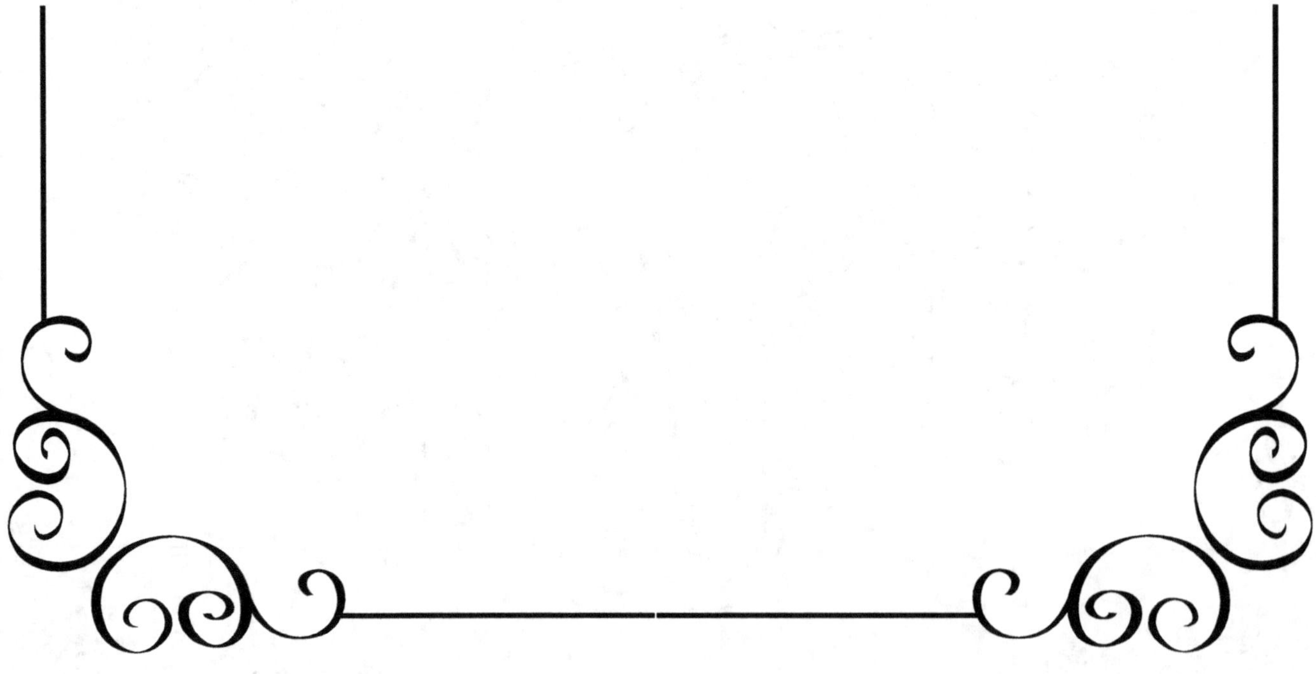

*Exercise:
Imagine designing and constructing your inner
sanctuary, a space of peace and sobriety, as you color.

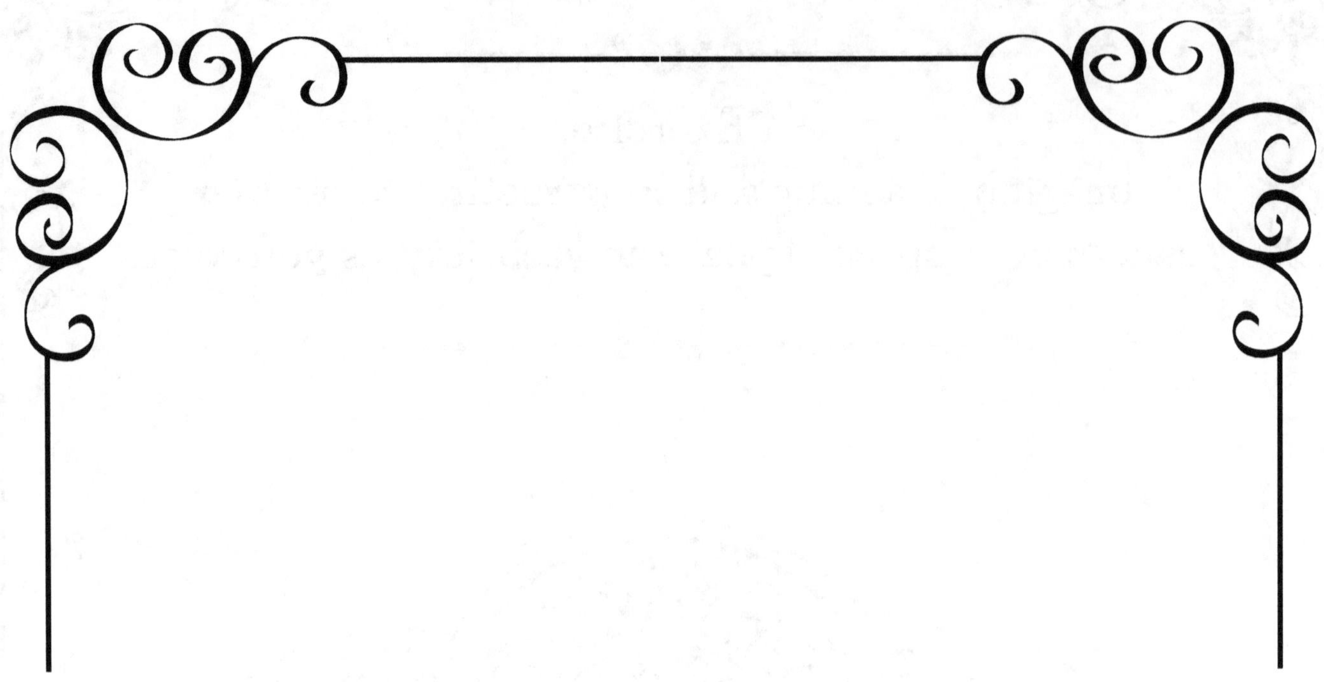

I visualize my
recovery as a mosaic,
each piece unique and valuable.

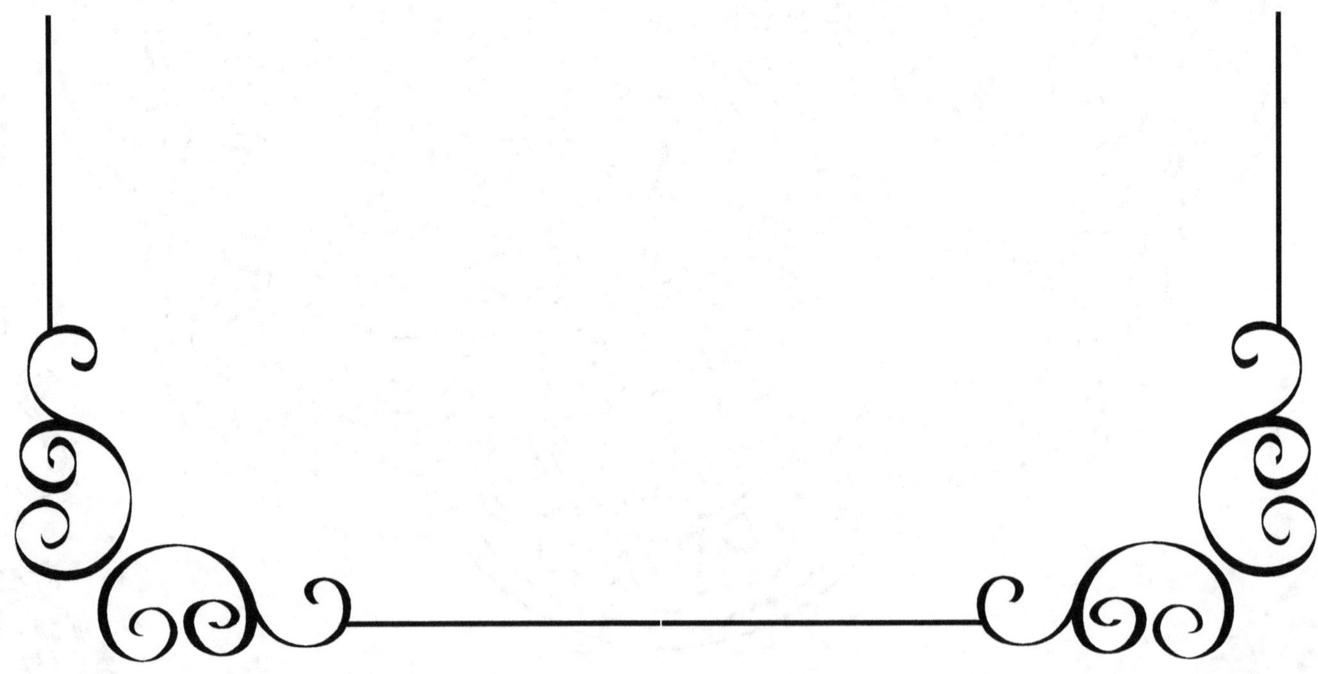

*Exercise:
See your recovery as a mosaic, with each color
choice representing a unique and valuable piece
of your journey.

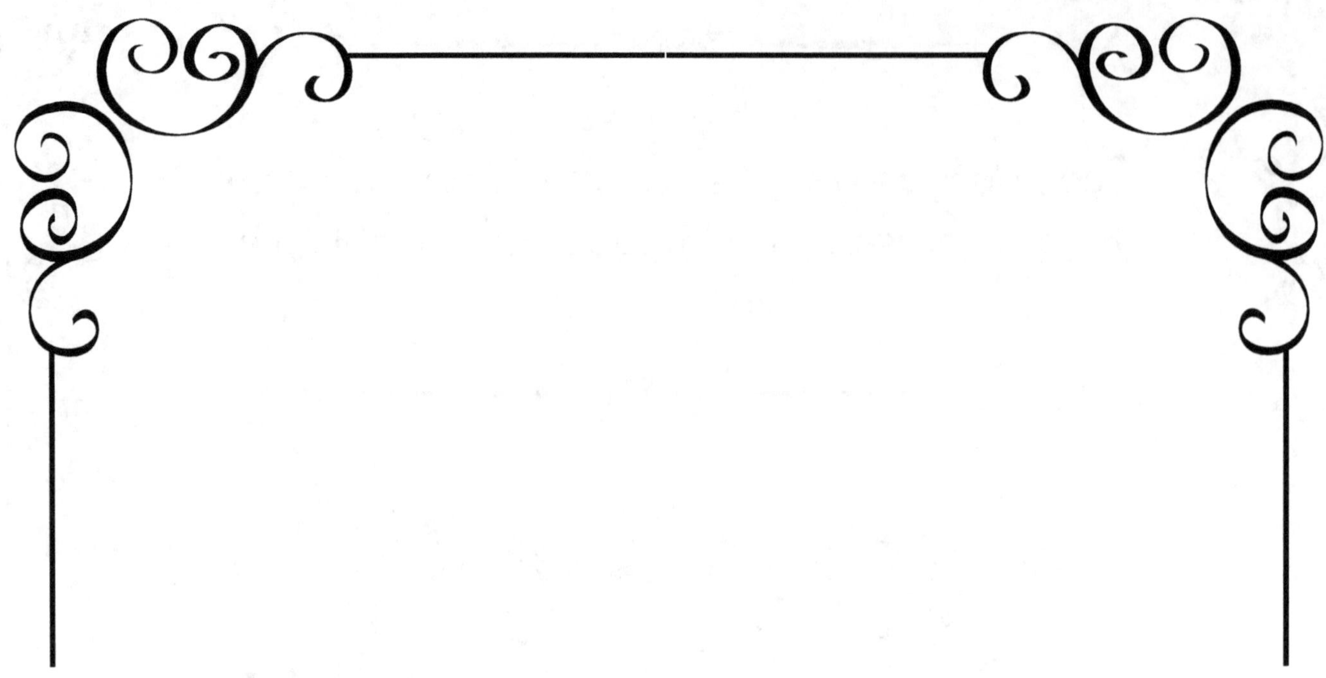

I visualize the
support
of my loved ones as I color.

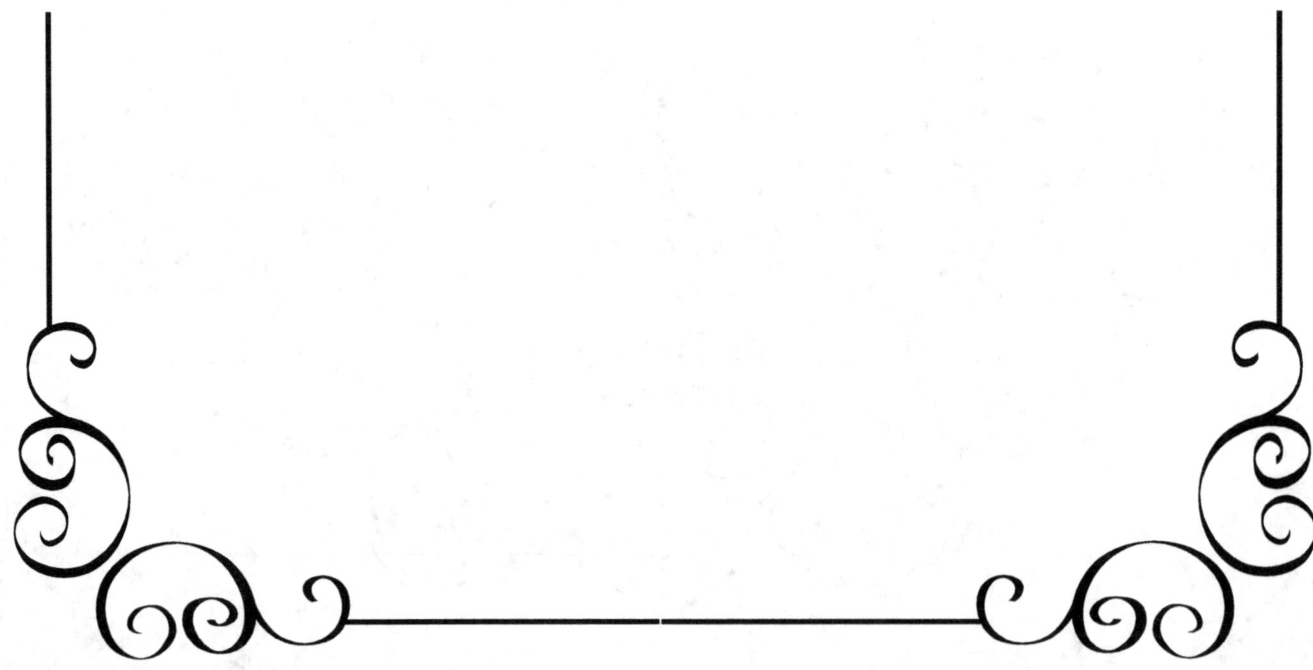

*Exercise:
Picture the faces of loved ones who support your
recovery journey surrounding you as you color,
feeling their encouragement.

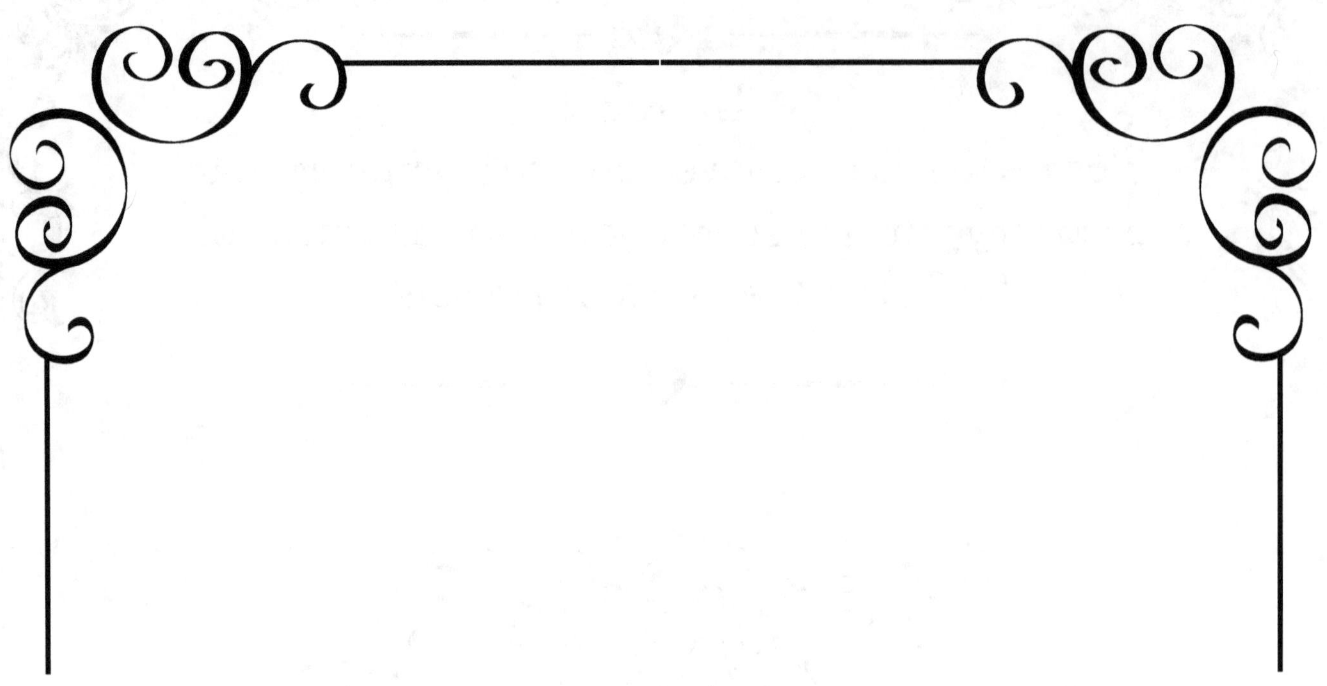

Sobriety is the key that
unlocks the doors
to self-discovery and genuine
happiness.

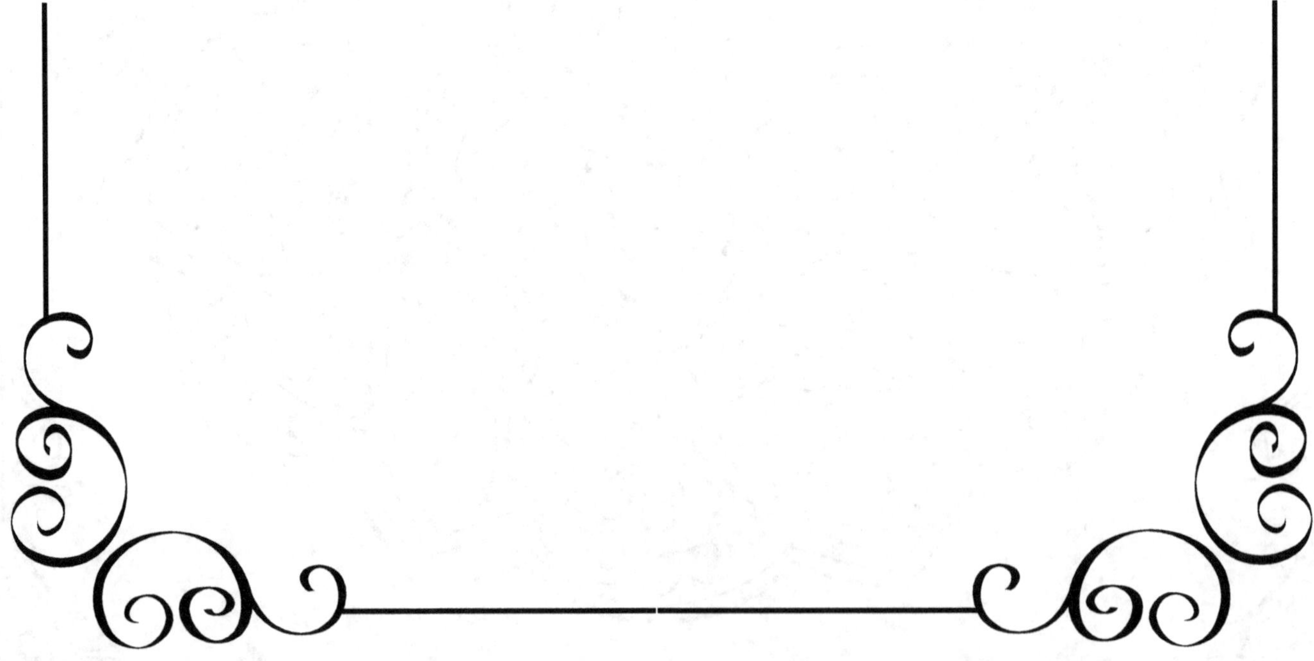

*Exercise:
While coloring, see each stroke as unlocking doors
to self-discovery and happiness in sobriety

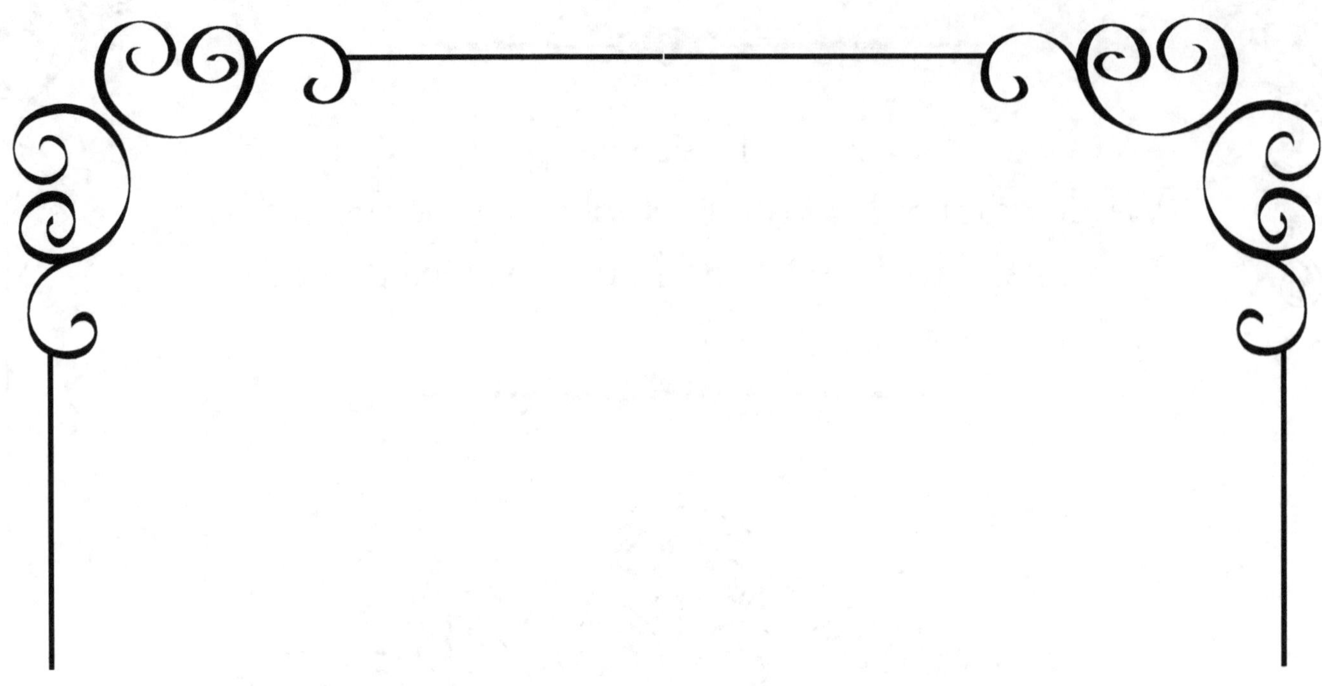

Alcohol masks pain
but doesn't heal it,
leaving emotional wounds
unaddressed.

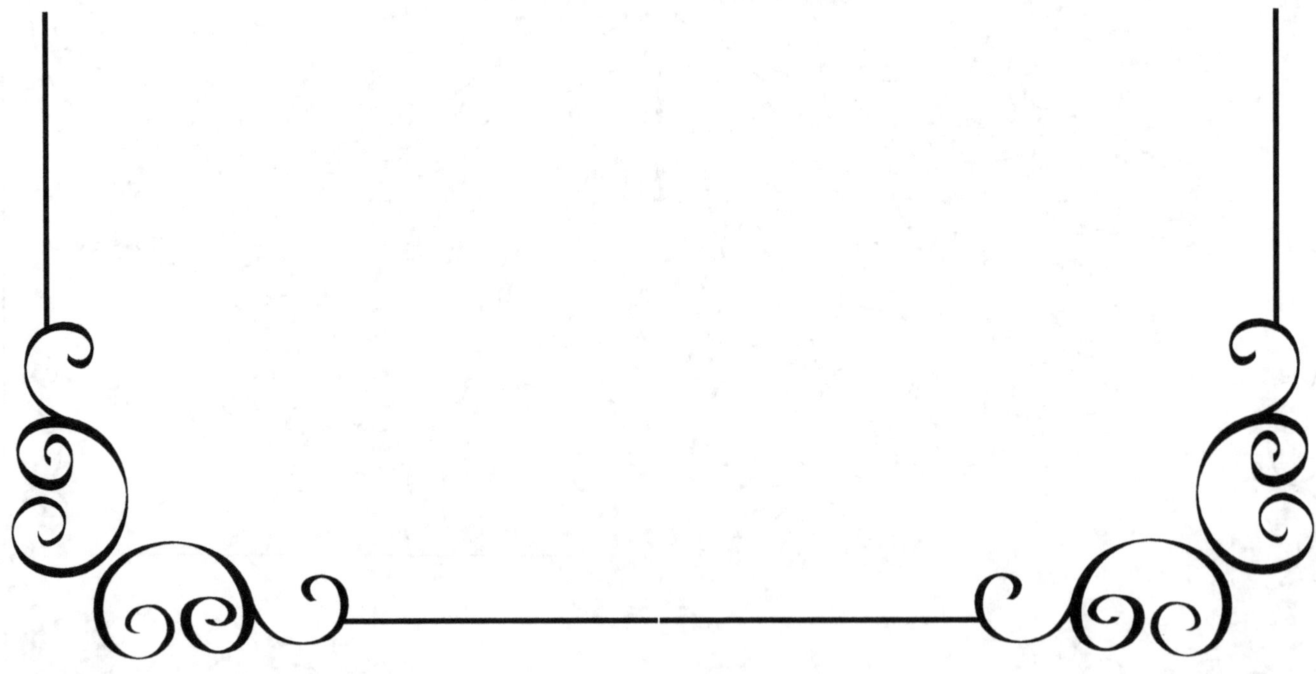

*Exercise:
While coloring, reflect on how alcohol masks pain
but doesn't heal it. Use each stroke as a step towards
acknowledging and addressing emotional wounds.

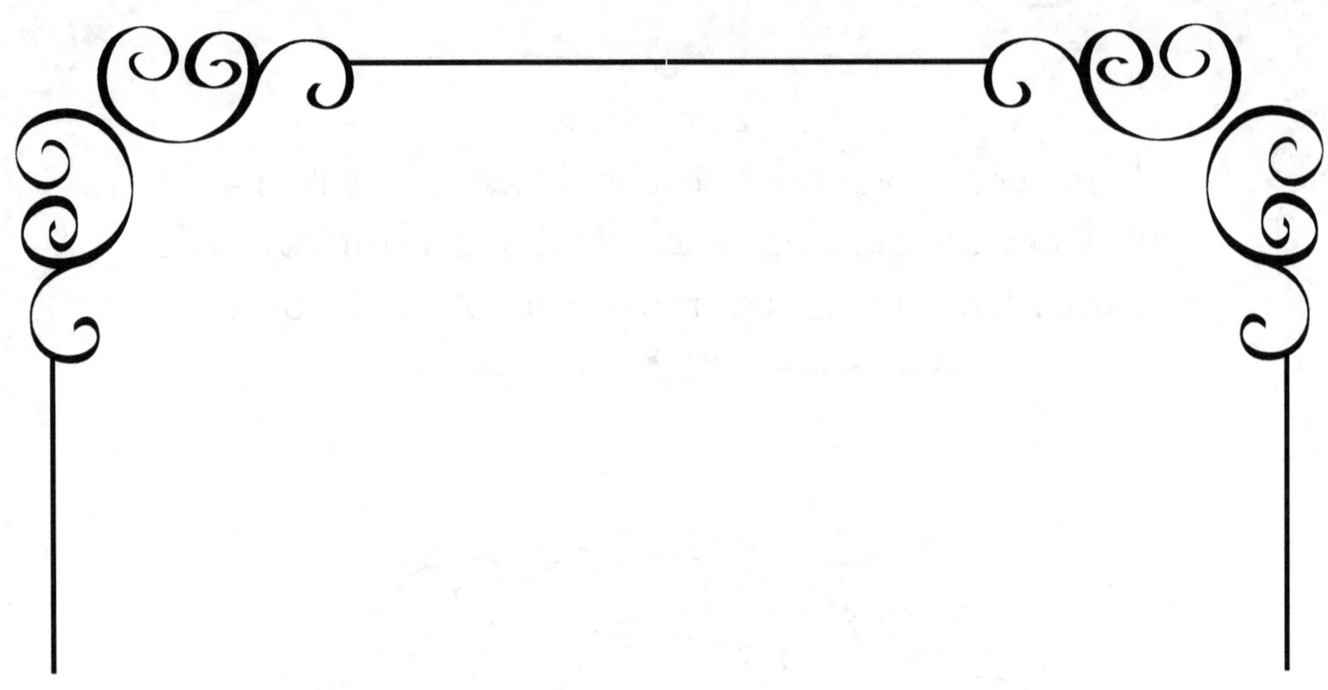

I find strength in the
tools that help me
overcome alcohol-related
thoughts.

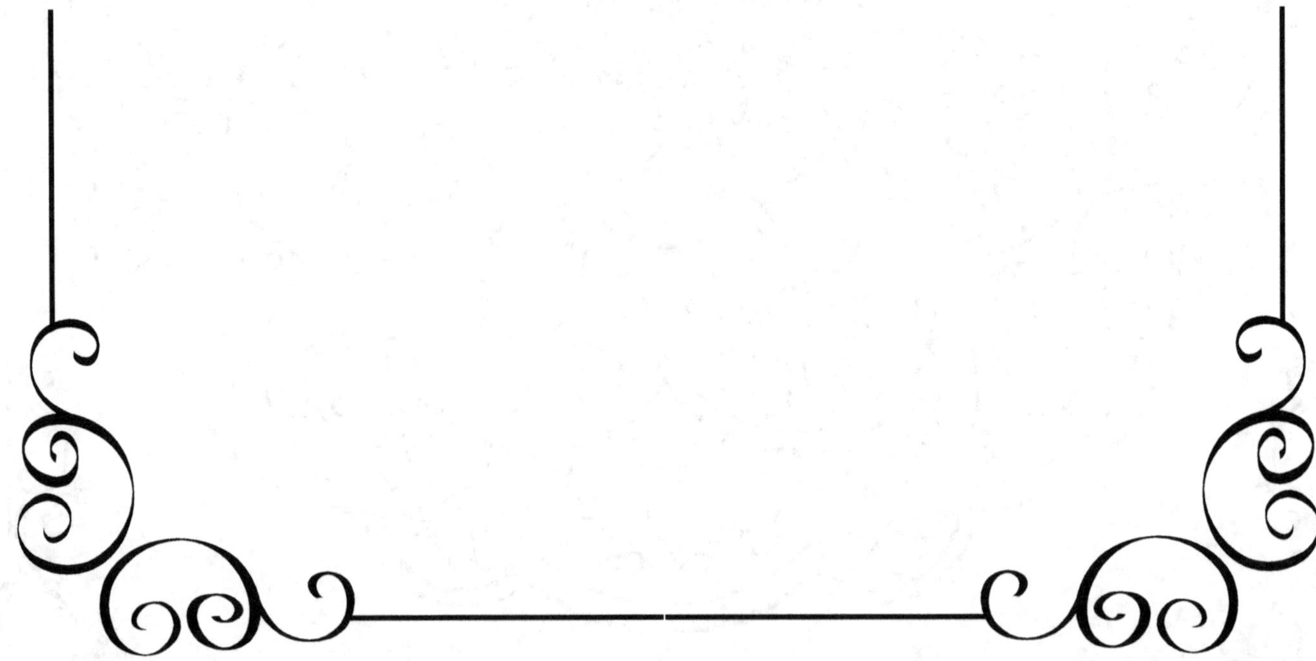

*Exercise:
Imagine a toolbox filled with strategies for managing alcohol-related thoughts, and visualize yourself reaching for the right tool when needed.

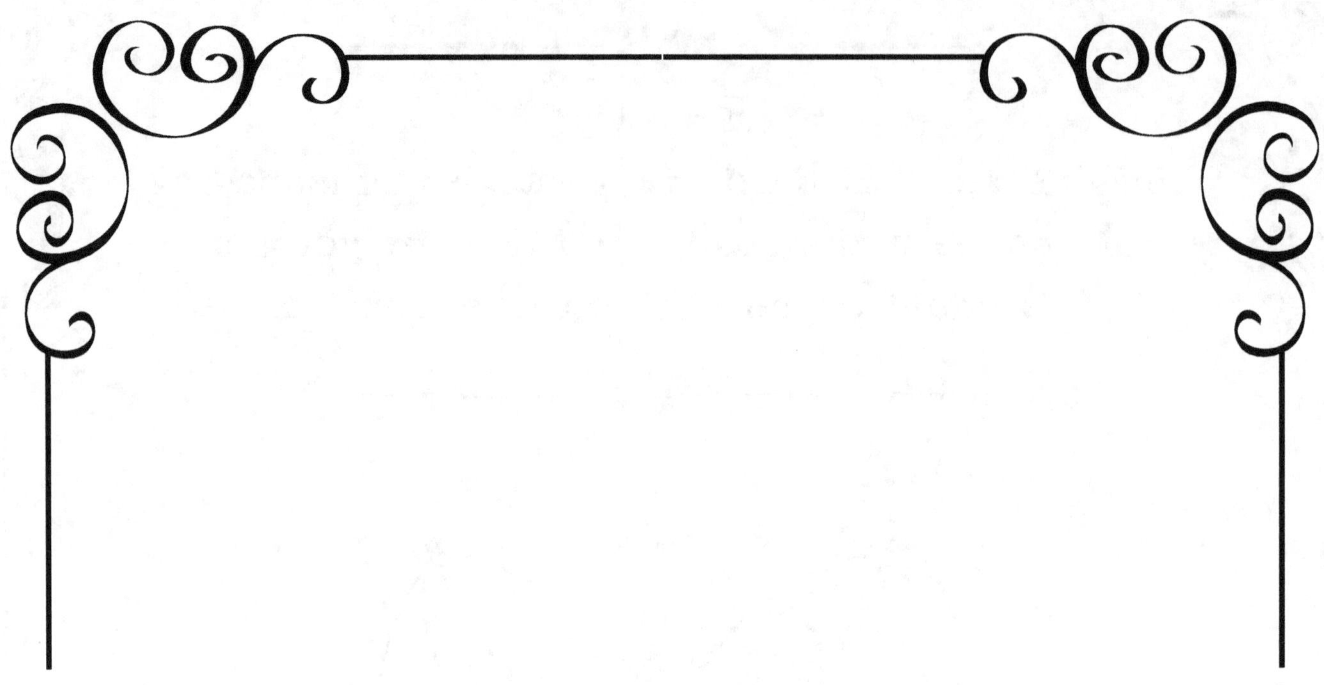

I stand firm in my
commitment to sobriety,
even in the face
of peer pressure.

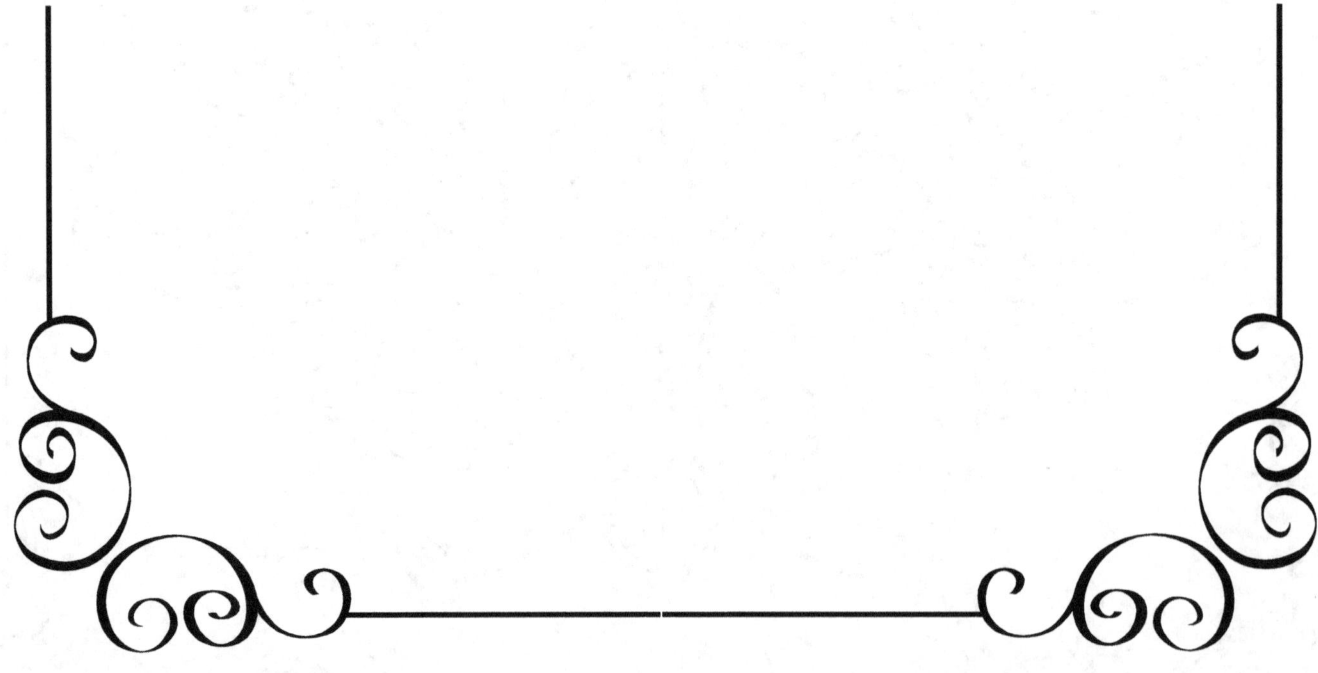

*Exercise:
Use bold strokes to symbolize your strength and resilience when confronted with peer pressure situations.

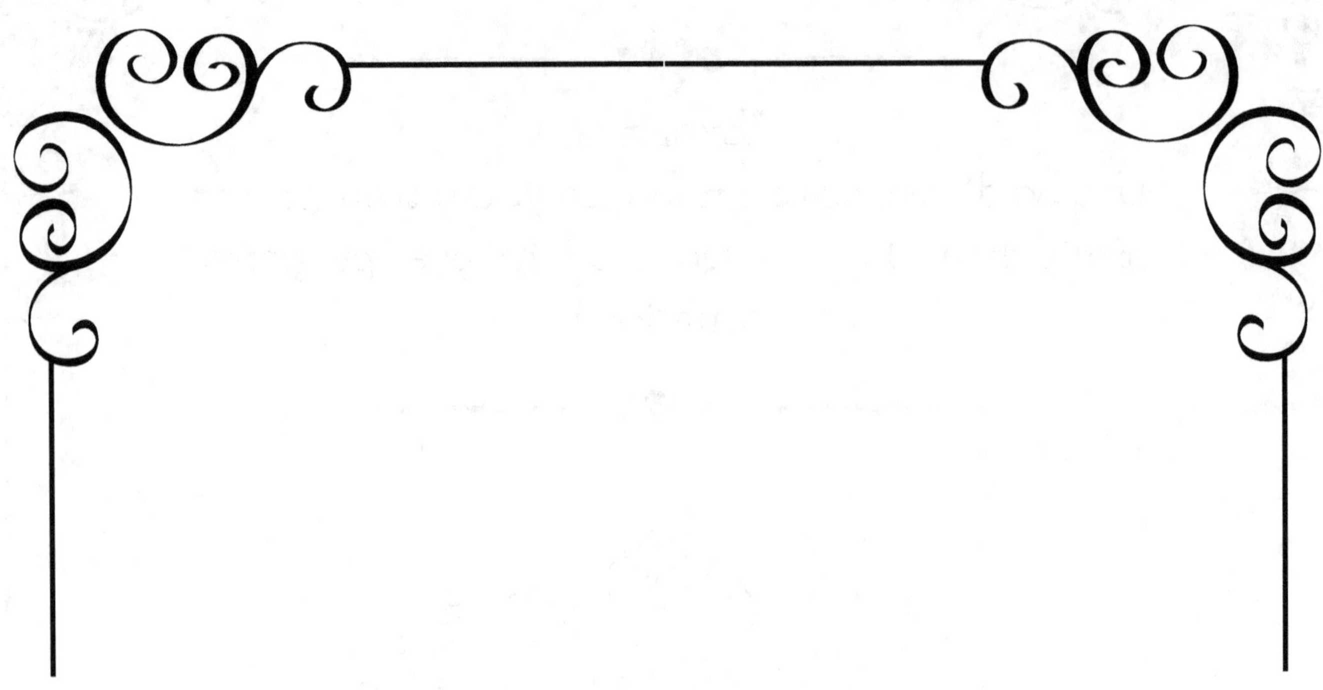

In seeking happiness
through alcohol,
we drift further from joy
and closer to despair.

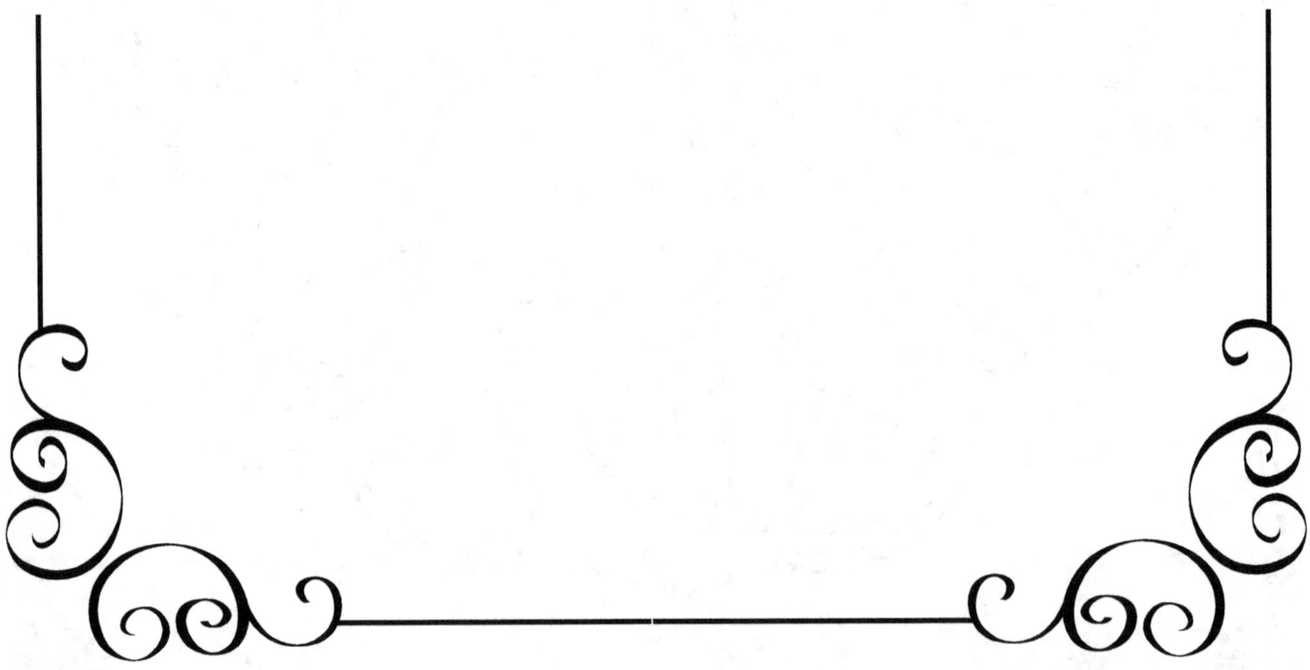

*Exercise:
While coloring, reflect on how seeking happiness through alcohol often led to despair. Use each stroke to envision a path towards genuine joy and fulfillment.

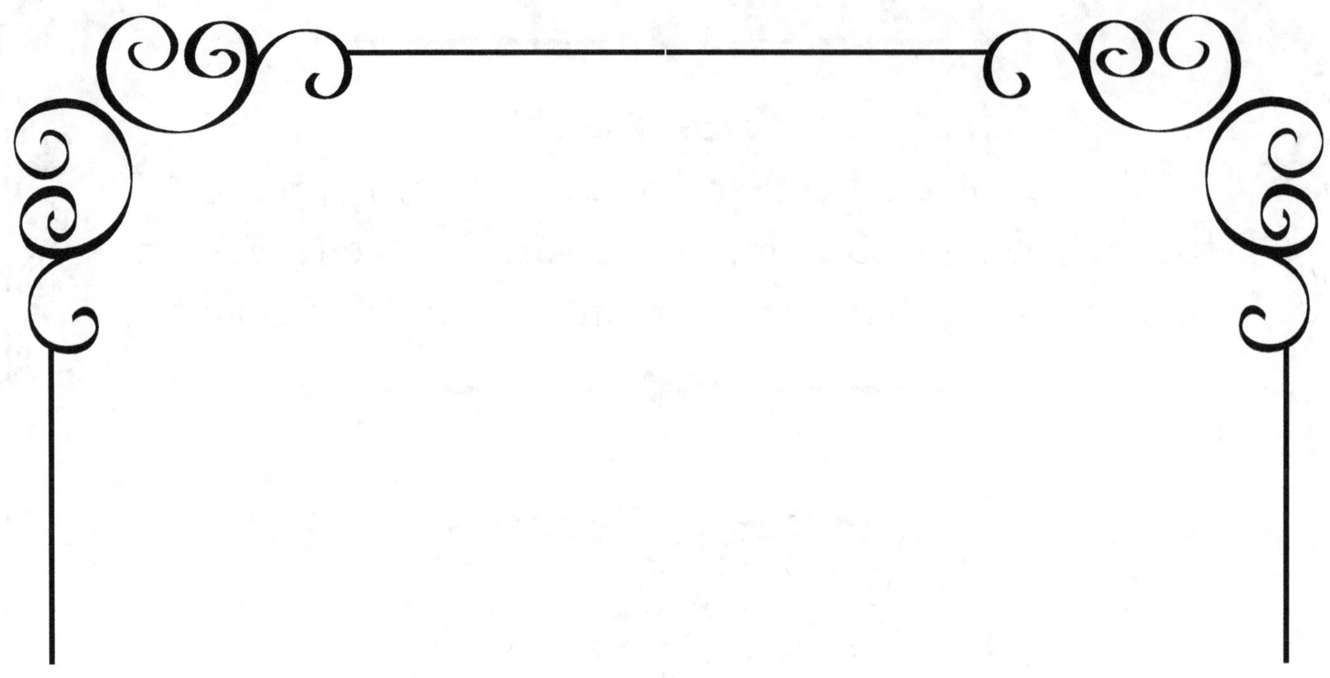

Over time, the soothing
crutch of alcohol
becomes a heavy burden.

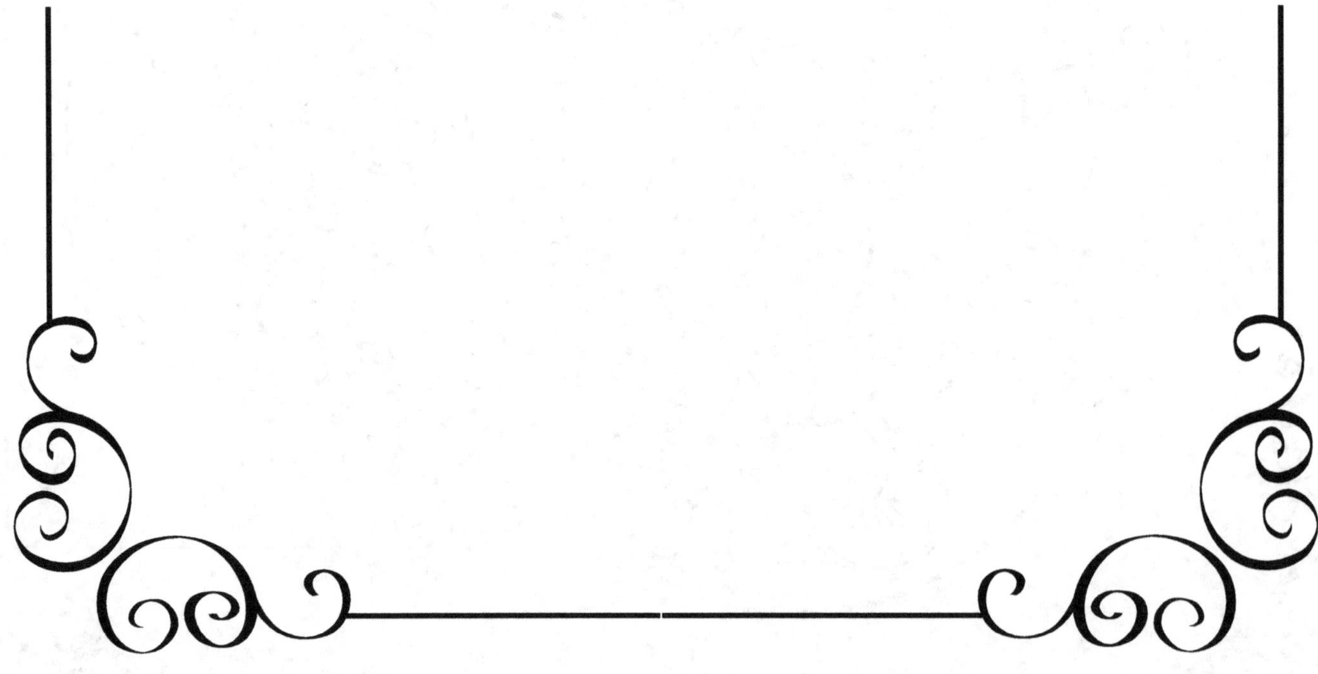

*Exercise:
As you color, think about how alcohol, once a soothing crutch, became a heavy burden over time. With each stroke, imagine shedding that burden and feeling lighter.

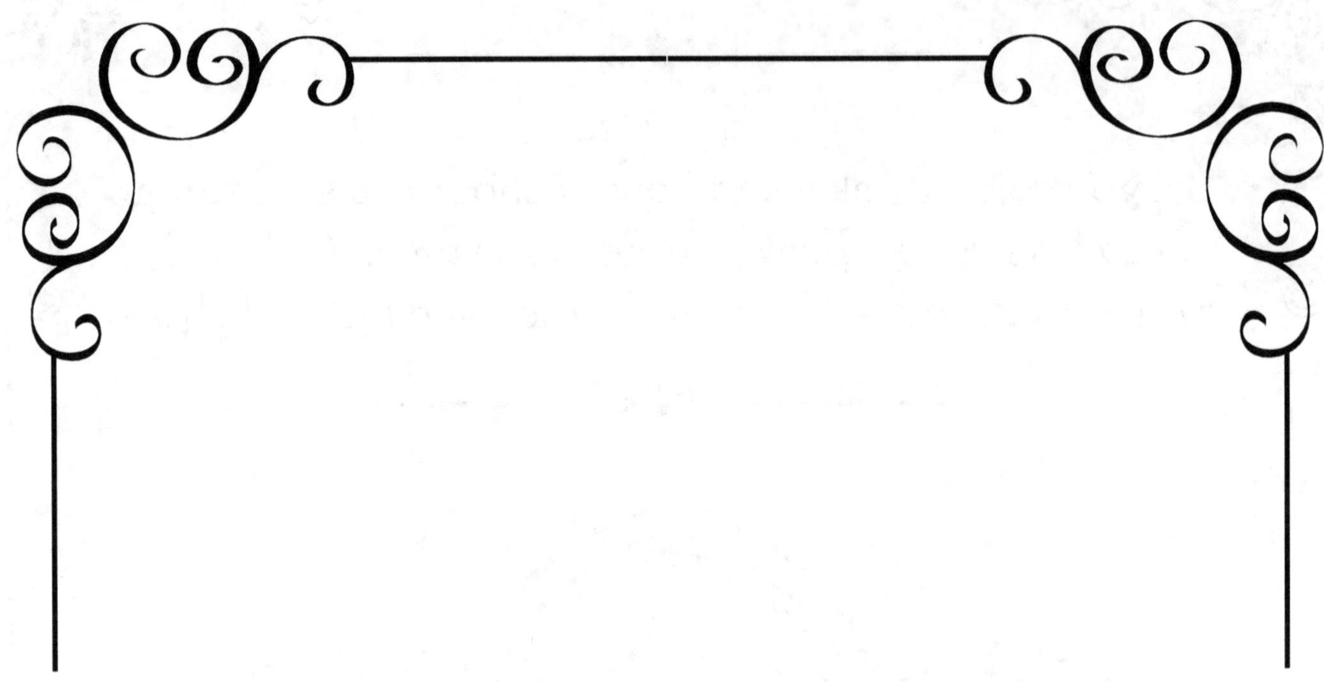

Alcohol turn the best
intentions
into broken promises.

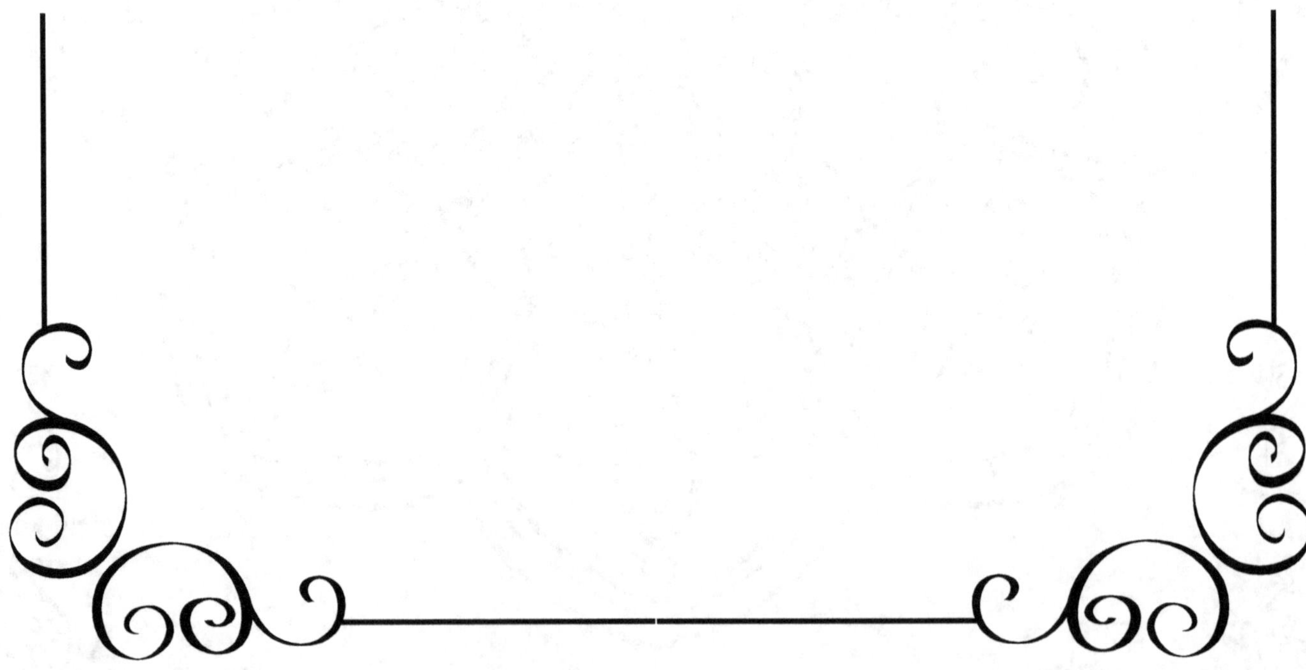

*Exercise:
As you color, think about times when alcohol turned your best intentions into broken promises. With each stroke, visualize renewing your commitment to keeping promises and making positive choices in sobriety.

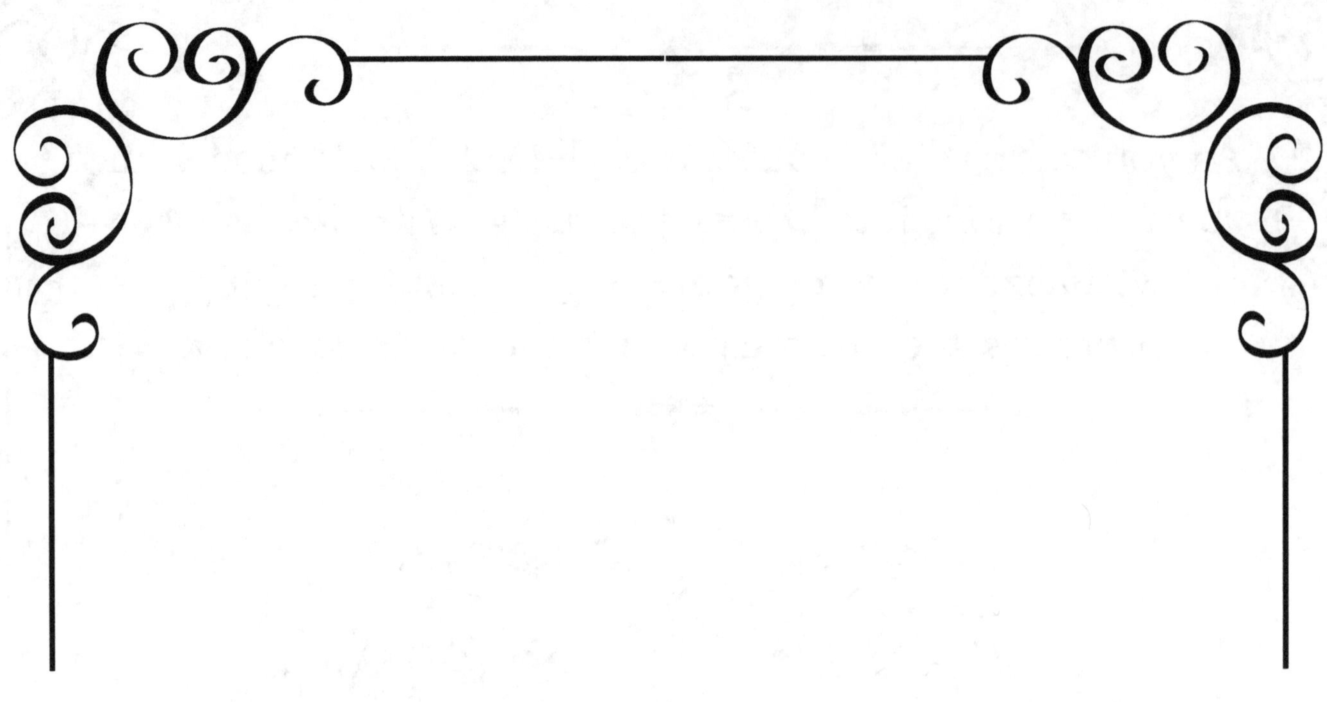

I nurture my body
with love,
knowing it's my
greatest ally.

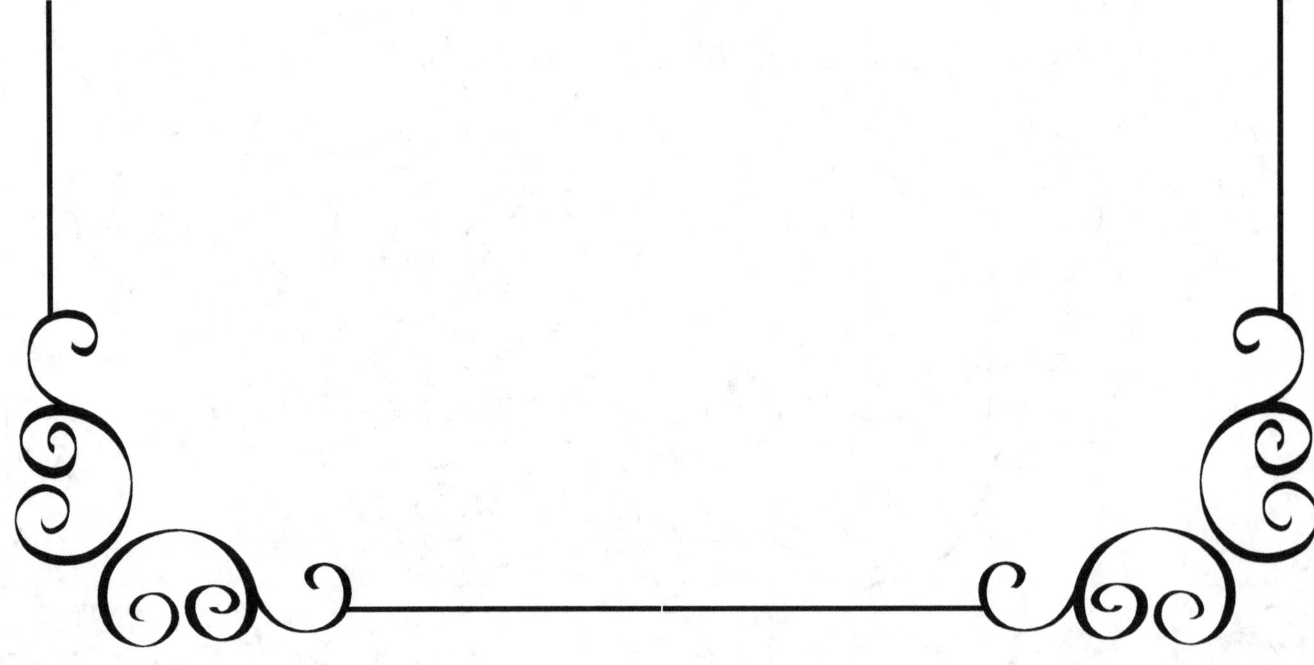

*Exercise:
As you color, imagine sending waves of love and
gratitude to your body, thanking it for its resilience.

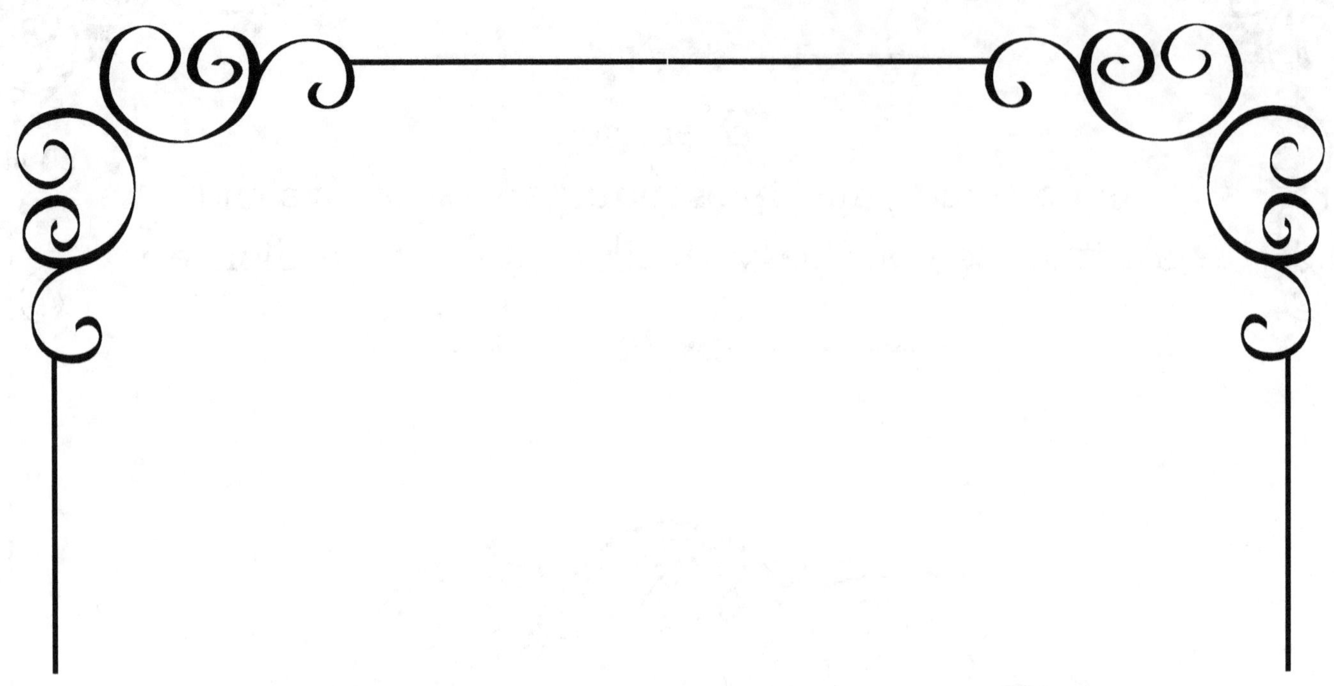

I release the past and
embrace the present
moment
with open arms.

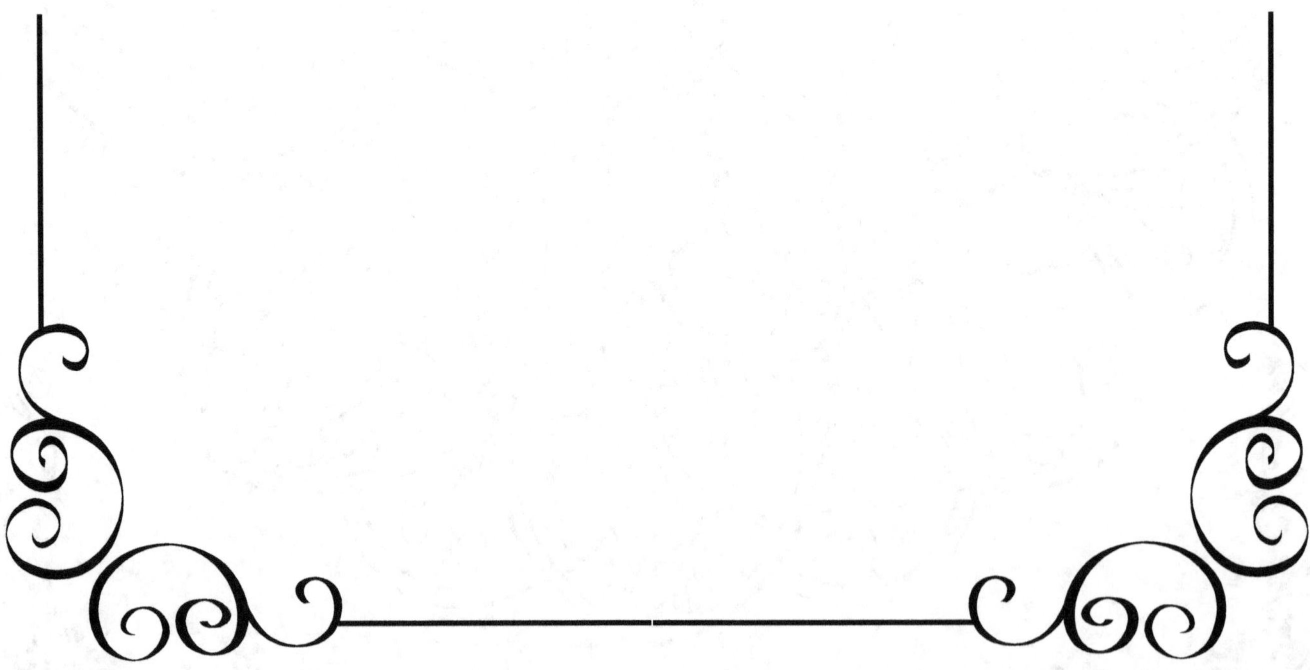

*Exercise:
While coloring, let go of any thoughts related to the past and focus on the present moment, enjoying the process.

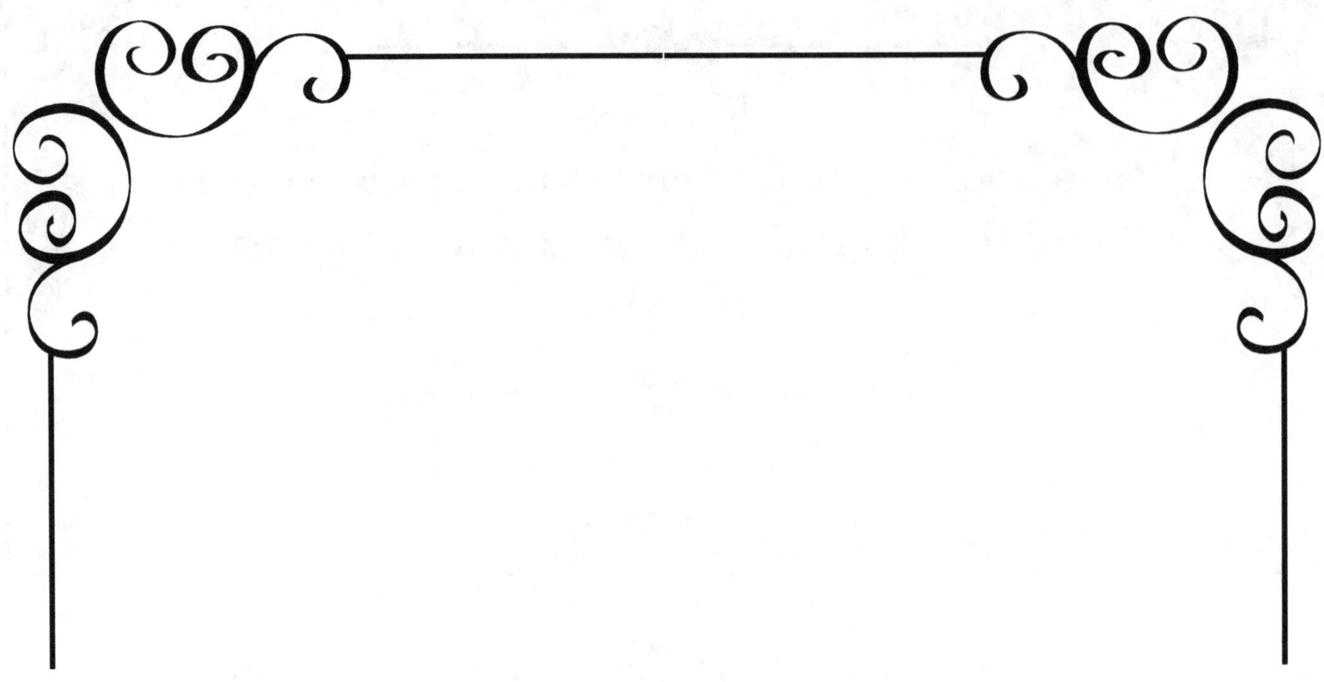

I choose empowerment
over alcohol,
painting a brighter future.

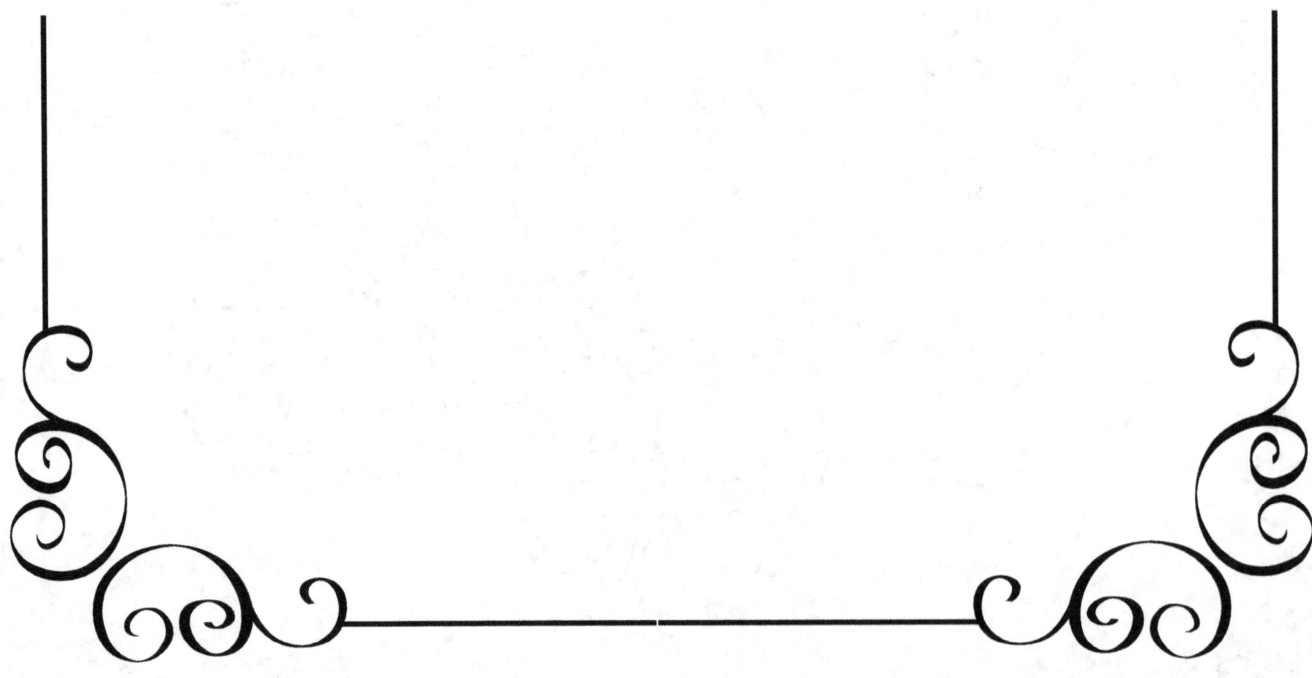

*Exercise:
Visualize your future as a bright and colorful
landscape, created by your choices to stay empowered.

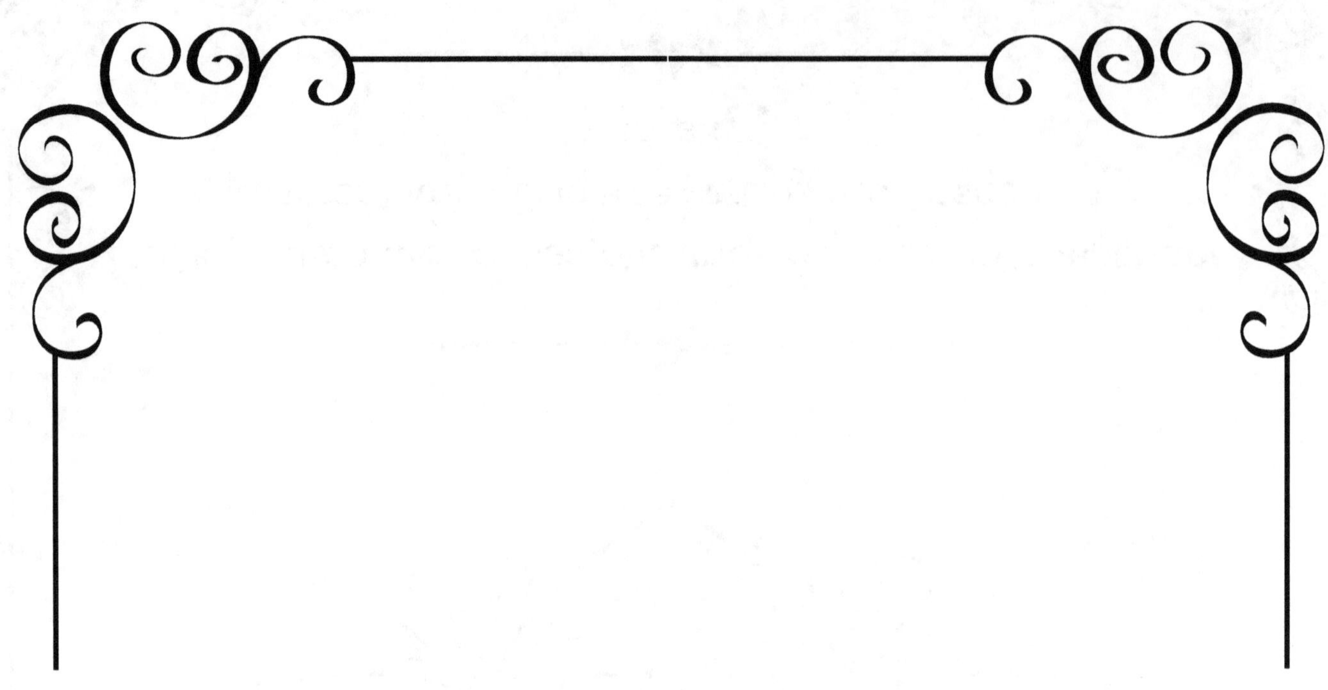

I see the beauty
of a life
without alcohol
in every shade.

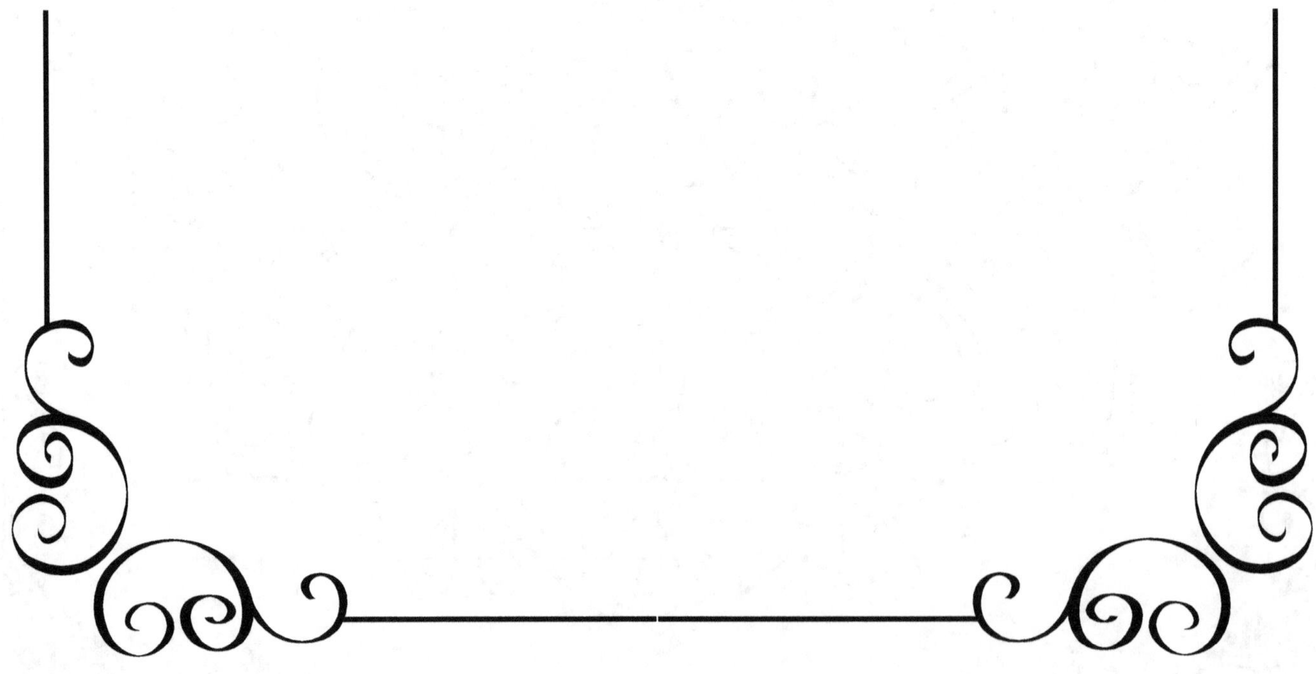

*Exercise:
Visualize the beauty of sobriety reflected in the colors you choose, making each shade a testament to your journey.

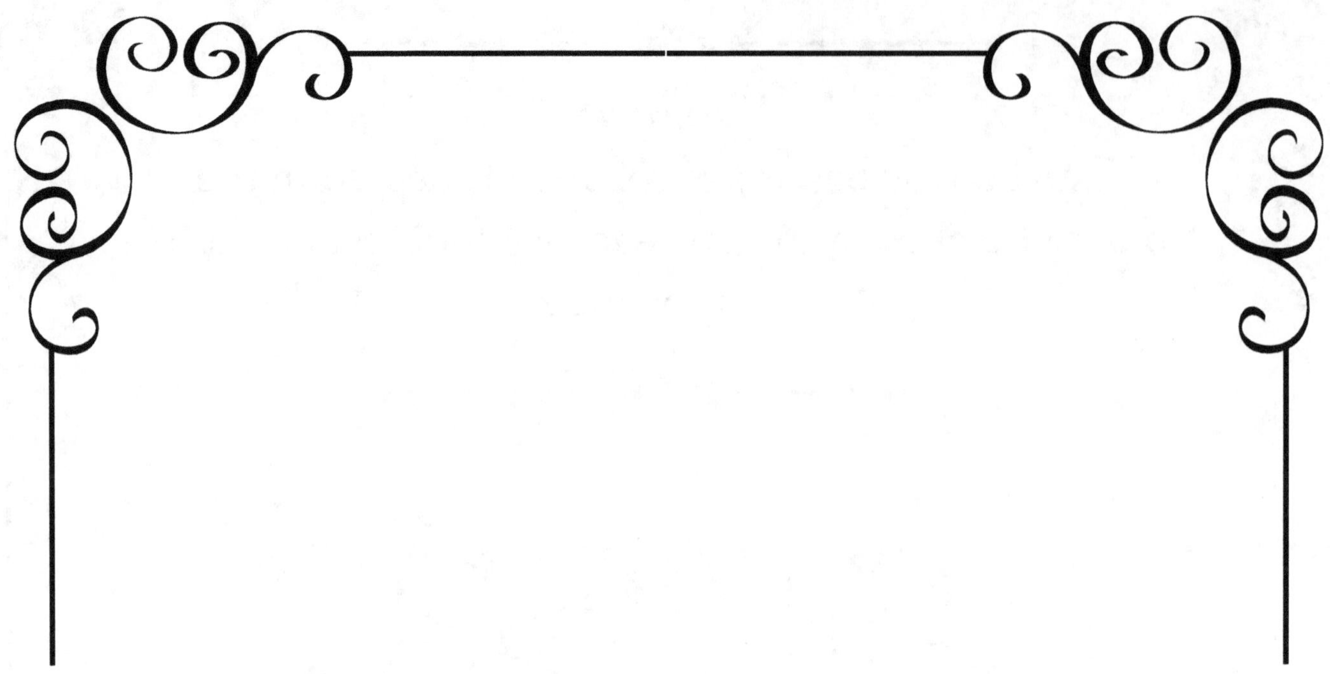

I visualize the negativity
drifting away,
making room for positivity.

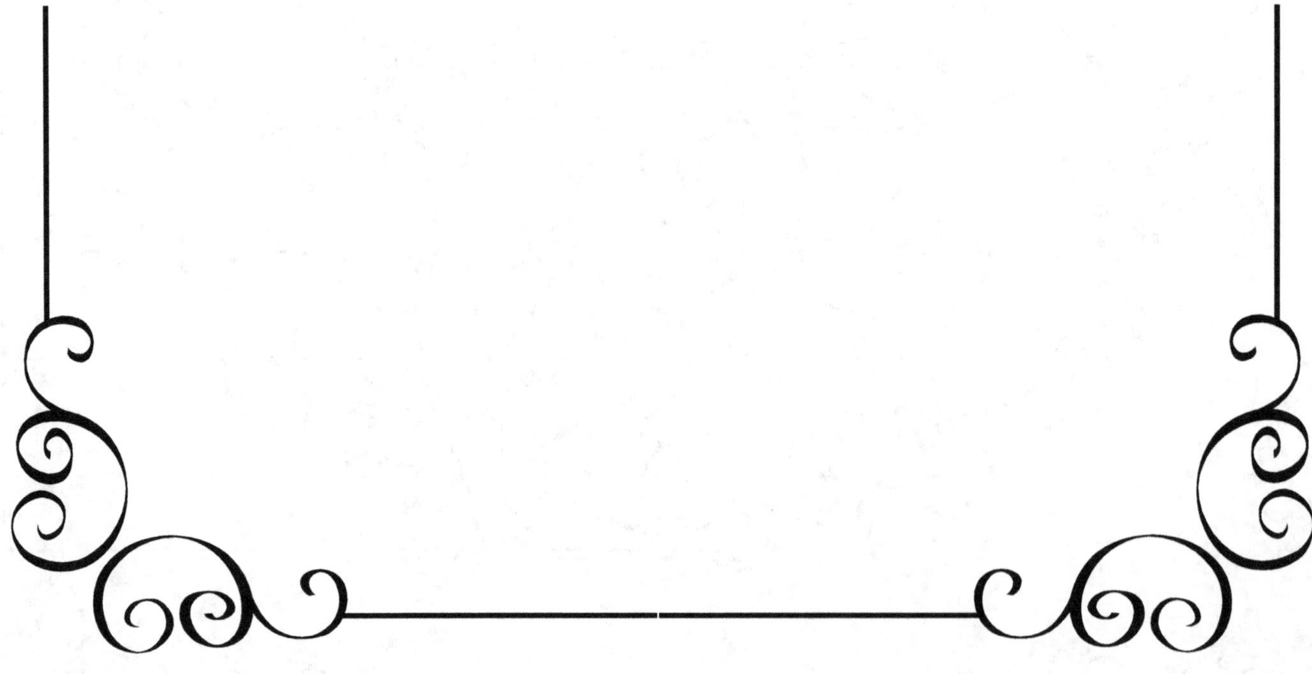

*Exercise:
As you color, imagine the negative thoughts floating
away like clouds, leaving behind clear skies filled
with positivity.

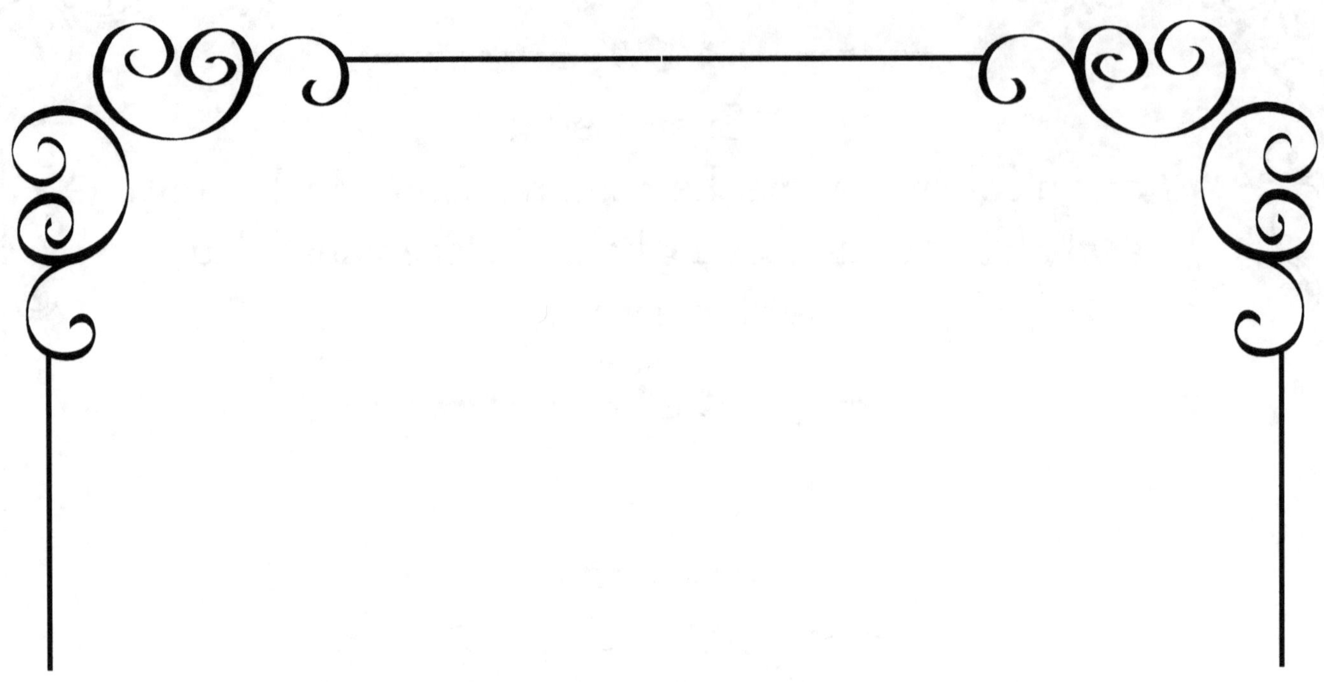

I find refuge in my
supportive circle,
guarding my sobriety.

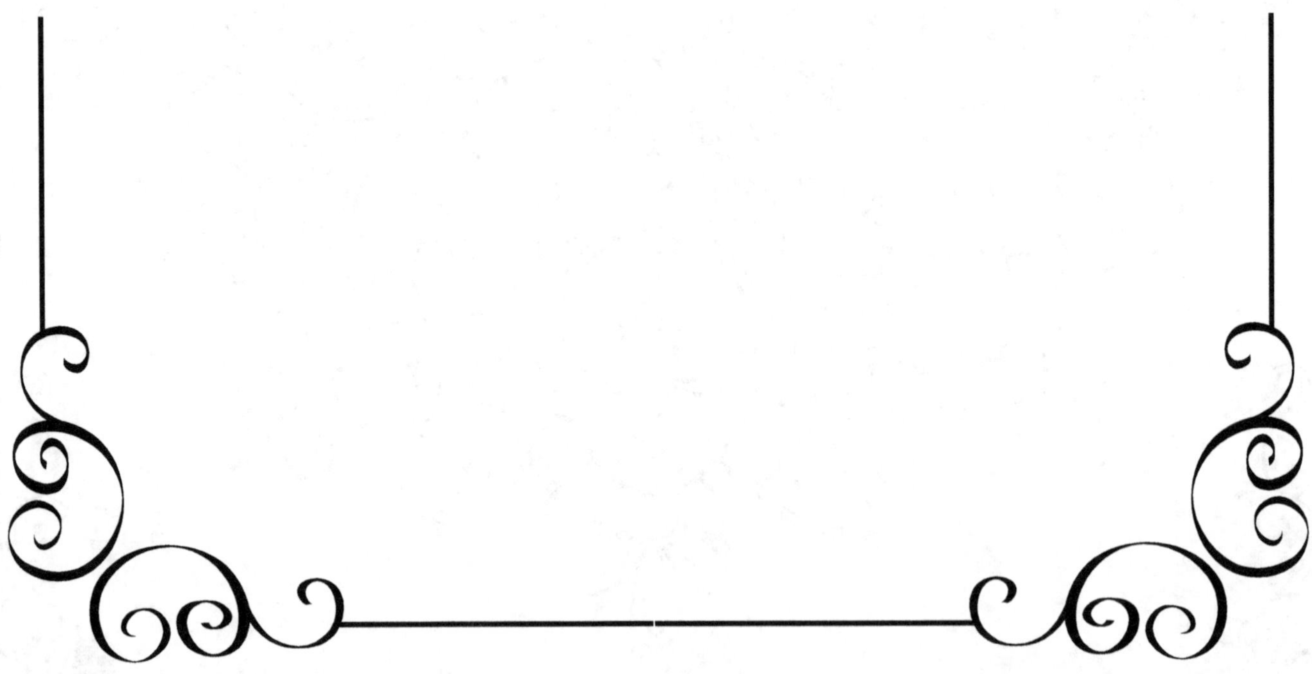

*Exercise:
Use colors that symbolize your supportive circle of
friends and loved ones, reinforcing their importance.

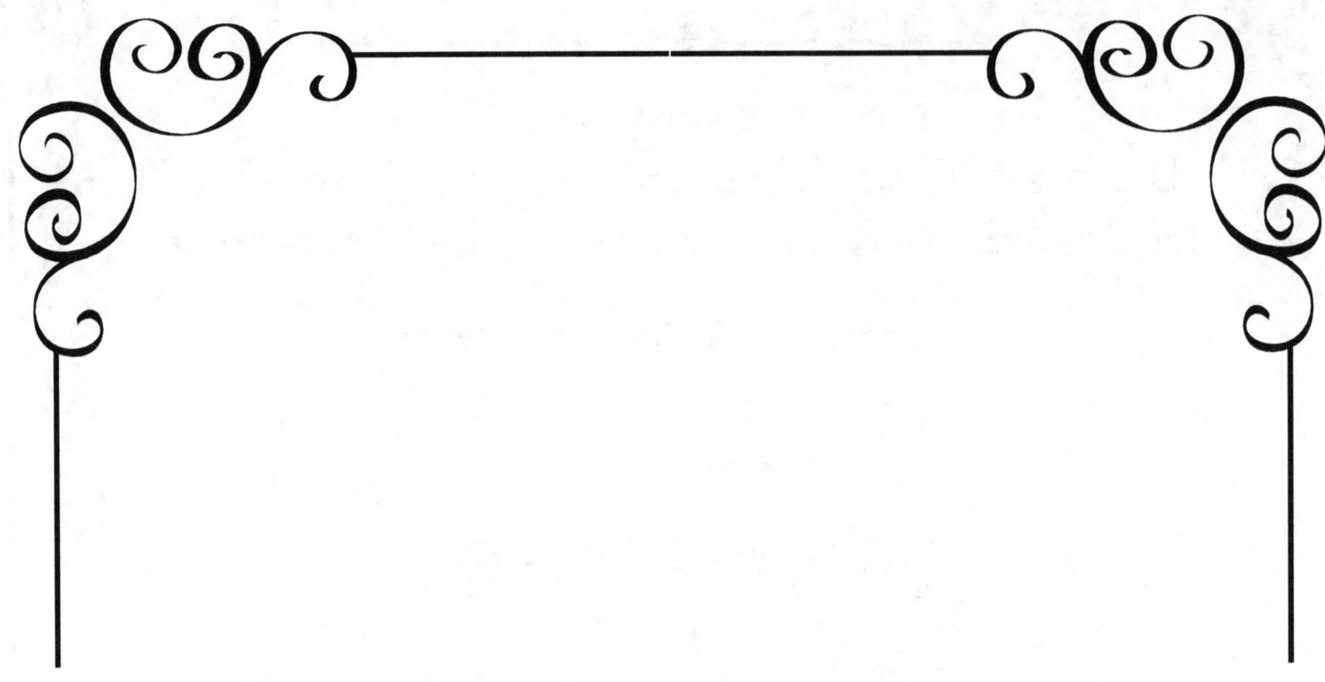

I am the captain
of my ship,

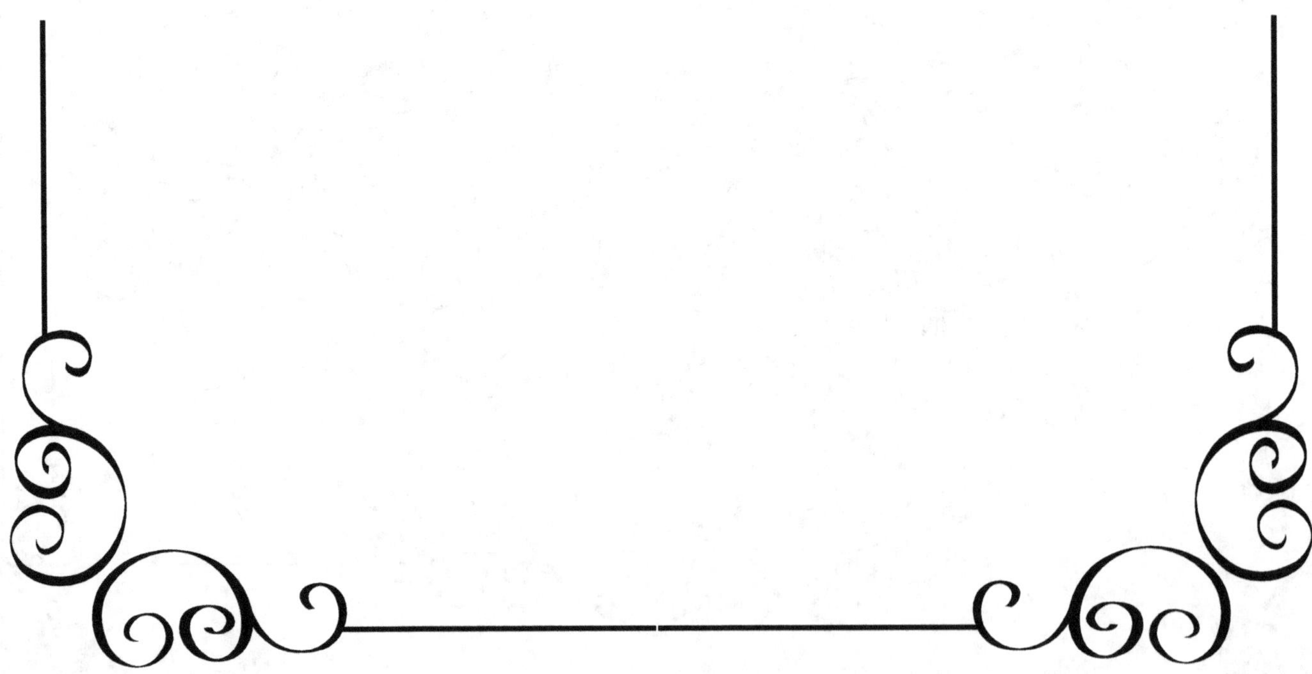

*Exercise:
Imagine yourself as the captain of your life's ship,
navigating it toward a brighter future, and use colors
that represent this journey.

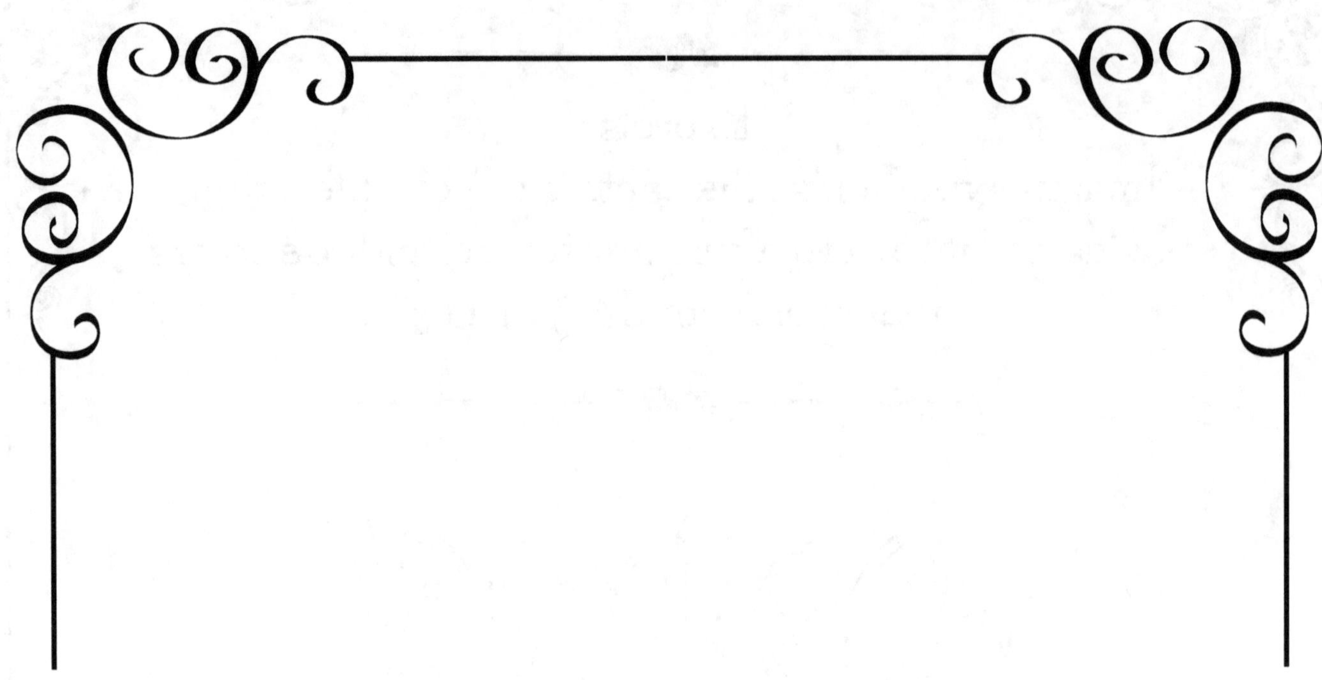

I am deserving of
good health
and well-being.

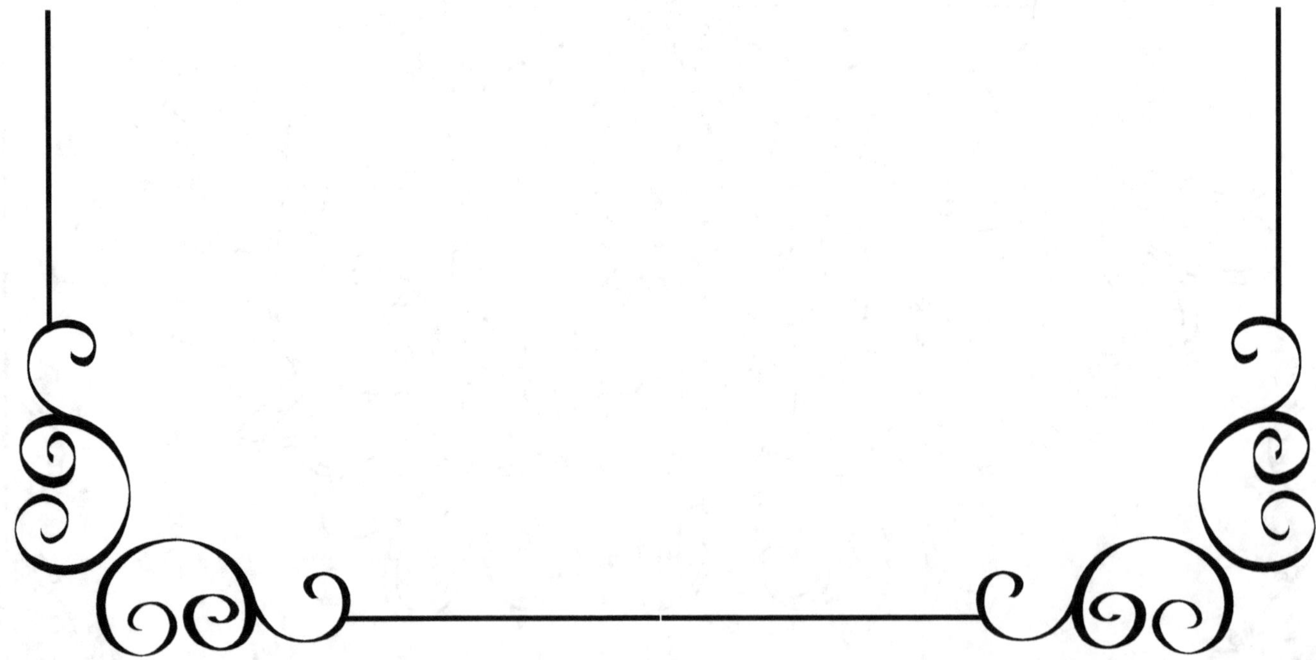

*Exercise:
As you color, feel yourself worthy of good health
and well-being.

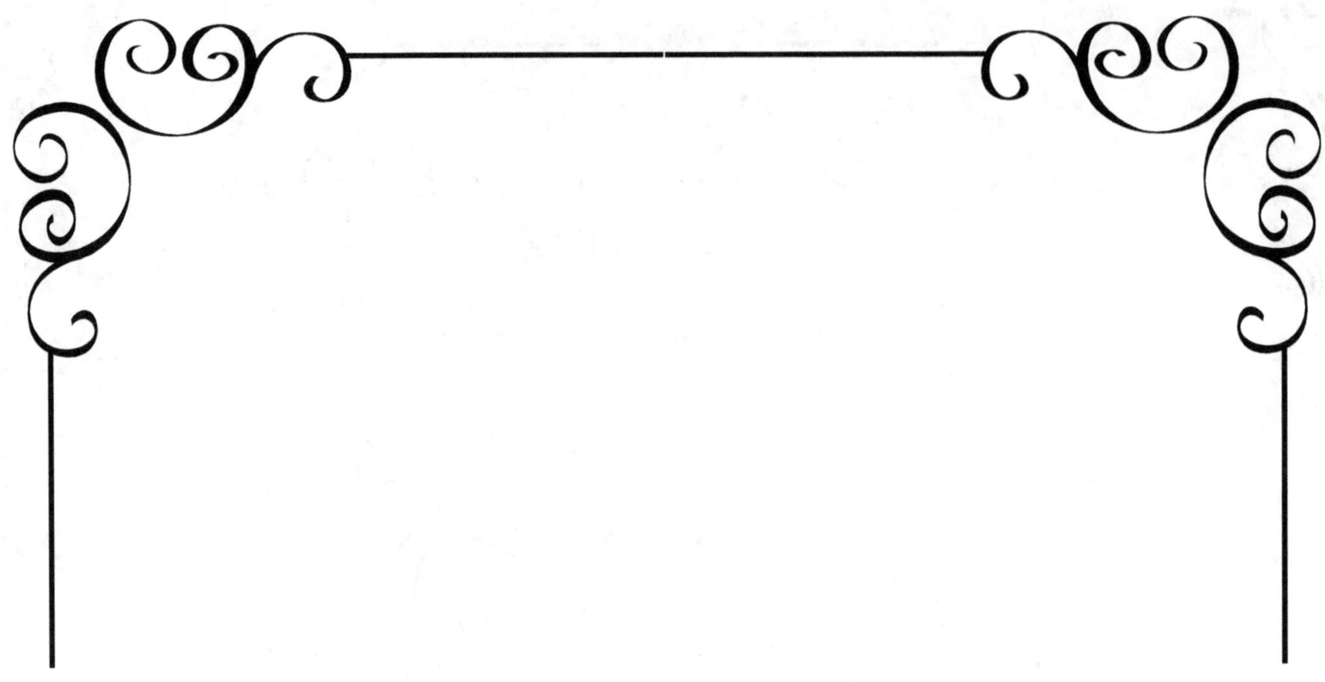

I find peace in
the quiet moments,
nurturing my soul.

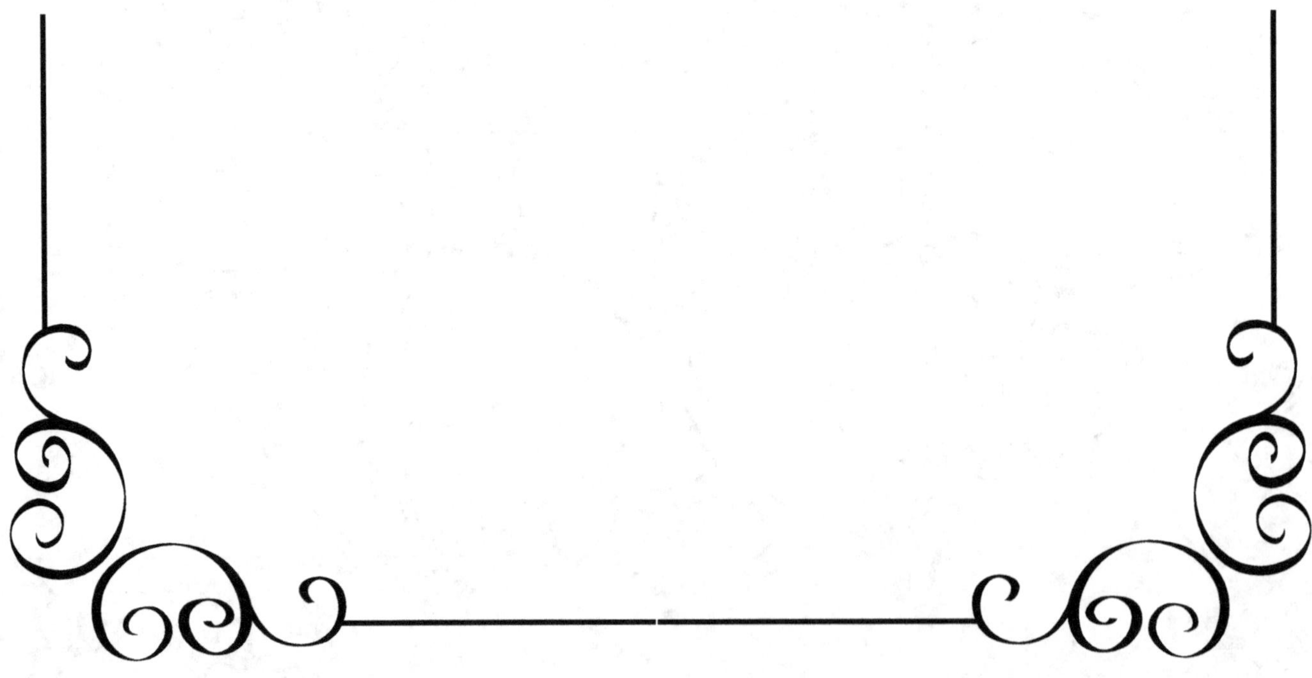

*Exercise:

While coloring, appreciate the peace and tranquility
of the moment, allowing it to nurture your soul.

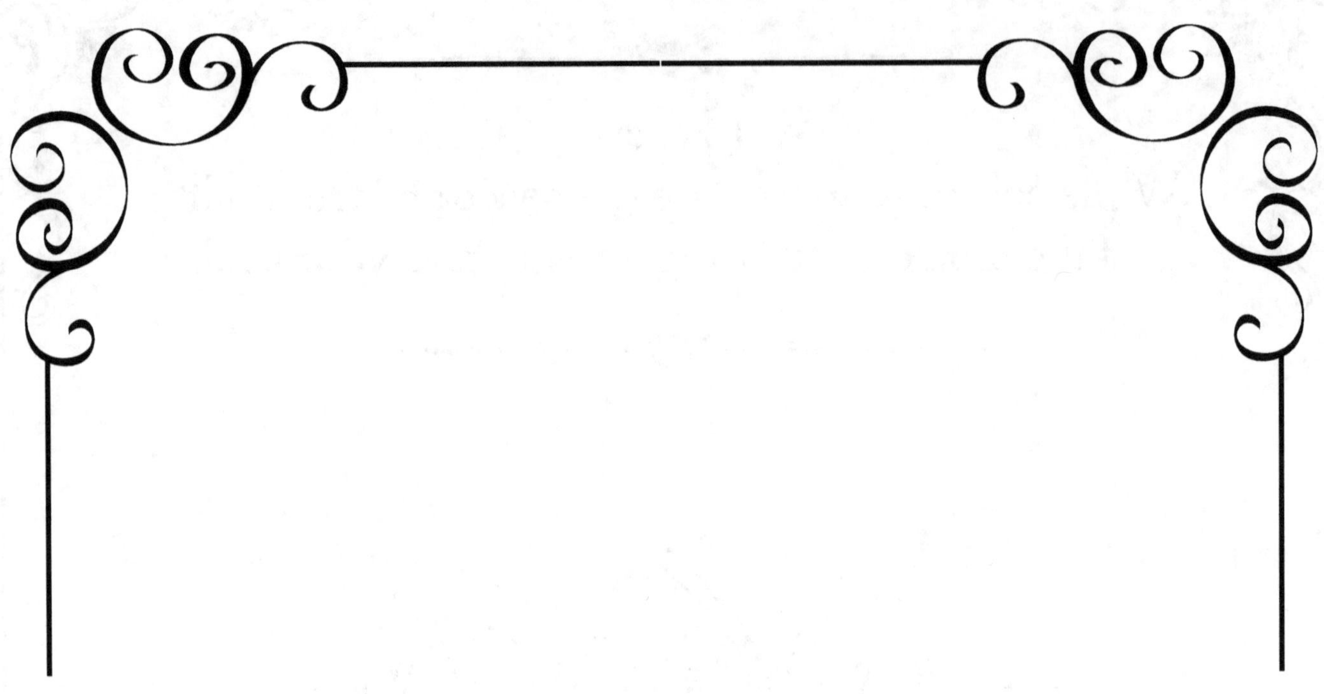

I am the author of my
own story,
and I choose to write it with
sobriety.

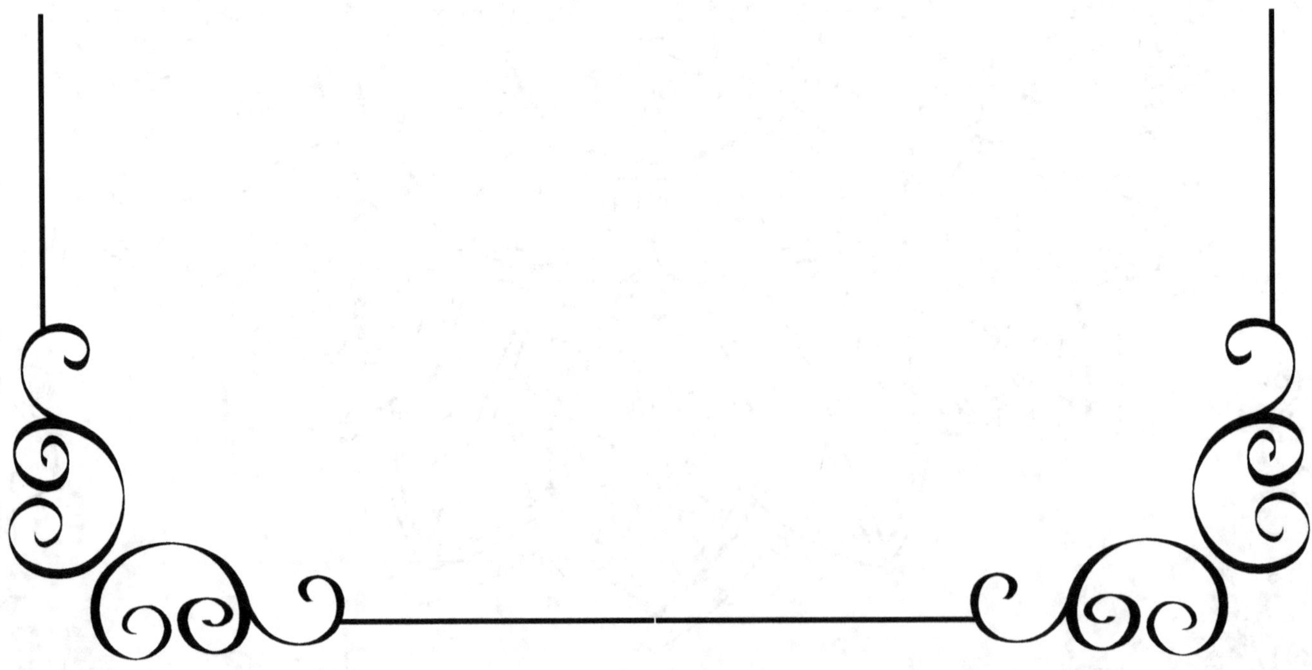

*Exercise:
See your life as a storybook, and each color stroke
as a word in the narrative of your sobriety journey.

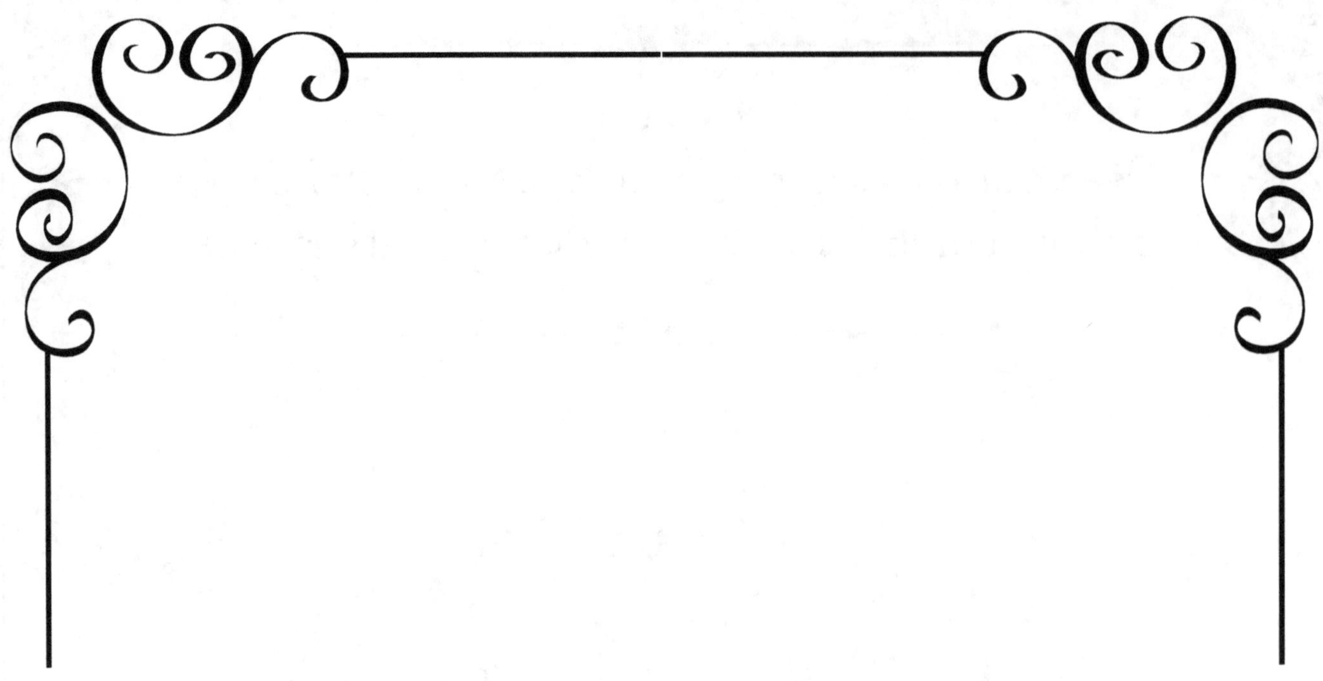

Alcohol is a
relentless thief,
robbing us of our health,
relationships, and self-worth.

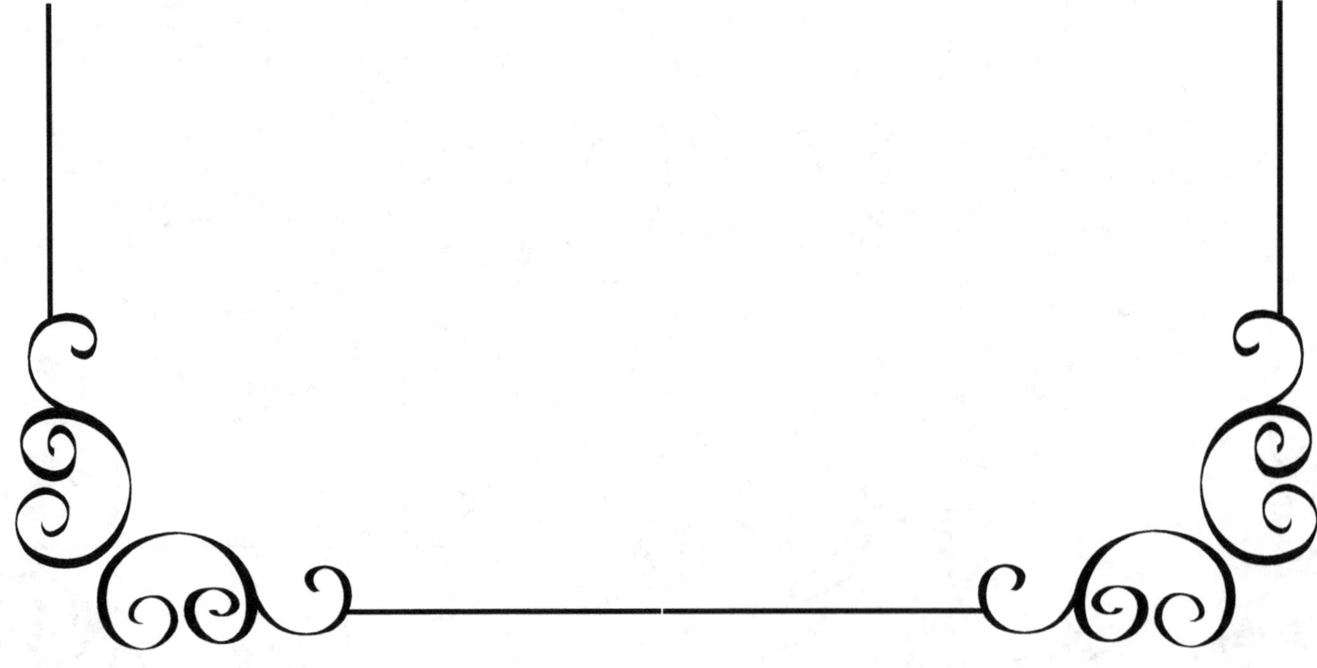

*Exercise:
As you color, contemplate how alcohol can steal health, relationships, and self-worth. Use your coloring strokes to visualize taking back what was lost and reclaiming your well-being

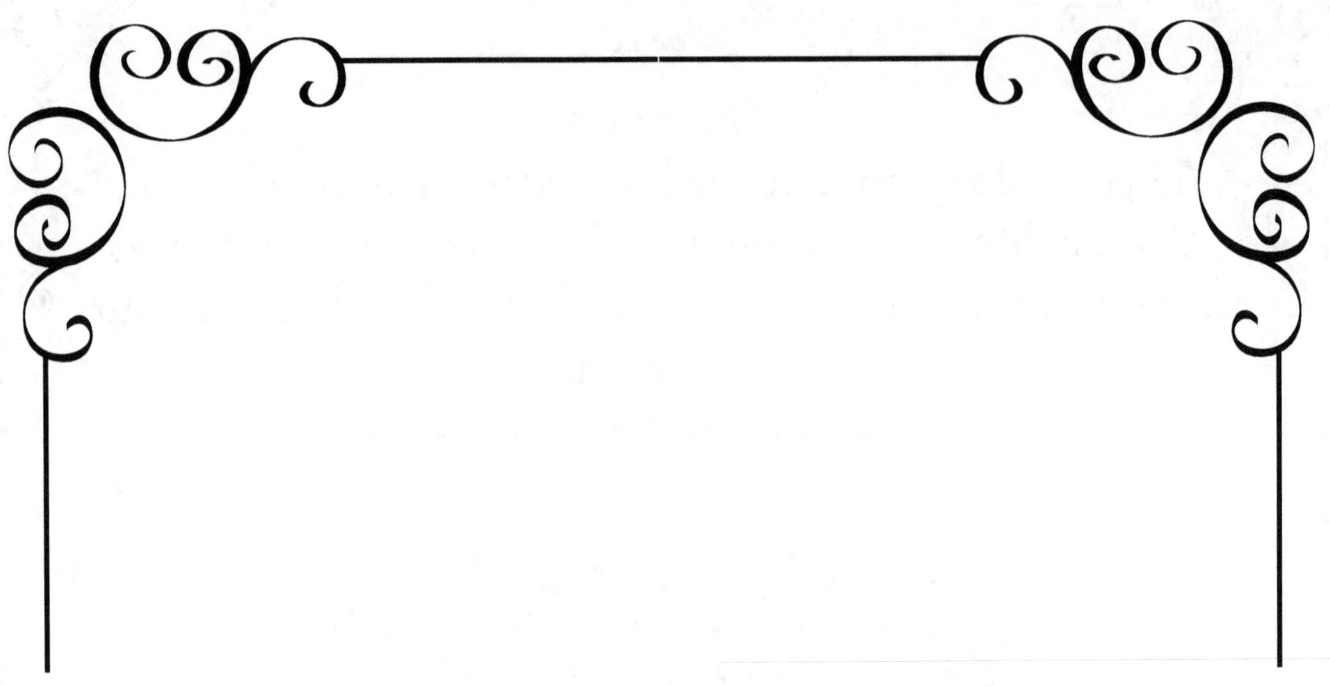

The temporary euphoria
of alcohol
leads to the lasting despair of
addiction.

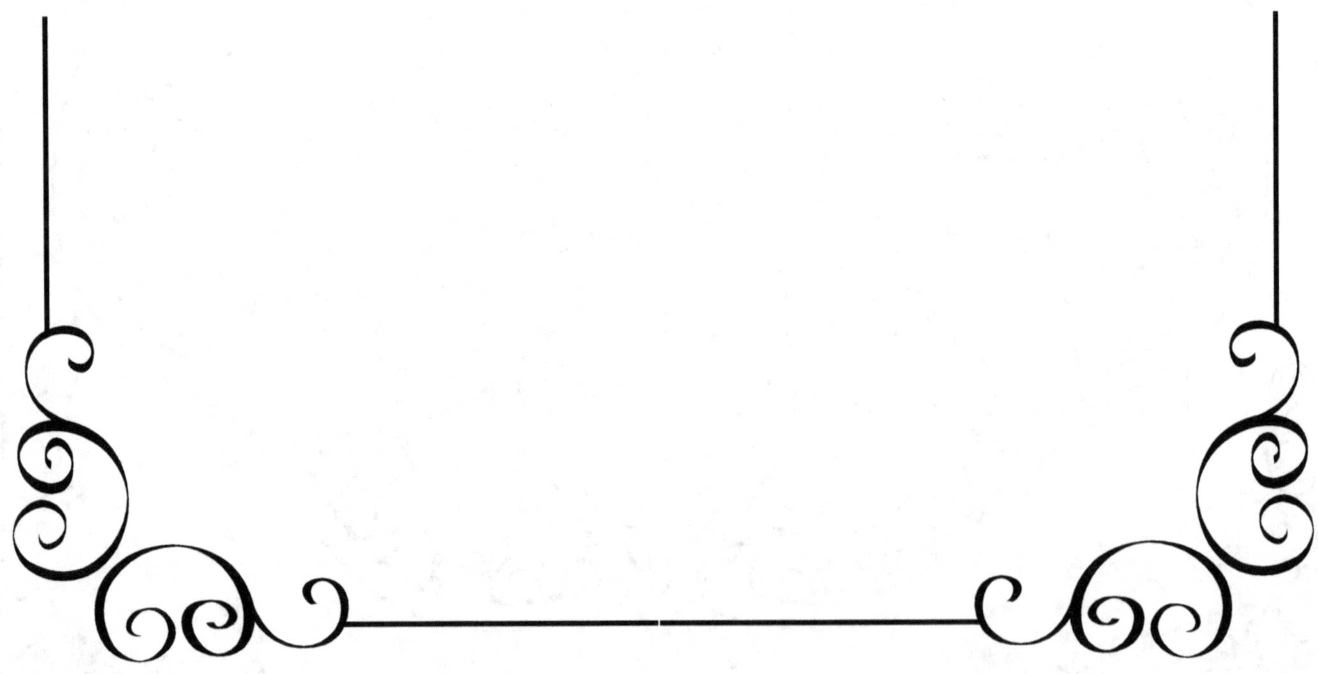

*Exercise:
Think about the fleeting joy alcohol may bring and its potential for lasting despair. Let your strokes represent your determination to break free from this cycle and find lasting happiness

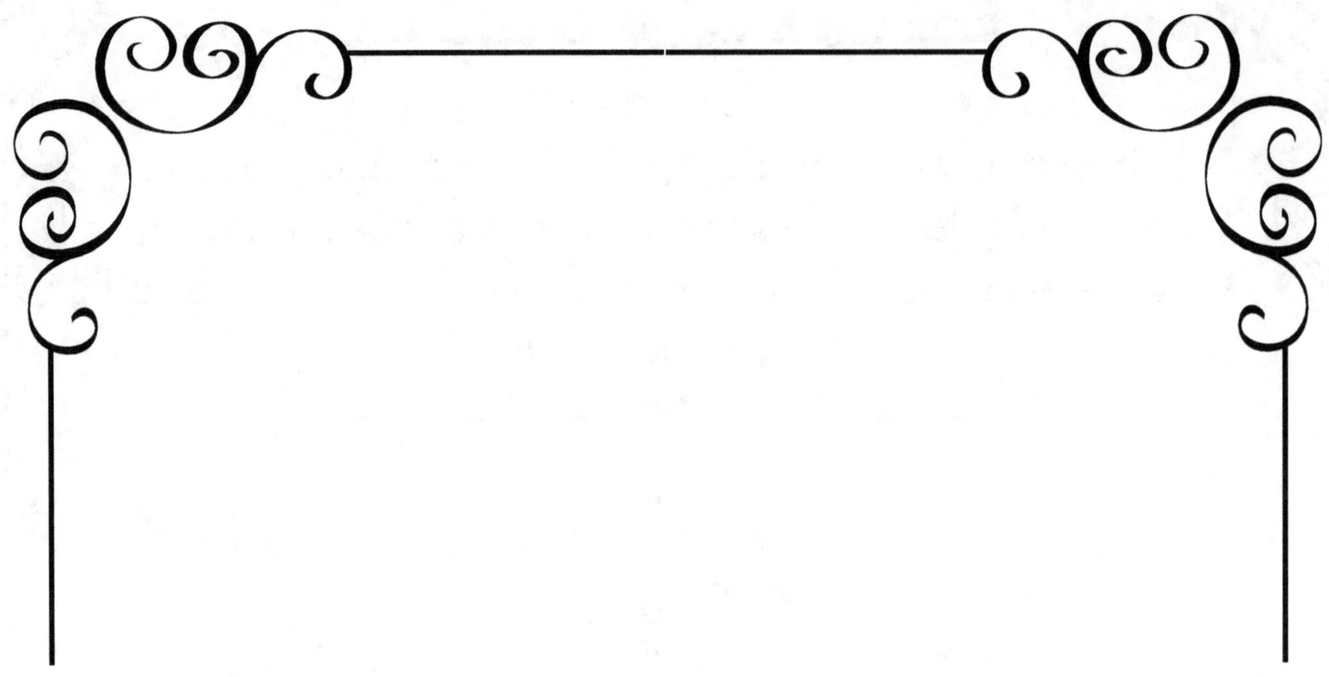

I choose to see the mirage
of alcohol for what it is
—an illusion of escape.

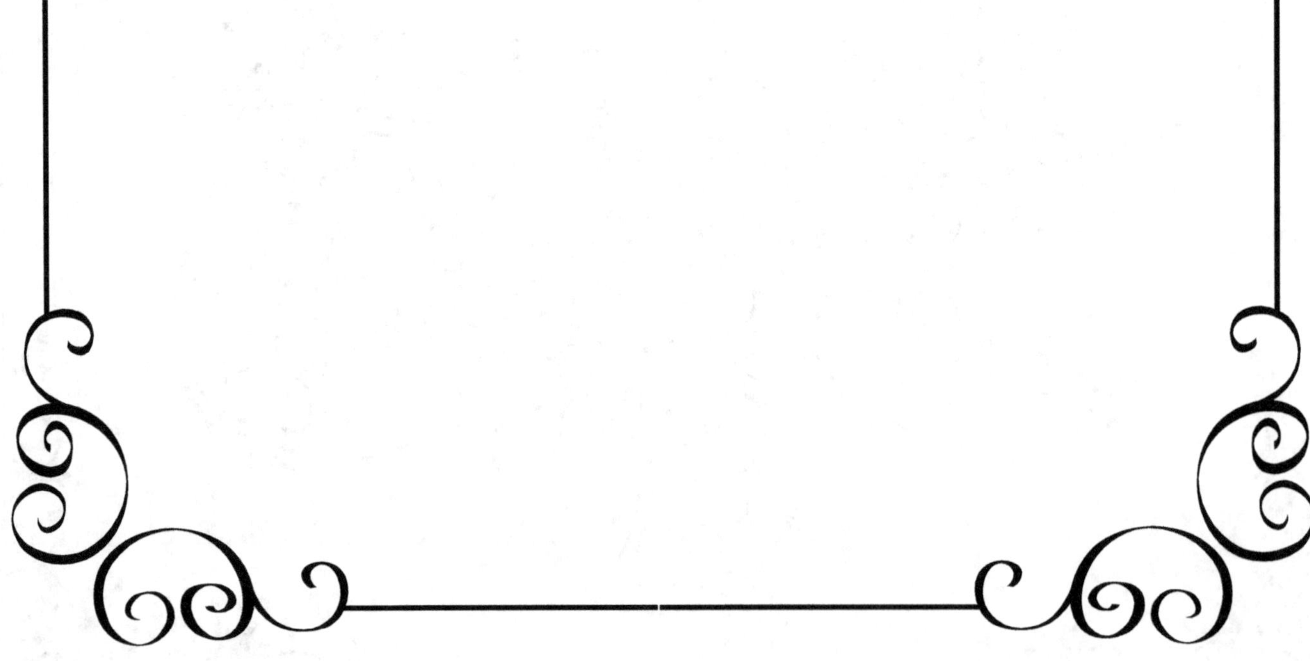

*Exercise:
Visualize a mirage in a desert, and as you color,
allow the mirage to transform into a solid path
representing a sober reality.

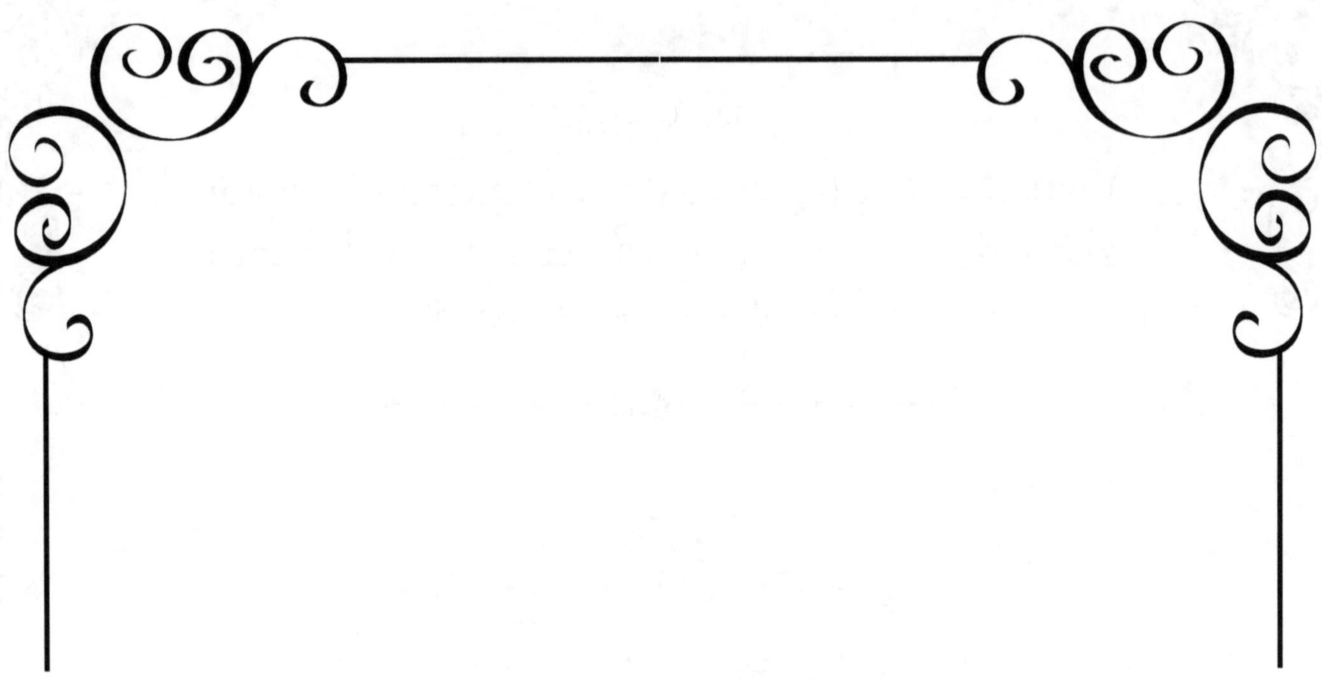

I remind myself that
sobriety is the true
path to joy and fulfillment.

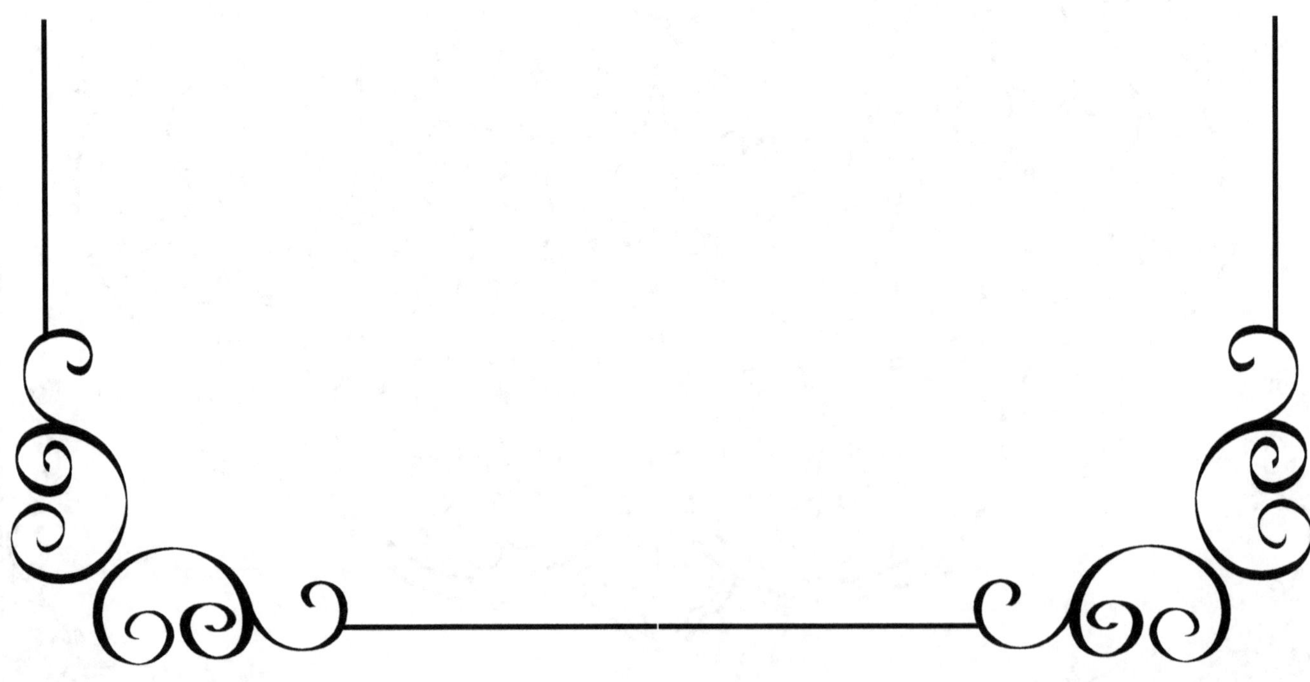

*Exercise:
While coloring, focus on colors that represent joy
and fulfillment, reinforcing your belief in the path of
sobriety.

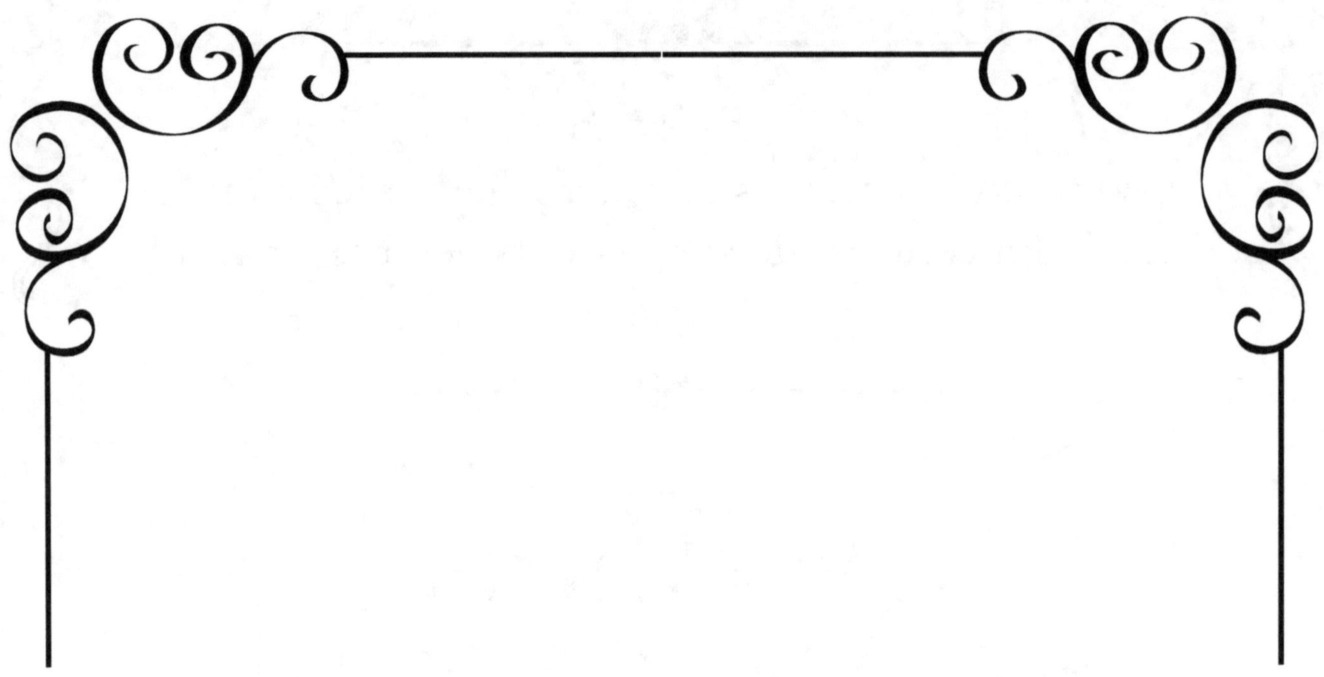

Alcohol is a thief
that steals joy
and replaces it with regret.

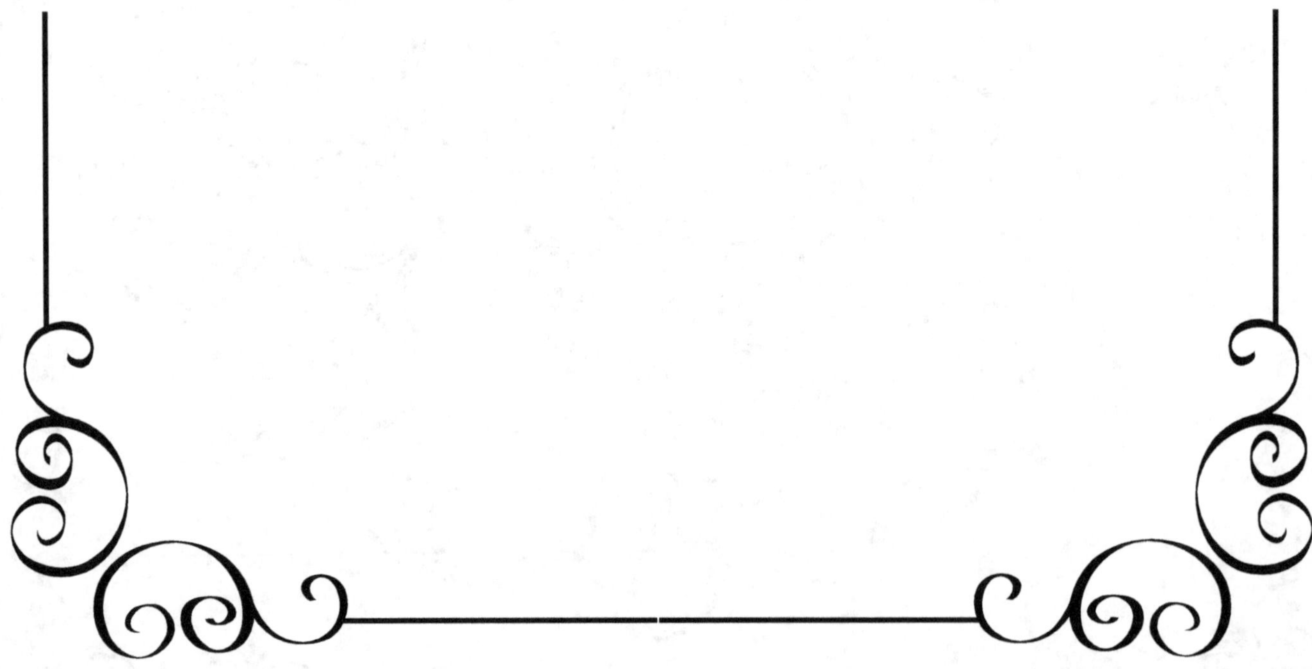

*Exercise:
While coloring, reflect on how alcohol may have stolen joy and left regret in its wake. Use each stroke to symbolize reclaiming your happiness, one color at a time.

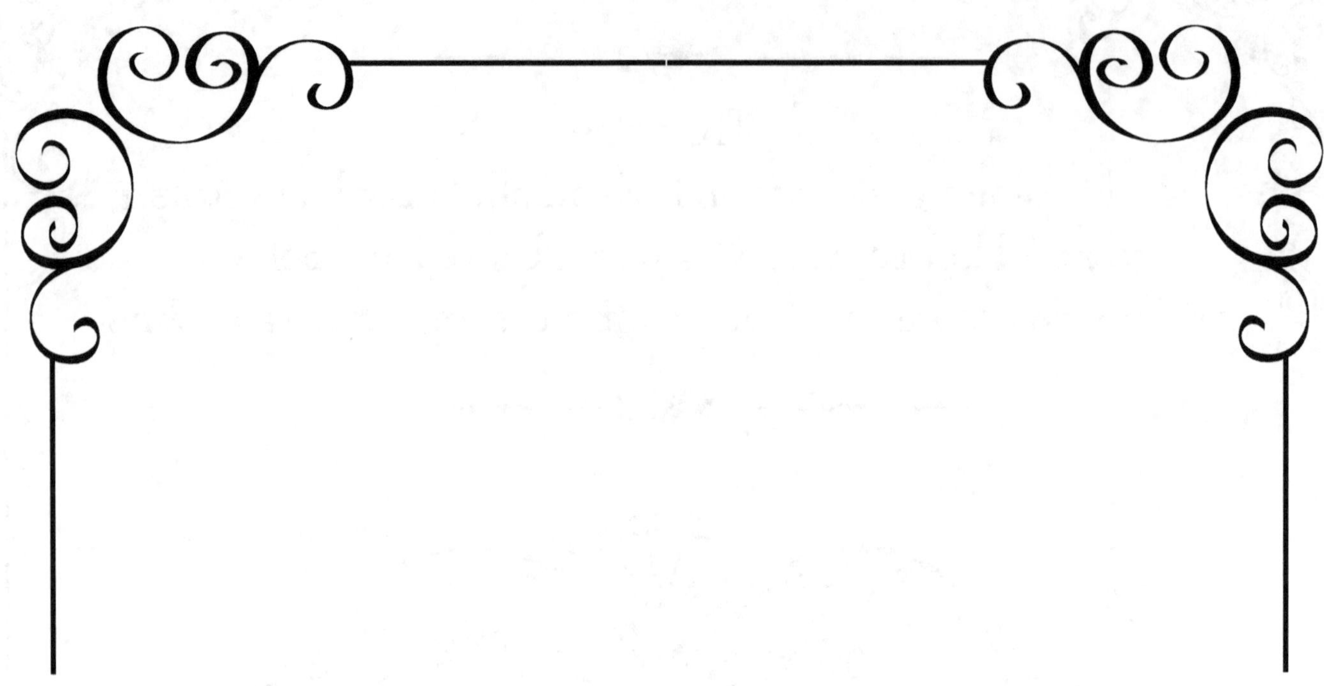

In the bottle, I found
temporary relief,
but in sobriety,
I discovered lasting freedom.

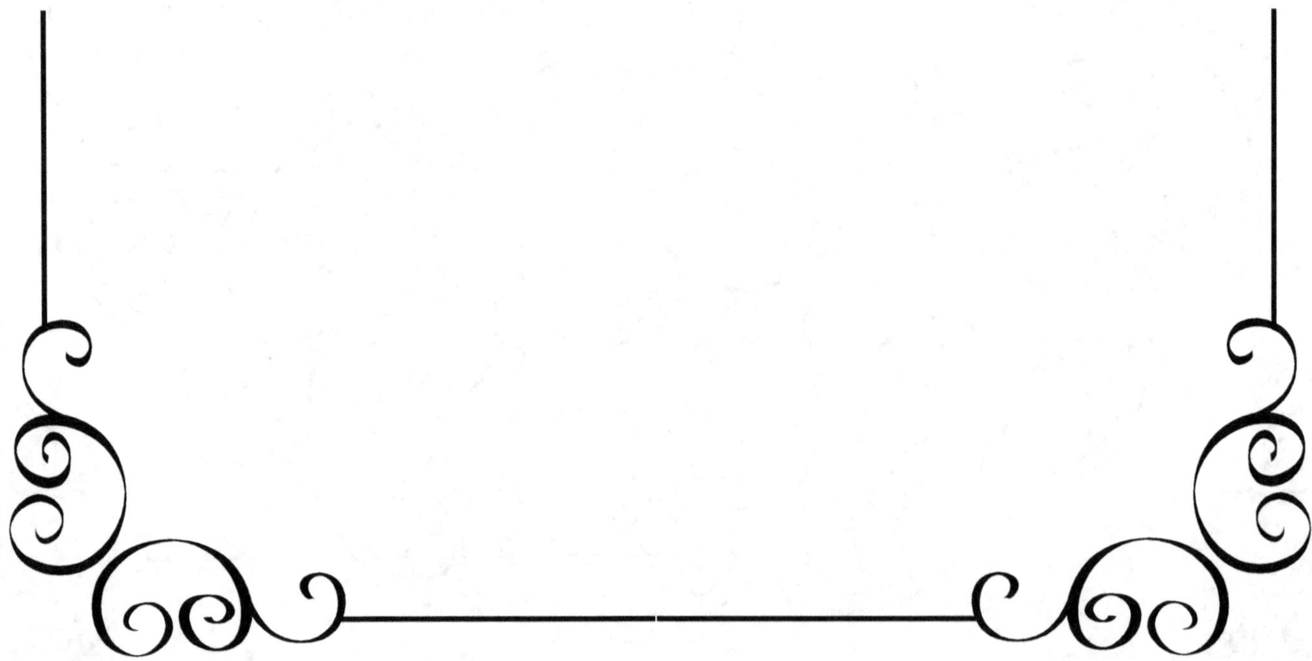

*Exercise:
As you color, contemplate how sobriety offers lasting freedom. With each stroke, visualize the chains of temporary relief breaking, and embrace the enduring liberation that comes with being alcohol-free.

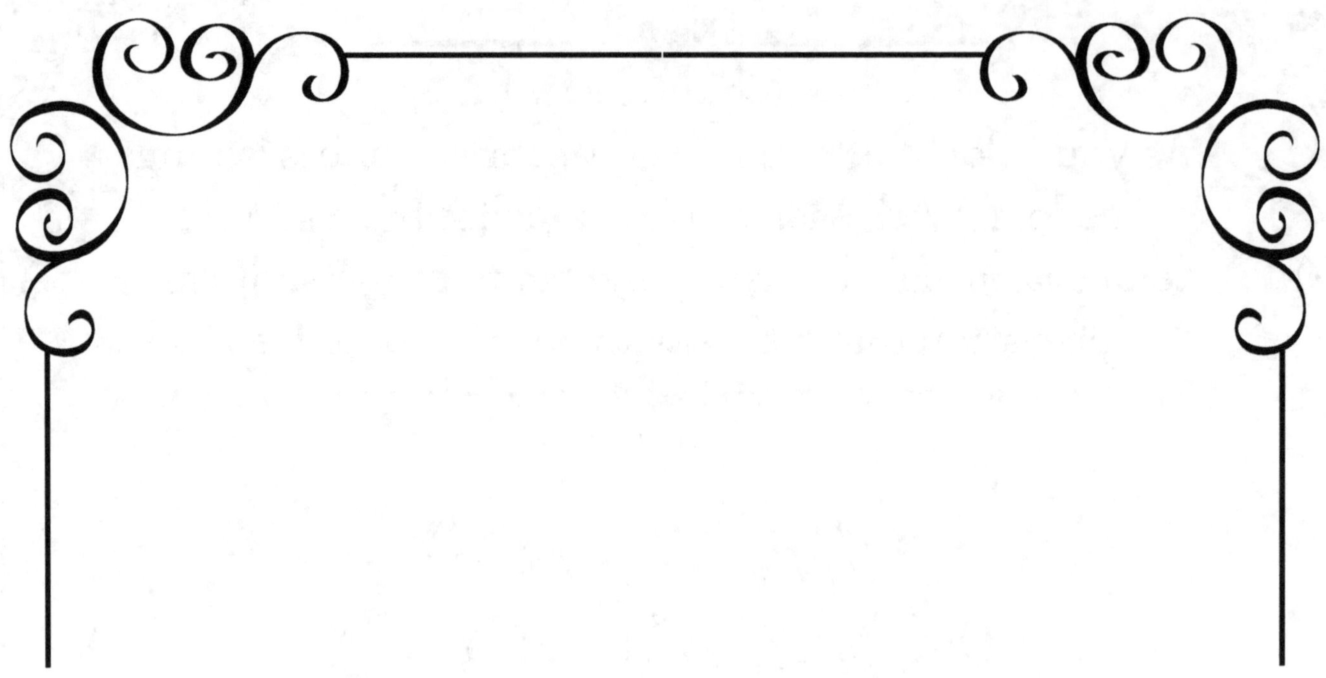

Alcohol promised an escape
but delivered a prison.

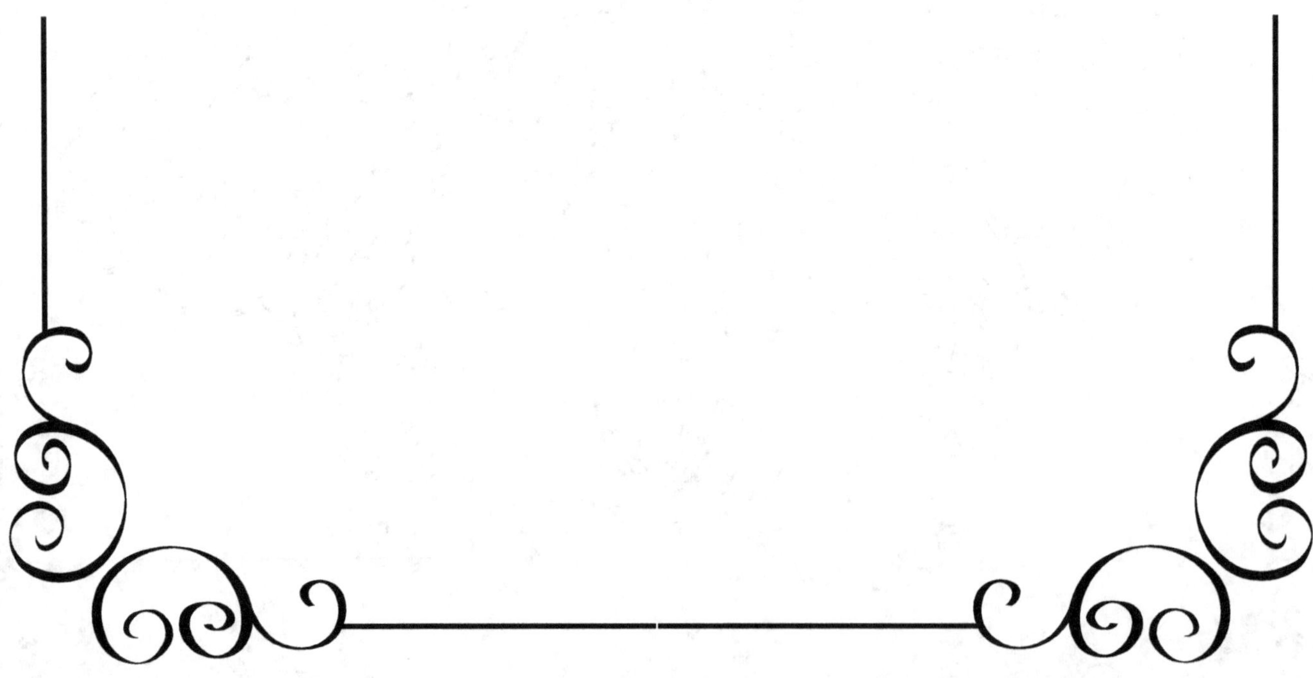

*Exercise:
Visualize alcohol cravings as dark clouds passing
overhead, and with each color stroke, imagine the
clouds dissipating, revealing clear blue skies.

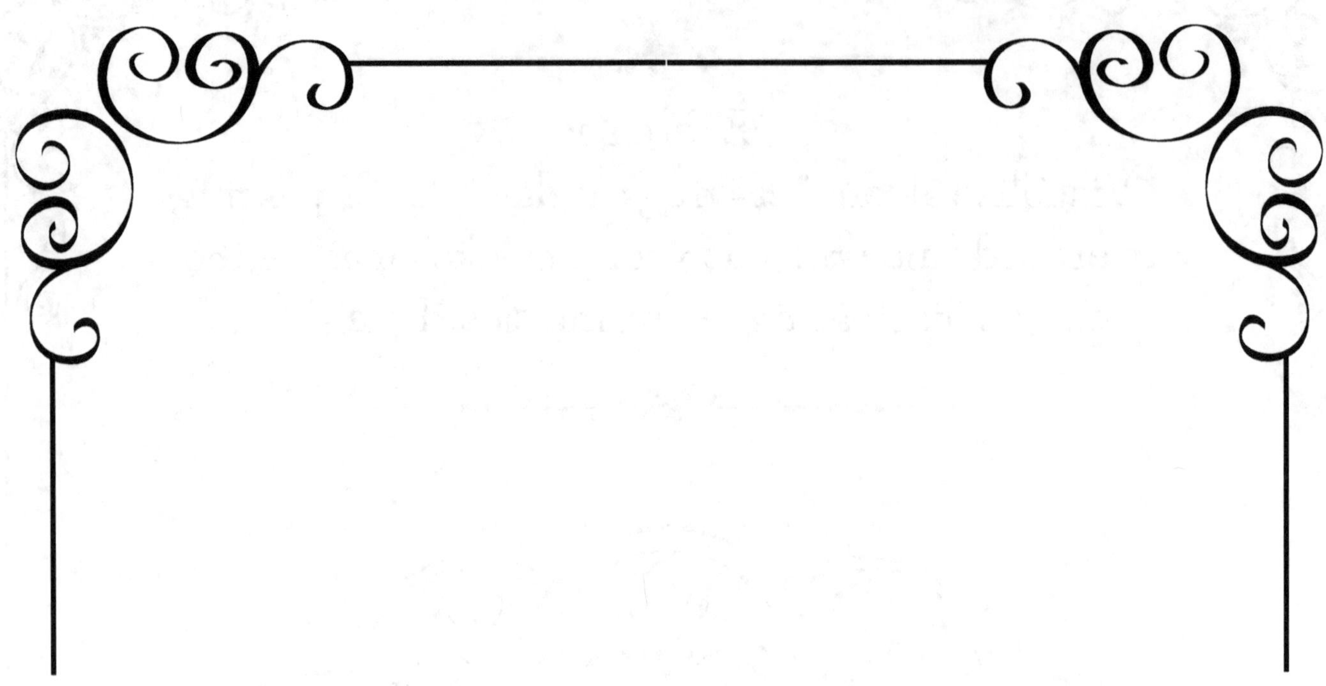

I visualize the weight of
alcohol lifting,
allowing me to walk a lighter,
happier path.

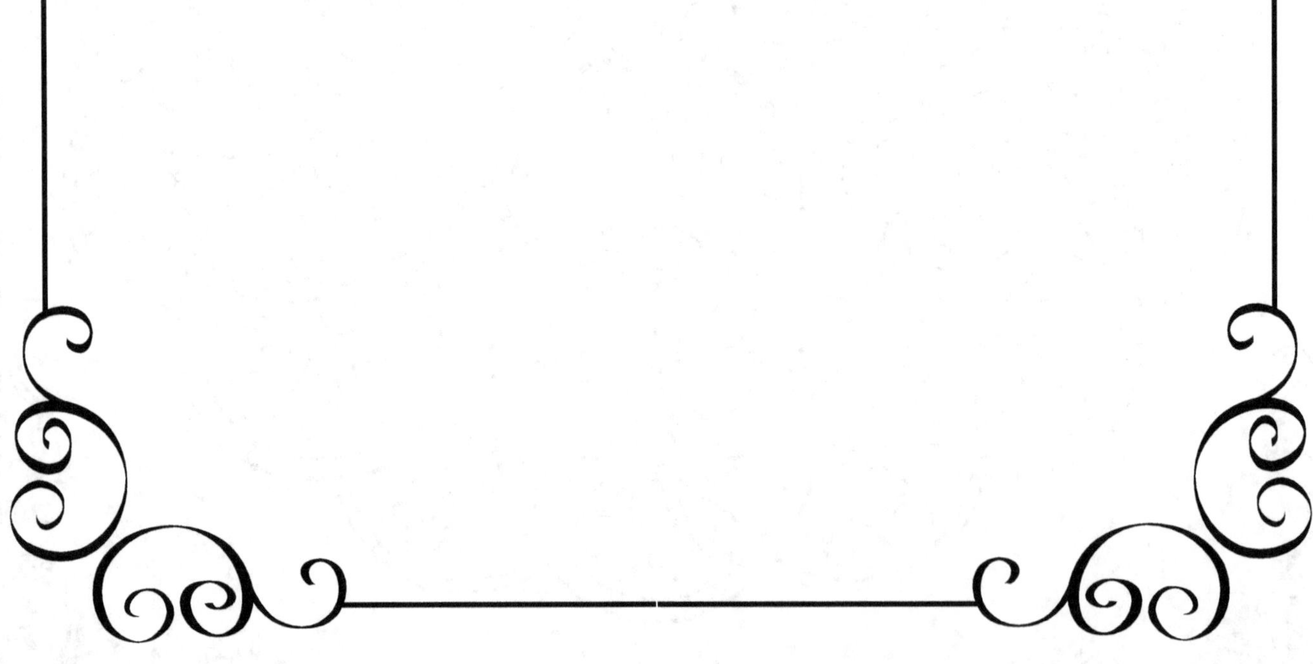

*Exercise:
Imagine yourself carrying the weight of alcohol, and
as you color, visualize it gradually lifting off your
shoulders, leaving you lighter and happier.

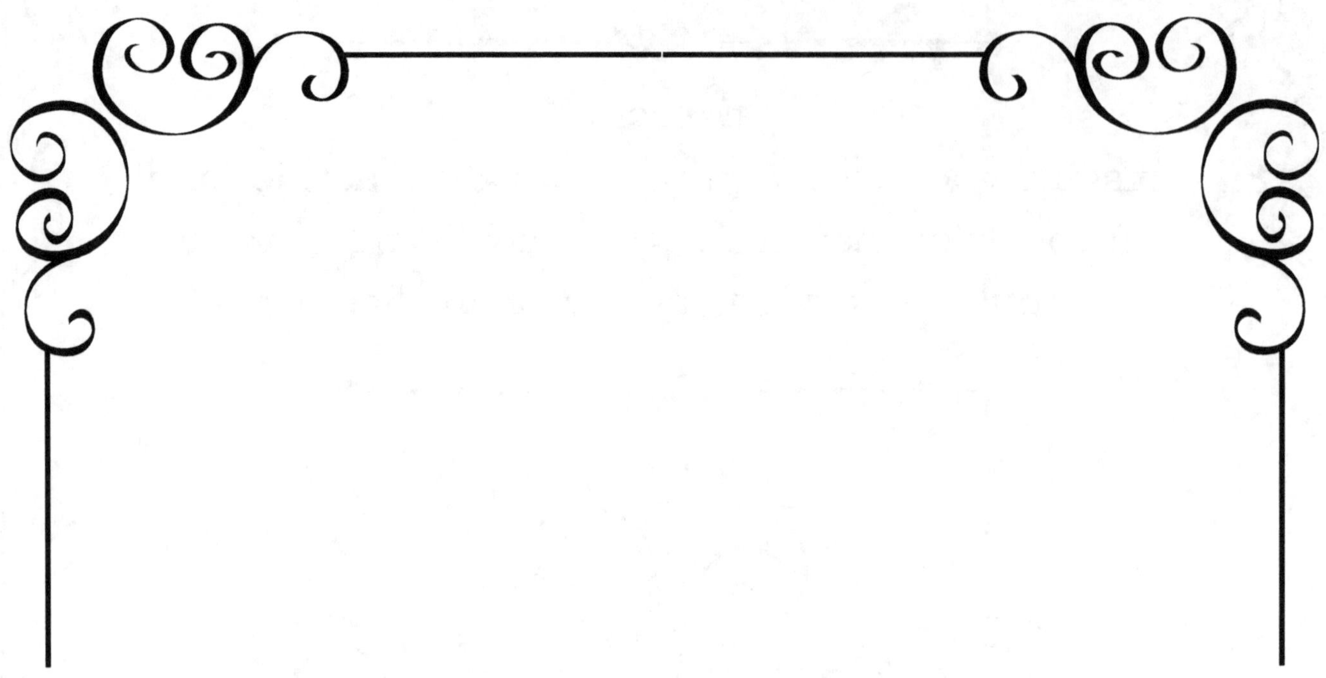

I see alcohol's temptation
as a mirage,
shifting my focus to the oasis
of self-improvement.

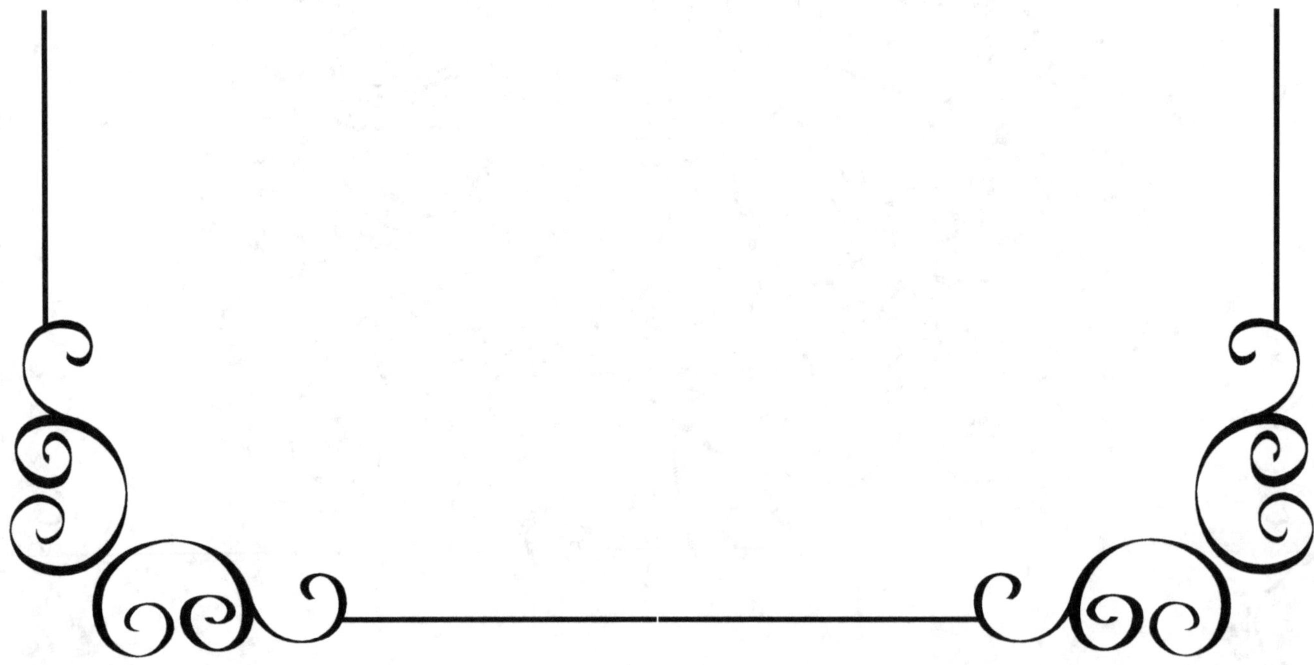

*Exercise:
Visualize yourself walking towards an oasis of self-improvement, leaving the mirage of alcohol behind with each color stroke.